WILLA CATHER

WILLA CATHER

Willa Cather

A MEMOIR

BY

Elizabeth Shepley Sergeant

UNIVERSITY OF NEBRASKA PRESS

Copyright, 1953, by Elizabeth Shepley Sergeant

Copyright © 1963 by the University of Nebraska Press

Library of Congress Catalog Card Number 52-13732

"Going Home," "Prairie Spring," and "Spanish Johnny"
reprinted from *April Twilights and Other Poems*, by
permission of Alfred A. Knopf, Inc., copyright 1923 by
Willa Cather, renewal copyright 1951 by the executors of
the estate of Willa Cather.

First Bison Book printing May, 1963
Second Bison Book printing April, 1967

Manufactured in the United States of America

For Pauline Goldmark

in memory of our trip to Greece

Contents

Foreword to the Bison Book Edition

IT IS A PLEASURE to have this memoir reprinted by the University of Nebraska Press, near the fiftieth birthday of the novel with which I had the most intimate connection in my thirty-seven years of friendship with Willa Cather—*O Pioneers!* My copy of the book was, as I have said in the following pages, inscribed "to the first friend of this book." To share the breakthrough of a genius into its rightful path is an incomparable privilege to one who has always had a special interest in how the creative process works, why it falters, how it eventually finds itself. I must not repeat this story here but refer the reader to Chapters Three and Four of my book.

Miss Bernice Slote, in her imaginative scholar's introduction to the Bison Book edition of Cather's original *April Twilights*, her single book of poems, as she first published it in 1903, quotes the author as saying that the artist finds himself through the wisdom of the intuition, not the wisdom of the intellect. This was eminently true of Cather herself; she was speaking for herself, as she always did. Parenthetically, I have found that it is sometimes another faculty— possibly thinking or feeling or the reality sense—that is dormant, undeveloped, in the unconscious, that comes to the aid of the true artist from the shadow side of himself.

Certainly Cather did not have at all, when I first knew her at *McClure's Magazine* in 1910, the rather vague dreamy atmosphere of one guided by intuition. She did have something inside that the New Englander or urban New Yorker had lost several generations earlier—a kind of clarion, buoyant pioneer promise that life was taking her to a certain goal. But she was, as a personality, crisp, blunt, attentive, practical, intellectual—not tactful or deeply aware of the other person, as born intuitives frequently are to a disconcerting degree. She was sagaciously living as an editor, seemingly with her whole self, solidifying the walls and foundations of her business life. But as we quickly became literary friends she let me know that all this practical side of her career was directed to getting together enough money to retire and write fiction.

Now, seen in the perspectives of time and fame, Willa Cather stands out as closer than any other writer of stature I have known to living Goethe's dictum: "We approach the world through art, and art is our link with it."

Both Mildred R. Bennett in her *The World of Willa Cather* and James R. Shively in *Willa Cather's Campus Years* have made us aware that, astonishingly, the unfledged girl with the stiff starched shirt waists, short tailored suits, and cropped hair—in an age of feminine furbelows, long skirts, and high pompadours—brought this philosophy with her to the University of Nebraska from the small prairie town of Red Cloud, and offered herself as a conscious compulsive victim to "art." How did she already know—perhaps through her buried intuition?—what she set forth rather brashly in her first printed collegiate essay—on Carlyle—now familiar: "Art of every sort is an exacting master, more so even than Jehovah. He says only 'Thou shalt have no other gods before me.' Art, Science and Letters cry 'Thou shalt have no other gods at all.' They accept only human sacrifices."

Already in college, Mrs. Bennett tells us, Cather chose friendship as the only tie valid for her, though the sophisticated part of herself certainly was aware that most artists, great and small, have linked themselves almost desperately to wives, husbands, children, lovers or mistresses, as if to avoid being devoured by art. She wanted to be so devoured, and only in age came perhaps to feel the human cost.

A primarily intuitive type of human being, who lives in the present and the future, would long before the age of thirty-eight have wiggled through the barriers of prudence which Cather had to overthrow to find herself and her own path, separating herself from *McClure's* to write what turned out to be *O Pioneers!* Years of journalism, teaching, editing were behind her. One cannot, however, view this patience as a loss or error, for no concrete, factual or sensuous detail of the Nebraska Divide that was, she felt, the real hero of this story had been lost—rather had gained in poetry and universality.

In her patience and lack of self-belief, Cather resembled her heroine, Thea of *The Song of the Lark*, who was so slow to grasp that the voice was her medium, that her fate was not to be that of a drudging teacher of piano and church singer in a small town, but an exemplification of the dream she harbored even as a child while kicking her baby brother Thor around in his go-cart—a secret, warm sense of a personal destiny totally different from that of her family and friends, bound to overtake her somewhere, sometime. We know now how close Thea's history is to Willa's own. To me the childhood and adolescent part of this book is one of the most poignant of Cather's pieces of semi-autobiographical writing, and deserves to be published by itself, divorced from the more "plotted" and sophisticated story of the singer's mature years as an opera star. The author later herself cut much detail from her novel and pointed out that the story of struggle was more interesting than that of success.

When I first knew her, Willa Cather would say disparagingly, ironically, that she could never write stories of Nebraska—Swedes and Bohemians were just a joke in New York—everybody would laugh. She was apparently still holding down the lid of her deep reservoir of regional memories, which Sarah Orne Jewett had begged her to tap and use in fiction. She was thinking of what "people might think" instead of what she had to say.

Writers have always differed from other artists in having to train themselves and make their own way from scratch. One cannot imagine Cather receiving a Guggenheim fellowship or going to a school of creative writing. She had, when she went to the University of her home state, taken every possible English course and written for almost every possible newspaper and periodical, besides her classical and language studies—yet had not even thought of living by fiction writing when she was ready to face life on her own in Pittsburgh. Every step of the way was taken with honest effort and passionate interest. But once through with these steps she left them behind except for the human ties they had fostered. She made nothing of them when I had one talk with her before writing my first portrait of her in the twenties.

The only conception I could have had about her campus years then was the symbolic version from the pages of *My Antonia*:

"There was an atmosphere of endeavor, of expectancy and bright hopefulness about the college that had lifted its head from the prairie only a few years before," says Jim Burden, the narrator, who is unquestionably the author's alter ego. Jim goes on to make an important point: the classical studies and mental excitement he was experiencing were not turning him into a scholar: "I could never lose myself for long among impersonal things. Mental excitement was apt to send me with a rush back to my own naked land and the figures scattered upon it." Jim learned that these figures (the Swedes and Bohemians that Cather wrote of in her college days) were so alive to him inwardly that "I scarcely stopped to wonder if they were alive anywhere else, or how." In other words, the attitude of the mature novelist, who has to be free of the fear that his subjects will recognize themselves and be hurt, was already born.

Seventeen years—not yet the twenty-five some biographers say are needed for adequate detachment—have passed since Cather's death; ten since my book was written, and already the vital and so gifted personality which I was trying to keep alive for myself is fading into the novels which scholars and critics are studying as works of art. If I were writing a new book I should want to study the mysterious process by which Cather more than most novelists used and transformed her own personal experience into the stuff of those great books that are taking their permanent place in American history and literature.

Recall, for instance, her many brief and fleeting revelations of herself in childhood and adolescence—besides the more lengthy and complete narratives of *The Song of the Lark* and *My Antonia*. There is the observant little girl who witnessed the dignified return of the slave girl from Canada in *Sapphira and the Slave Girl;* the growing adolescent girl, so eager for European culture, who visits her Jewish neighbors in that touching late story *Old Mrs. Harris*, a story to my mind as fine as Flaubert's *Coeur Simple*. The tomboy who hung around in the moonlight at the edge of a dusty road to listen to two leading small-town business men talking politics and quarreling about Bryan in *Two Friends*. There is the young teacher who loved her brothers so dearly in *The Best Years*.

Critics sometimes assume that Cather had a conscious plan—as to write a series of Nebraska novels. Though her unconscious self may have had such a purpose all along, I am sure she was not aware of it when she began to write *O Pioneers!* in 1912. She described the experience with wonder, as something that just "happened to her." Here I quote from my book:

"She said that she could only describe this process [the coming together of two pastorals written separately] as a sudden inner explosion and enlightenment. She had experienced it before only in the conception of a poem. Now she would hope always for a similar experience in creating a novel, for the explosion [she would not have used this word had she lived to feel pressed by the "population explosion"] seemed to bring with it the inevitable shape that is not plotted but designs itself. She now believed that the least tinkering with the form—*revealed* from within, the better." Coordination and simplification were part of the process.

She did not speak mystically, nor is there anything in her posthumous volume of critical essays collected by Miss Edith Lewis—*On Writing*—to suggest that attitude. But for a creative writer, especially a poet, almost a poet, like Cather, anything like a dream or an overpowering insight which seems to be Truth itself is close to a religious experience. The cluttering petty detail of life of which Willa Cather was so afraid, is eliminated.

Tom Outland, the young man in whose face and behavior, his creator wrote, was "a fine disregard of trivialities," is portrayed in *The Professor's House* as having one of those precious moments of inner realization and spiritual enlightenment when alone on the Blue Mesa where he had had the great adventure of being the first to discover the cliff-dweller ruins. Tom's long effort to clear them and make them known to his government had failed; his friend had, under a false conception, sold the ancient pottery artifacts to a European collector; everything human and material connected with his selfless struggle had been taken from him. Yet it was just then that he came into possession of his material. He understood what it meant in the history of man on this earth to have had the fortitude to make homes and decorated pots and a long brave history on the cliffs of Arizona.

Nineteen twelve was indeed the turning point in Willa Cather's life as a writer. No longer would she fear her own overpowering love for the red grass of the prairie of her early childhood on the Divide and for the men and women who broke the soil, or talk in New York about dying in a cornfield. She had fenced off a piece of the prairie, given it arcadian beauty and meaning in the human sense, and henceforth had a share in Nebraska—and the wide world—that was all her own. Surely her finest books —not all her books or just her Nebraska novels—fulfil Malraux's definition of art: *La monnaie de l'absolu.*

E. S. S.

Piermont, New York
December 1962

Foreword

IT WAS NOT MY FATE to know Willa Cather until 1910, and this memoir deals chiefly with the years from 1910 to 1931 when I saw her most frequently. The reason I set myself to write a memoir at all is that I happened to be present at the critical turning point when, casting prudence aside, she took the veil of final dedication to the art of fiction.

She had no inner certainty as to the consequences. Some of her letters, which I have preserved, reveal her humbleness about her great powers. I cannot quote from them for her will forbids the printing of letters. The prose she used in friendly correspondence was colloquial, vivid, frank, at times emotional, more like her casual talk than like the subtle, sober, equable prose she developed in her finest novels and stories. She feared the betrayal, in print, of the heat and abundance that surged up in her. In her art she transformed heat to a plasticity that made her characters and her landscapes live as if one actually saw and touched them. And abundance supplied its opposite: that grace of simplicity, directness, tautness, which she strove to attain without destroying the emotional aura which, as she always said, is more felt than actually present on the page.

Miss Cather talked both in print and in private—sparingly enough—of her great passion, the literary art. The most interesting and impersonal side of our affectionate friendship, the place where it "clicked" was concerned with this art. An editorial incident first brought us together: ardent talk of books, people, places followed. That I, too, loved and knew the fair land of France and the works of Flaubert made a difference at the very first meeting. I had at Bryn Mawr College been given passages of *Madame Bovary* to imitate in my Descriptive Writing class; just as Willa Cather had recommended similar readings to the young students whose themes she corrected in the preparatory course at the University of Nebraska.

> In my prep course at the University of Nebraska [wrote Alvin Johnson, who came to the university straight from the cornfield] I had to produce "themes". . . My themes were passed on by a rather mannish young woman with a head that seemed vast under her jungle of hair—Willa Cather. She did me the great honor of calling me to her office. "You write not badly," she said. "But you don't *see*. Learn French, a little French and read Flaubert or even Maupassant. They *see*. *Madame Bovary:* the book is worth committing to memory."

American literature had no place in the Bryn Mawr curriculum in my time—no Melville, no Hawthorne, no Poe, no Dickinson, no Whitman. Henry James and Edith Wharton were the only modern fiction writers; expatriates, you see; and we read them for pleasure, not for study. When, ten years after my graduation, I told one of my English professors that I had discovered a genuine, first-class work of American fiction, in which a young woman of prairie background had conceived her world with new eyes and had made of it a work of art, she looked at me skeptically. Even *My Ántonia* failed to move her.

My knowledge of Willa Cather's life before 1910 came to me largely in the fragmentary reference of her own talk. Feeling when I wrote her "portrait" in 1926 her sudden reticencies I did not even ask her for a complete Vita. She was still spending much time in Pittsburgh when I first knew her—going there to write. Always she was shooting out to Red Cloud. More than once she described visits to Virginia, and sometimes she told me that the most valuable experiences of her life came to her before she was twenty years old.

So it has seemed pertinent here to take a swift look back to her Shenandoah Valley origins, her Nebraska childhood and girlhood and to her Pittsburgh years. This I have done briefly in my introduction, drawing considerably and gratefully on the reports of others named in the acknowledgment.

E.S.S.

The MacDowell Colony,
Peterborough, New Hampshire,
July 1952

Introduction

WILLA CATHER was born December 7th, 1873, in the Back Creek Valley of the Northern Neck of Virginia—a beautiful part of the Shenandoah Valley now called Gore, not far from Winchester. She was named for her father's dead sister, but considered her name a link to her two grandfathers, William Cather and William Boak, both descended from families associated with pioneer days in Virginia: with its farm lands, its legislatures, its problems of slavery, states' rights and secession. Though deeply a Southerner, her grandfather Cather in his youth fought on the Union side in the Civil War. An unusually perceptive, impressionable child, and a very observant one, Willa Cather was aware of the surges and conflicts of feeling and the economic insecurity that confronted her Southern elders.

The Cathers, her father's people, descended from a certain Jasper Cather, who was believed to have emigrated from North Ireland to Pennsylvania, then to Virginia in the eighteenth century. Jasper cleared and settled land; and fought in the Revolutionary War. Willa's grandfather, William, was the grandson of this original Irish pioneer from the old world, who perhaps had also Welsh blood.

The old brick house with the willow grove and the ever-flowing spring described in *Sapphira and the Slave Girl* was built by him and when he went into the Union Army, was used as a Union rendezvous during the Civil War. His two sons, George and Charles, Willa's father, were too young to be conscripted.

Charles Cather, who had married Mary Virginia Boak, a girl of a genteel Confederate family whom he had known since childhood, moved from his mother-in-law's house—where his eldest child, Willa, was born—to his father, William Cather's substantial brick house, Willowshade Farm, when his little girl was three years old. Here Charles Cather started in the business of fattening sheep for the Baltimore market; and here the young growing family lived until Willa was nine, and the future novelist acquired the memories and stories which make the background of *Sapphira and the Slave Girl*. We know from the presence of an attentive little girl of five, in the last chapter of this book, when the runaway slave girl returns in high dignity from Canada, that on this child's heart and memory life's deep currents were to be recorded like musical themes.

But Nebraska and its pioneer promise had come into the lives of the Cather tribe as early as 1873. George P. Cather, Willa's uncle, who had married Frances A. Smith, a Massachusetts girl recently graduated from one of the pioneer New England colleges for women, then called Mt. Holyoke Female Seminary, took up a homestead in Webster County. Mrs. George P. Cather, Willa Cather's beloved "Aunt Franc," thus became a cultural influence in a region that was still "frontier"—in her niece's stories recognizable

as "my Aunt Georgiana" in "A Wagner Matinée," and as
Mrs. Wheeler, the mother of Claude, in *One of Ours*.

In 1877, four years after his elder son's move to Nebraska, William A. Cather, Willa's grandfather and his wife,
Emily Anne Caroline Smith—Caroline's Virginia ancestors
had had land grants from Lord Fairfax—also pulled up old
roots to migrate to Webster County. In a photograph reproduced by Mildred R. Bennett in her book, *The World
of Willa Cather*, grandfather William Cather is very impressive: a devout, experienced, wise, white-bearded patri-
archal man. He was a Baptist, prayed and read the Bible to
his grandchildren, and seems a proper ancestor for a novelist
who believed that creative art derives from passion, and that
art and religion have a common inner source.

In 1883, ten years after the family exodus, Willa's father
decided to follow this migrating trend to the fallow Middle
West that was now stirring the old Virginians with its
potentialities. A second family home had been established
twenty miles from Red Cloud, in Webster County, and
ten miles from the Kansas line. Young Mr. and Mrs.
Charles Cather, who by now had four small children, went
out by the railroad. Mrs. Cather took along her widowed
mother, Mrs. Boak, and an unlettered poor-white servant,
who was probably the touching model for Mandy in "Old
Mrs. Harris" and for Mahaili, one of the lesser personages
and greater characters in *One of Ours*. For Willa Cather's
first impressions—she was now ten—of the untamed country, and the homestead we must look to those classic first
chapters of *My Ántonia*, which seem to contain pristine
experience—remembered in maturity with meanings no
child could fully apprehend. There, too, are the grand-

parents; the stalwart, kind grandmother, so quietly responsive to the need of a lonely child; and the grandfather with his biblical authority.

It is usually assumed from the legend of a childhood spent on ponyback, on the prairie, visiting Scandinavian and Czech neighbors, in their sod houses, that Charles Cather and his gay, firm, Southern wife, lived on at Catherton, as the region was already called. But, in fact, Willa's father sold his agricultural machinery and moved at the end of the first lonely year into Red Cloud; he had had some legal training, and felt drawn to what was then believed to be a town with a future. It had twenty-five hundred inhabitants at that time; four trains east and four west stopped daily at the station—a division point of the Burlington and Missouri Railroad—which was a mile from the center. Even nowadays prairie children are drawn toward a railroad station, as to a banner. Willa Cather's ten-year-old imagination had but to make one leap over the steel rails to arrive in Chicago, San Francisco, or Boston where her Aunt Franc came from. When the road companies of actors, weaving back and forth across the continent, burst from the teeming cars, with all their glitter and fustian, to shine in the local theatre, she was enraptured, carried into a land of dreams that was better than the hard realities about her.

But one year on the Divide—as the region was called—had been enough to make an indelible impression on a nine-year-old. In the year of the publication of *The Troll Garden*, 1905, Willa Cather explained this to a future colleague on *McClure's Magazine*, who had queried her as to how she came to know the West and why her stories were so bleak.

She said, as if surprised by this impression, that she had

lived in Nebraska ten years. The move at such a tender age from the damp, shady, mountainous beauty of the Shenandoah Valley to a raw, treeless and nearly waterless land had been cruel for a child.

Eighteen miles from the tall, gaunt homestead house which she had described, almost literally, in "A Wagner Matinée," was a stagnant creek, all but dried up in summer. A few ragged, forked cottonwoods grew along the banks. Yet to this meagre travesty of running water the Cather children were determined to go to play. They had become frantic tree-worshippers. When they drove in to Red Cloud for supplies, as they had to do, over a naked land, they were halfway along before the tops of some Lombardy poplars planted for crop protection, showed against the sky. Then the children burst into a tumult of joy. Perhaps the worst moment of all was when at Christmas the Virginia youngsters, used to sturdy pointed firs, were taken to the Norwegian church and asked to admire a pindling box elder, decked with cut green tissue paper for needles. Later Willa Cather considered the cottonwood, planted by the pioneers, the most beautiful tree on the plains, and fought against its replacement by the maple.

In the small crowded house where there were, eventually, seven children, Willa was very much the devoted elder sister. Her care of the younger ones, her story-telling gifts, early recognized and called upon, were parts of her life that she talked about. She always said that she got her best education from the foreign women on the Divide and from her grandmothers, who read her the Bible and Shakespeare. An unforgettable picture of the childhood-adolescent years of a girl, who privately nursed a deep sense of personal

destiny, is given in the first book of *The Song of the Lark;*
where it is also suggested that a youngster who is brilliant
and avid for culture in all forms could find elements to fill
her need even in a town like "Moonstone."

Willa's parents, especially her mother, evidently encouraged her strenuous, untiring, hungry efforts to extract
the essential facts and implications of knowledge and culture from a storekeeper, a druggist, or an old German
musician, like Professor Shindelmeisser, or shall we say Professor Wunsch, Thea Kronborg's first piano teacher. Willa
was given, as a little girl, an unusually good chance to learn
to play the piano. But, evasively, she climbed on her
teacher's lap and plied him with questions about the European background and the European languages. She wanted
him to play to *her;* and she listened with rapture to the
Norwegian mother of her best friends—the little Miners—
when she played on her piano. The Miners' grandfather
had played the oboe in Ole Bull's Royal Norwegian Orchestra. Willa Cather had a true musical ear, and she started
her connoisseurship and her listening to the classic repertoire in adolescence and before.

An interesting phase of her early education, taking education as she herself did, in the broad sense, was her concern
with medicine. In her mid-teens, she called herself Willa
Cather, M.D., wearing her father's Civil War visored cap
(bearing his initials W. C.) over cropped hair and boyish
shirt and jacket. Mildred R. Bennett's book gives some
charming photographs of this driving, frank-faced young
person who, intending to study medicine when she went
to the University of Nebraska, defended vivisection at high

school; and went so far as to dissect frogs and even dogs and cats.

In 1890 this promising if puzzling young woman entered a university preparatory course for one year at Lincoln; and then, in 1891, the Nebraska State University. At that time she threw herself headlong not into science but into studies like Latin, Greek, French, German, English, and likewise into college activities, so-called, where they were cultural; as dramatics, and writing for the college publications.

Here, too, according to James R. Shively, who was the first to comment on Willa Cather's college years, she continued her boyish trend in dress, wearing her skirts short like her hair, and her shirtwaists stiffly starched. Her manners are described as bluff and aloof. She was a girl everybody respected and nobody knew very well, for she avoided intimacies and flirtations. Like most bright college girls she was popular with her professors, and bowed before these older minds with their stores of wisdom. She did find special friends in a German musical family in Lincoln, the Westermanns, who have admitted themselves to be the German family called Ehrlich whom Claude so loved in *One of Ours*. Dorothy Canfield, later Mrs. John R. Fisher, the daughter of the Chancellor of the University, James H. Canfield, was a college friend who remained a lifetime friend, though their paths diverged early in the century. After Willa had gone to Pittsburgh, they met in England one summer, making literary pilgrimages occasionally, like the one to see A. E. Housman, which Mrs. Fisher has recalled in print.

The late Professor E. K. Brown, the sound authority on

Willa Cather, in a contribution to *The Newberry Library Bulletin* on the Benjamin D. Hitz Collection of Cather items at this Library, cites as one of Hitz's treasures her first known appearance in print, an article on Carlyle,

> which came out in the State Journal, on March 1st, 1891, with the accompanying note—"The article on *Some Personal Characteristics of Thomas Carlyle*, which appears in this issue of the Journal is original work from the literary department of the University of Nebraska. The writer is a young girl sixteen years of age who comes from Webster County. A careful reading will convince any student of literature that it is a remarkable production, reflecting not a little credit upon the author and the university." The article [Brown continues] was published without Willa Cather's knowledge; the pleasure she had in seeing herself in print was what directed her away from science, the principal interest she had brought with her to the University, and determined her to become a writer.

In this essay on Carlyle, Willa made a pronouncement on art, which was in fact a remarkable definition of a lifetime philosophy:

> Art of every kind is an exacting master, more so even than Jehovah—He says only "Thou shalt have no other gods before me," Art, Science and Letters cry, "Thou shalt have no other gods at all." They accept only human sacrifices.

She was already, Mrs. Bennett says, enjoying the isolation, and laying foundations for her life as a dedicated novelist.

Those who wish to see Willa Cather's early contributions to *The Hesperian*, the student magazine, and to *The Sombrero*, the University annual, and to *The Lincoln Courier*, a weekly edited by Sarah B. Harris, for which she had written pretty steadily while in Lincoln, and wrote regularly after going to Pittsburgh, will find the files in the Hitz Collection.

Shively, in his *Writings from Willa Cather's Campus Years,* has reproduced some of the collegiate pieces, notable among them "Peter"—from the *Hesperian,* November, 1892—her first published story, which had appeared a few months earlier in a small Boston literary journal, *The Mahogany Tree.* This is the story of a Bohemian fiddler who had played in an orchestra in Prague, and migrated unwillingly to southwestern Nebraska to take up a homestead. Peter's son, Antone, drove the old man so hard in the fields that he broke his fiddle and committed suicide by pulling the trigger of his shotgun with his own toe. The story is deeply moving, humane, and is close to the tragic death, in *My Ántonia,* of old Mr. Shimerda, who also had a hard son, a better man than himself.

Another fine story of delicate feeling in the campus collection is "Lou, the Prophet," the story of a farmer who went crazy in a mystical way: possibly a true happening of the time of terrible drought which, during Willa's university years, dried up the land and imperiled the mortgages of her former Scandanavian neighbors on the Divide. Among the Norsemen, as Willa Cather called them, were outbreaks of insanity and suicide. She especially grieved over the effect on the children.

Even when she returned to Webster County from Pittsburgh and found that the ultimate survivors of this era of disaster had bought oak furniture and Brussels carpets and parlor organs, it was hard to forget this grim picture. She almost assumed the unbeautiful and the tragic, she said. We know, in fact, that it took her seven years, after the publication of "The Sculptor's Funeral" and "A Wagner Matinée" to picture Alexandra's victory over intolerable obstacles, in *O Pioneers!*; and still longer to tell the story of the Shimerdas in final perspective and to present the harsh landscape in evocative, lyrical prose.

Before Willa Cather left the University of Nebraska, she had, through her stories and newspaper work, given solid proof of unusual promise in the literary field. Though in her correction of student themes she crossed swords with her superior, Professor L. A. Sherman, whose methods were peculiar and dogmatic, she impressed the unusual young people who came to her. I have mentioned one, Alvin Johnson, a Danish farmer's son, later highly distinguished as economist, editor, and educator and founder of The New School for Social Research.

After taking her degree in 1895, Willa, seemingly discouraged and tentative as to how to get a start, spent a restless year in her family home in Red Cloud. Like many another young college graduate, she may have found her independence and her great hopes challenged. Parents of large families with many children and small means recognize gifts, but rarely discern that far more inconvenient and aggressive thing, genius. In any case Willa carried with her to Pittsburgh one of the—like it or not—precipitants of genius: a desire to "show" them, a passionate determination to carry out her inner will to do the very best she could as a writer.

The Red Cloud Chief of June 26, 1896, records her departure. She went to Pittsburgh because she had, through friends, obtained the post of editor on *The Home Monthly*, a family magazine of Presbyterian fireside trend, which hoped, with the aid of new blood from Nebraska, to achieve *Ladies' Home Journal* status. Willa is credited by her Pittsburgh commentators as looking eighteen at this time. Was it because she seemed so young and fresh-hearted? Because she had such an exquisite brow and eyes— that brow, those eyes—sometimes grey sometimes blue—that were her rare beauty to her death? According to the birth date, 1873, now accepted as established by a family letter —Virginia records were sketchy—she must have been twenty-two, a more normal age to assume such a responsible stringent career.

The Pittsburgh years formed a decade: the first five of them, especially, were years of education, experiment, apprenticeship, as a writer's twenties should be. The young woman's vitality, her eagerness to extend her horizons, her unsparing industry and level-headedness, in carrying tough responsible jobs, and living low to achieve high thinking, impressed all her associates. It was now that her favorite saying from Michelet: *"Le but n'est rien: le chemin c'est tout,"* was lived in full. The road was all, and the end could be left to take care of itself. George Seibel, a librarian, a contributor to *The Home Monthly* found her more eager to learn from humankind than from books. Some of her earliest poems, short stories and critical reviews were written for her own monthly in her modest, not too cheerful lodgings, and helped her when she resigned from the *Monthly*, to find a more stimulating job on an evening paper, *The Pittsburgh Leader*.

According to a short memoir by John P. Hinz, she was

assistant on the *Leader* to the telegraph editor, Edward P. Course; one of several dramatic and operatic reviewers, under Hezekiah N. Duff; and the best of several contributors to the weekly book-review. In addition she was writing "The Passing Show" (signed Sibert, an abbreviation of her grandmother Boak's maiden name, Seibert), for the Nebraska readers she had left behind. This column appeared first in *The Nebraska State Journal*, then in *The Lincoln Courier*, whose editor had forecast for her a great literary future. It was filled, in part, with personality sketches of singers or musical celebrities, for instance, Ethelbert Nevin, and Harold Bauer, whom she had come to know through her Pittsburgh newspaper job. This connection with Lincoln and the past was evidently of utmost meaning to her, and when she went back to Nebraska in her holidays, to be guest editor of *The Lincoln Courier*, and with the kudos of the home-town girl who is making good, she was indeed joyous, as she reveals in a little free-verse poem of which I quote the third verse:

Going Home
(Burlington Route)

How smoothly the trains run beyond the Missouri;
Even in my sleep I know when I have crossed the river.
The wheels turn as if they were glad to go;
They run like running water,
Like Youth running away . . .
They spin bright along the bright rails,
Singing and humming,
Singing and humming.
They run remembering,
They run rejoicing,
As if they, too, were going home.

While working on the *Leader*, Willa Cather established another editorial connection with an ephemeral magazine, *The Library*, which lasted only six months but gave her a winter in Washington, with opportunities to see Sarah Bernhardt and to enlarge her experience still further. In *The Library*, July 1, 1900, appeared "Peter Sadelack, Father of Anton," a revision of her "Peter" sketch. But the magazine and newspaper experience had been insecure as a means to earning a living, and Willa now decided to make a great change in her life: to take a position as high school teacher of English and Latin—another hard-working job—and to accept the invitation of Isabelle McClung to live in her father, Judge McClung's household, and write seriously on her own account in her spare time, her week-ends and holidays.

To transfer from the quasi-bohemian, hard-driving life of a newspaper woman living in a boarding house on a plebeian street to that of a guest in a distinguished Pittsburgh family was a change with many psychological and spiritual implications. Willa had more natural affinity for *la vie de famille* than for *la vie de bohème:* after her long bout with uncongenial surroundings she enjoyed the protected, delicately nurtured life of the well-to-do. At the McClungs' her personal liberties were respected. Isabelle McClung, the daughter of the house, beautiful, intelligent and identified with the arts herself, rather than with the social round of the rich young lady, had read Willa Cather's work in the newspaper, and had met her in the dressing room of an actress. If not herself an artist, Isabelle, as a patroness of the arts, could help to create one. The relationship was one of joyous companionship, registered best in a little poem which dedicates *The Song of the Lark* to Isabelle McClung.

> On uplands,
> At morning,
> The world was young, the winds were free;
> A garden fair,
> In that blue desert air,
> Its guest invited me to be.

The two young women shared a room with a view. Willa worked a long day at the high school, yet was able to spend her evenings with Isabelle, reading Flaubert and Tolstoy. Week-ends, if school papers were not too numerous, the guest worked in a little study in the attic, transformed from a sewing room; and if a delightful At Home was in process below in the parlor, she need not come down if the divine fire flamed.

Out of this tightly disciplined, organized life of teaching, and writing, came the first, ephemeral magazine stories, like "Eric Hermannson's Soul" and "Jackaboy," which the author quickly outgrew and dismissed. There, too, were written both the ephemeral and the final stories of darker strain in *The Troll Garden*, like "The Sculptor's Funeral" and "A Wagner Matinée." When there were enough poems, Richard G. Badger, at The Gorham Press in Boston, brought out the first edition of *April Twilights* (1903). When a volume of stories was ready *The Troll Garden* was sent, on a venture, to McClure Phillips in New York.

Elizabeth Moorhead, a friend of Miss Cather's Pittsburgh days, says, in a small book of intimate reminiscence of Louise Homer and Willa Cather, *These Too Were Here*, that this manuscript was lying on S. S. McClure's desk, tied up for the post, with a rejection slip inside, when he came back from one of his distracting European trips. McClure immediately reopened the parcel, read the manuscript, and on one of those hunches that were final with him, sent a telegram and made tracks for Pittsburgh.

A passage from the *Autobiography* of Lincoln Steffens, of the earlier group of *McClure's* editors ("the first of the muckrakers"), gives a clue to why and how this could happen:

> Blond, smiling, enthusiastic, unreliable, he [McClure] was the receiver of the ideas of his day. He was a flower that did not wait for the bees to come and take his honey and leave their seeds. He flew forth to find and rob the bees. He was rarely in the office. "I can't sit still," he shouted, "that's your job. I don't see how you can do it." One reason he could not stay in the office was that we checked him. That, too, was my job, the job of all of us to hold down S. S. But his nerves drove him too; his curiosity, his love of being in it, his need to wonder and be wondered about. He followed the news, especially big personal news. If a new author rose on the horizon, or an explorer started for it, or a statesman blew in over it, S. S. went forth to meet him and get him into *McClure's*.

McClure saw Willa Cather rising on his horizon, like a new moon. Finding her at the McClungs' where she was cherished and loved, he promised to publish her book, to print some of the stories in the magazine—he chose "The Sculptor's Funeral" and "Paul's Case," which came out during the year of the book's publication, 1905.

A year later this emotional editor who started as an Irish farm boy translated young to the Midwest, persuaded a prairie girl—who, like himself, had made her own way—to resign from her English teaching position at the high school and join his staff which had recently been seriously depleted. This was a hard decision to make (she used to tell me) because of Willa's now established Pittsburgh roots and affections and, above all, because of her love of teaching the young. But make it she did, with Isabelle's blessing.

Willa Cather's success was immediate in this new rôle and this new climate of a popular magazine, where fresh ideas were challenging the stuffiness of the older monthlies. S. S. McClure needed her capacity, her insight, her loyalty, enthusiasm and her fine literary taste. He was to discover that he had taken on an editor whose ultimate loyalty was given to the service of an art more unbending than Jehovah in its demands. But this he respected in her; if anyone had to bend the knee, he did it. In two years Willa Cather had risen to the managing editor's desk where I found her in 1910.

Part One

—◄{ }►—

*It was as if she had an appointment to meet the
rest of herself, sometime, somewhere. It was moving to meet her and she was moving to meet it.*

The Song of the Lark

—◄{ }►—

—◄ CHAPTER I ►—

Encounter at McClure's

THE PRELIMINARY SKIRMISH between a nascent writer and her first editor is likely to be memorable to the novice. Young people are sometimes luckier than they know. Perhaps I did instinctively divine, on that January day in 1910 when I timorously presented my article on sweated tenement workers to the Managing Editor of *McClure's Magazine*, that Willa Sibert Cather was a matchless being—unique in her kind, in her age. I have never in truth met anyone at all like her.

In the restless, reforming times that engulfed us after my graduation from Bryn Mawr College, *McClure's* was esteemed, especially by social workers, the best of the popular "uplift" magazines. S. S. McClure, astute, naïve almost to credulity, whether you regarded him as a genius or as a genii, was an animating spirit: he invented the popular, fifteen-cent magazine, and his nose for the significant in news and personality set his magazine apart from its ready imitators, like *Everybody's* for instance.

Even so, the winter wind whistled an invidious word in my ears as I made my way along East Twenty-third Street from Madison Square. "Muckraker" it was, a name—I knew—plucked out of *Pilgrim's Progress* by President Theodore Roosevelt in the days when Lincoln Steffens, of the *McClure's* staff, was writing on *The Shame of Cities.* I was bringing in "muck" myself, the fruit of a long social study but—I didn't want to be a *muckraker!* The Bostonian in me, nourished on *The Atlantic Monthly, Harper's, The Century,* shivered at the very thought.

So I rushed blindly around and around the block, murmuring to myself three lilting names: *Willa Sibert Cather.* They had a sort of ballad ring and Pauline Goldmark, a social worker *sans peur et sans reproche,* who sponsored my facts, had given me a letter of introduction to her. But my wide beaver hat had blown off, my manila envelope had slithered from under my arm into the slush, before I made up my mind to enter the featureless door of *McClure's.*

Magazines did not pamper their contributors in 1910. No soft lights or stuffed armchair received me. I was led to a golden-oak bench on the edge of what seemed—and indeed was—a big noisy business office. Divested of my talisman, the letter of introduction, I sat there nude and minute. The aspirant's bench was like a sand spit on an alien ocean full of strange creatures.

Harried people, mostly female, were fluttering typescripts, dodging in and out of editorial sanctuaries. Above them, penetrating my spinal cord like the rumor of hornets on the war-path, hung a sharp, angry, clicking sound: the emanation of madly typing secretaries. Or was it the emanation of an editorial point of view?

Here, right here, I said to myself excitedly, was Mary Baker G. Eddy divested of her halo. Here was that great

American business god, John D. Rockefeller, the doler out
of dimes, the creator of Standard Oil, knocked from his
pedestal by quiet Ida Tarbell. I had met Miss Tarbell at
Professor William James's in Cambridge. As she had for-
merly been an editor of *McClure's* I, in my innocence,
fancied that Willa Sibert Cather must resemble her.

So I looked hard for someone tall, grave, imposing,
middle-aged, authoritative, dignified, spinsterish, dressed in
the long, dark, plain, "tailor-suit," the stiff starched shirt-
waist, as we then called them, and the mannish necktie of
the strong-minded woman with a job.

The only woman I could spy, however, coming in my
direction was youngish, buoyant, not tall, rather square.
No trace of the reforming feminist in this vital being who
smiled at me, her face, open, direct, honest, blooming with
warmth and kindness. Her eyes were sailor-blue, her
cheeks were rosy, her hair was red-brown, parted in the
middle like a child's. As she shook hands, I felt the freshness and brusqueness, too, of an ocean breeze. Her boyish,
enthusiastic manner was disarming, and as she led me
through the jostle of the outer office, I was affected by the
resonance of her Western voice, and by the informality of
her clothes—it was as if she rebelled against urban con-
formities.

Her blouse was bright with stripes, her Irish tweed skirt
was chromatic. Though the fashion was for long skirts,
hers cut her sturdy legs in half. And then those halting,
admiring words about Pauline Goldmark. Miss Cather
had recognized her as a dedicated person, authoritative as
Jane Addams in the social movement, yet also charming as
a wood nymph. Her raven hair, her camellia skin, her

Viennese-Bohemian beauty, her vivid mind—Miss Cather re-created my old friend in a few ardent words. Their accidental shipboard meeting in April, 1908, and their dinner in a Neapolitan fish restaurant under the glow of Vesuvius were described like a bit out of a story.

But now, all at once, we were in Miss Cather's private editorial office. The door closed behind us with a click bringing me face to face with—an adversary? In the sudden hush and aloneness, like animals in a wood, we stared, making the secret circle around one another. Was it the circle of acceptance? A lively sense of clash and curiosity rose between us, like smoke from a new fire.

Miss Cather now motioned me to a chair, and her gesture was philosophic and noncommittal. The ballad lady was gone, like a wraith, and what remained was a powerful, almost masculine personality, who had taken many tyros through a first interview. This Miss Cather filled the whole space between door and window to brimming, as a man might do.

Watching her with beginner's tremor I felt the impact of something beneath her editorial mask: crude oil, red earth, elemental strength and resoluteness. Her sheer energy was alarming to a shy New Englander, full of self-doubts. I happened to know that she came from Red Cloud, Nebraska, named for an Indian chief. Nebraska had been mere geography to me till I met this tense dynamic person, with her homespun brilliance. Now I wanted to know where she ended and Nebraska began.

Huddled into the depths of my Paris cloak, I watched her eyes narrow to sharpness, as they swam over my paragraphs with hummingbird speed; her square-tipped fingers flipping the pages of "my" manuscript—now hers. My chances seemed to vanish into thin air.

I was counting to a hundred by tens when a voice from the empyrean remarked:

"The tone of your article is good, Miss Sergeant."

She was smiling at me again. Her mouth had such generous sweetness. She explained that she meant my "tone" was objective—and this was important when facts were grim. It was not only what one did but how one did it that mattered to *McClure's*. Her Chief, she remarked, was the first, the very first editor to insist on and pay for solid research. He had made a new tradition by starting with the premise that many of those who wrote well were hazy about facts, and many of those who "knew" unable to express themselves clearly.

With this comment, Miss Cather again turned to the manuscript, and I began anxiously to ask myself—is this exasperation she is feeling? Is it dismay? Is it the bald disclosures of misery that make her push back her straggling lock of hair and stare out of the window? Her chin is so dogged . . . she is bored.

"Tell me," Miss Cather suddenly exploded, "why you joined the reforming pamphleteers? This all has its place—it's good—but aren't short stories more in your line? I don't mean tenement stories—you look like a Jamesian—am I right?"

Tears rushed into my eyes, and Miss Cather looked sorry for me. I had tried so hard, climbed so many tenement stairs, and had spent so many tense hours pounding my typewriter. A Bryn Mawrter raised by President M. Carey Thomas must try to right these terrible social wrongs

that blistered and festered under the shiny urban surface
of Manhattan Island. Didn't Miss Cather care for reform
except as part of her job?

"What happens," I demanded—rhetorically I am sure—
"when two million peasants from Southern Italy and Sicily
get dumped on the Bowery and settled in vile, dark tenements below Washington Square? Why didn't they go on
West, like the earlier streams of immigrants?"

Miss Cather gave an involuntary start, and looked at me
almost suspiciously. But she still sat there mute as a statue
and I found myself—as if determined to break through her
defences—speaking in the same harsh emotional tone with
which I sometimes addressed the guarded remoteness of my
conservative father on the unwelcome topic of the rights
of the worker. Though the "Welfare State" was barely
stirring at this time, my own college-educated generation
was all sails set for social change and very self-righteous
about it, too.

So I spluttered: "Just those same women that you and
Pauline admired sitting in the sun, by the fountains in
Naples, brushing their long black hair, and bending over
their lace-pillows—*they are here, in New York!* Using their
exquisite, inherited gifts for handicraft to 'finish' crude
coats and suits for the garment trade. To make artificial
flowers for the ten-cent stores. To embroider fine shirtwaists for the department stores. Fifty cents a day—that's
what a whole family gets for a twelve-hour day! Grandmothers, mothers—school-age children, playing truant!"

My editor turned to look at me squarely—she seemed
hurt or angry, and I drew a sigh of relief: she *did* sympathize with the underdog, then?

"I know those Italians," she answered quietly.

"Have you really *seen* the sick babies thrashing about in the artificial cornflowers on the beds? *Smelled* the nauseous stench on the stairs of those flats? A mixture of out-door-privy smell and Chinese pigtail smell—they cook them right there. . . ."

"*Cook* them?" Miss Cather ejaculated.

"Pigtails cut from Chinese criminals, to be made into rats for the Gibson girl to wear under her pompadour," I glibly answered. "I, too, used to wear a rat—but now . . . !"

"Chinese *criminals?*"

"So the workers say. The women who make the flowers and roll the cigarettes do not know a word of English—but they understand my bad Italian."

Miss Cather brooded and rather gruffly replied that she knew the Italian children, because they splashed in the fountain in Washington Square of a summer evening when she often sat on a bench with a book. She lived in Washington Place, right up against the Italian Quarter I was talking about, and she loved the big brown eyes, dark smooth skins and Latin voices of the youngsters.

She finished with an aggrieved sound as if I'd spoiled her fun and good humor by forcing her to look into those obscene tenements that crowded up to the Hotel Judson.

Then she turned back my pages, absently slipped the manuscript into its envelope. Refused? Accepted?

She laid it down again, said she would read it thoroughly at home.

Was she ready to dismiss me? Apparently not, so I just sat quietly watching her profile, rather wistful against the twilight. On an impulse I began to tell her about my trip

to Greece with Pauline, in May, 1908, just after her meeting with my friend, and how we met Anatole France with
a gay little white-haired old lady in the Athens Museum.

"Madame de Caillavet?" she asked, all curiosity.

I did not know. But I described how Monsieur France
looked, holding the treasure of Mycenae—one of the im-
memorial gold goblets with the bulls—in hands that clutched
greedily . . . tenacious . . . fastidious. . . . His eyes pene-
trated right through us—American tourists. What were we
doing in the *Royaume* of Greece?

Tourists we were . . . we had just come from Mycenae, a
red-gold ruin, standing above fields where peasants were
harvesting wheat—golden wheat that was blowing and rip-
pling in the hot wind.

Willa Cather looked as if gilded herself by that burning
Mycenae sunshine. She had been brought up in wheat
and cornfields. When she first saw a great French wheatfield she had cried with nostalgia.

She was silent a few moments, decided something and
began to tell me her own editorial aspirations for *McClure's*.
Her Chief backed her in an effort she was making to increase the literary and cultural range of the magazine. It
had always had good fiction. Perhaps I didn't know Mc-
Clure had, through the fiction syndicate that preceded the
magazine, enrolled from the start writers like Robert Louis
Stevenson, Thomas Hardy, Sarah Orne Jewett, O. Henry,
Kipling, even Henry James? Gifted writers valued him
because, she said with feeling, he recognized the sacred
flame, was ready to be burned by it.

Then she spoke of the moment in 1906 when he called
her to *McClure's* from Pittsburgh. Practically his whole

staff—Lincoln Steffens, Ray Stannard Baker, his partner Phillips, worst of all, perhaps, Ida Tarbell, his devoted friend whom he had discovered at the Sorbonne studying the methods of the French historians—had walked out on him because of his erratic ways. Willa Cather said she herself greatly admired Miss Tarbell—but it was clear that she regarded the "walk-out" as disloyal to McClure.

"You must meet the Chief," she said, rising abruptly to lead me into the big office where she tapped on a door.

Inside it, a high-strung, sad-looking, middle-aged man snapped out of a chair, smoothing a sandy moustache. His eyes were tired and mystical, went up into points like a wise, observant setter's. He had on his feet the white sneakers people laughed at. On his desk was a milk bottle: that too was derided in 1910—before stomach ulcers became part of the editorial tradition.

"Miss Sergeant has brought in something up our alley on the sweated workers in the tenements—maybe a 'First.' We must find her some more assignments," Miss Cather said cheerfully.

Thus I learned that my piece was accepted. S. S. gave me a swift, narrow, blinky stare—then looked at the warm, hearty young editor who had brought me in. If she liked my piece so would many others, he figured aloud, his worn face, half bored, half asleep coming sharply alive.

Clearly the two of them were partners in an alliance that had tang and motion. Their Midwest voices harmonized, their seething inner forces supplemented each other. There was an inspirational quality about the dynamic unspoiled assistant that kept the older editor afloat on his sea of discovery—the only sea he was interested in navigating. This

I imagined in a flash, and it made me happy that my first editor—who to my New England eyes was on the forceful side—could second such a man without his feeling diminished by her powers. She was not a wily female, a diplomat, she was one to stand to her colors like a trooper, and fight her battles in the open.

"He reveres genius," said Willa Cather in an intimate, admiring tone, as she led me toward the elevator. "He's lost more money on Joseph Conrad than any editor alive!"

Now I knew how she felt. There was journalism and there was art. The first could be respected, if it were honest. But the second—that was what one really cared about.

"There are only three or four people in the whole world with whom I can talk about books," Willa Cather said to me with a confiding look and that hesitation in her voice which I already associated with emotion.

Did this potentate really care what a shy Boston girl thought about books? Quicksilver filled my veins.

Flaubert, Balzac, Tolstoy, Henry James, Edith Wharton, Sarah Orne Jewett—we were deep in them in two seconds, so deep that when the elevator stopped Miss Cather motioned it imperiously on its way. She must know, especially, how I felt about Sarah Orne Jewett—in her opinion outstanding as a writer of New England stories. The best woman writer our country had produced. Dead only last year—from the way she spoke I divined that a rare literary influence, a deep personal friend, someone who cared for Willa Sibert Cather, someone who kept "Letters" alive, had been lost from her life.

When I said I'd given *The Country of the Pointed Firs*

to a French critical writer and he had compared it to
Turgenev's *A Sportsman's Sketches*, her eyes sparkled.
She must tell that to Mrs. James T. Fields. . . . Did I know
Miss Jewett's friend, this exquisite survivor of the Golden
Age of American Literature?

I shook my head, and she said thoughtfully, "Too bad.
. . . That long upstairs parlor on Charles Street in Boston—
those reflections, gleams, relics of the Past. . . . Think, Miss
Sergeant," she laughed, "what it is to know someone who
invited to her table Emerson, Holmes, Hawthorne, Howells,
James Russell Lowell—and who remembers and quotes what
they said there!"

I looked at her in amazement. It seemed very Western
of her to be such a hero-worshipper. New Englanders in
their twenties, like me, did not bow to the ancient and
honorable idols. They preferred Amy Lowell to James
Russell. I was about to say, "Come now, this is 1910!" But
Miss Cather persisted, quite gravely, that she was always
fearful of letting the flimsiness of the present age trouble
Mrs. Fields' protected literary Elysium! Mrs. Fields insisted on reading *McClure's*, and would ask, quite seriously,
whether Rex Beach belonged to "Literature."

My editor laughed ironically and said that Rex Beach
was one of her pet abominations. Yet publish him she must.

Then as the elevator insisted on coming to a full stop,
she gave me a little push, a sort of pat, and cried efferves-
cently, as the door slammed:

"To our next meeting!"

It was as if I had had a cup of champagne. The cold
snowy city, where my timid feet had stuck but an hour
ago, now bore me along a current of dreams. The shops

glittered, the "man in the street" who prodded my elbow would soon be reading my first attempt at being a writer—he smiled at me, as if my face were a bright leaf in the populous five o'clock stream. *McClure's* was a good magazine, a real friend to young people.

All at once, however, these personal considerations seemed to fade. High up, well above the crowd and the buildings, I saw Saint-Gaudens' Artemis, dancing out of the shining blue of the evening. Here was the symbol of that further reach, that transcendent thing which the passionate Westerner—unafraid to confess her literary faith to a fledgling—had pointed up for me as the true heritage of the writer.

Was Miss Cather a writer herself? I did not know. That was the mystery I was left with. My young heart was hungry to discover—to keep up with her, to follow her, to tag along and find out where she was going.

Not many days later, Miss Cather called me back to her office to tell me that my article was formally accepted. They would pay for it one hundred and fifty dollars. Would I consent to cuts? She said rather casually that all good writers did consent—they knew there were plenty more words where those came from.

I said yes, but what about *facts?* Facts take up room. Certainly, but I did not need to tell about every trade there was in those tenements. . . . I was to go back with a *McClure's* photographer.

"Don't lose your sense of fun," she urged me. If she seemed impatient with reform it was because so many ministering angels, so many fanatics with blood in their eye, came to her desk.

She confessed that my piece did make her low in her mind. In her Nebraska country Europeans from Northern or Central Europe were surely hard-driven. Most of them were handworkers to start with. And some failed and came to grief from drought or mortgages. But they were at ease in space and time, many labored, many prospered, and the corn and wheat sprang up and the girls grew along with the grain in the furrows.

But Italian peasants in New York—what a harsh fate— what an incredible anomaly.

Artists, lonely individuals finding themselves and their art, keep their typewriters and their fiddles on the bed and their suitcases under it. . . . That's all right. . . .

"I keep my own suitcases under the bed," she remarked with a quick affectionate smile—"Don't like it—would rather be a lucky Bostonian like you, living in a house, or going to Paris where the good hats come from."

She threw a pleased look at my *outré* sailor, resting like a shiny platter on top of a head that she would seemingly prefer to think giddy, rather than humane.

The July issue of *McClure's*, with "Toilers of the Tenements" surprisingly in the lead, and candid photographs in halftone of the family "home-worker" groups staring from the page, reached me in Paris, at an old bourgeois mansion above the silver windings of the Seine, where I was living *en pension* with French friends. A jolly letter from Miss Cather congratulated me on having my first article attacked in an editorial in *The New York Evening Post!* Defenders of my facts had arisen and now *McClure's* officially proposed an assignment in Germany.

Already deep, not in a magazine job but in a bit of comparative research on the Parisian artificial flower-maker, requested by the Russell Sage Foundation, I begged her to understand my dilemma: I was not at home in the German language, as in the French. It had been natural to fare forth under the white, scented cones of the horse-chestnuts, with a chic, disdainful Parisienne factory inspectress, who had led me into small well-ordered factories. Here the Parisienne, working as an artist, fresh roses and violets before her on the table, twisted velvet and silk into delicious replicas of nature's originals. Every flower made in this way was a *chef d'oeuvre* which *la haute mode* awaited and sold to *la femme élégante*. There was no market in Paris for crude lilacs and shoddy daisies like those thrown together in New York City.

Then I described Monsieur Arthur Fontaine, the very antithesis of the cigar-smoking Tammany boss who collaborated with the exploiters of Sullivan Street. Cultivated, knowledgeable, authoritative, this Permanent Secretary of the Ministère du Travail—which, with its polished corridors, its lackeys in green uniforms, suggested an embassy—had an impressive relation to the French worker.

Examining *McClure's* on a Louis Quinze table, Monsieur Fontaine, who had never heard of a "social" worker—strange term—expressed cautious surprise that the New York City home-worker should have no law to defend her. Only a new-fangled "magazine" and a few high-minded ladies "like you, mademoiselle?"

"Do not these poor women of Latin blood," he inquired,

commiserating their meek, beautiful, acceptant faces, "resent the unjust treatment they are getting from the *États–Unis*–from the State?"

How could I explain to Fontaine the velocity with which the industrial future unrolled *chez nous*–too fast for the laws to keep up with it?

Willa Cather, regulating the affairs of her periodical, struggling with inferior compositions in a city where, as she put it, most of the buildings I had left behind were being torn down, while all sewers and pavements were being dug up, wished me well in the tranquillity of an old, ordered, comprehensible civilization. She envied me, and with passion, Paris in the springtime.

No matter where I went or what I did, that rewarding French summer, I felt inwardly accompanied and spurred by a superior intelligence and a warm human heart, that were precipitants of nascent work and ideas. Willa was then thirty-seven, had been a journalist at intervals for a good half of her life. Though but eight years younger, I had been slow to turn life into copy. This was my third or fourth stay in France but my first with real jobs to do.

Willa had said to me before I left: "I'm so glad you are not the Thomas Bailey Aldrich kind of Bostonian–the kind who takes his own bed sheets to Europe and even his own drinking water!" That I was always being drawn into French life as lived by the native–whether the life of the poet or of the *fleuriste* and the *lingère*, who were also poets and artists in their fashion–was what she liked about me.

The price of a deep immersion in a foreign culture is the shock of return, but this was mediated for me by the sight of Willa Cather herself, with her blithe, made-in-Nebraska look, her lisle stockings, low-heeled oxfords, and easy sport coat, waiting for me, the day after I landed, by the fountain in Washington Square.

Neither then, nor later when everyone had them, did Willa have a car. But the topside trip on a Fifth Avenue bus from the Square to Central Park, where she followed the seasons as faithfully as the writers of today do in Connecticut—where she wrote many a letter on a bench—was for years an almost daily ritual and sensuous release.

Many such pleasure trips to Central Park did I share, but none with quite the flavor of the first one on that October day when, under white cottony clouds, blown across a blue sky by a lusty wind from the harbor—bus tops were open, then—we plunged into a whirl of talk. Willa loved weather, she esteemed me for having the patina of Europe, as she called it, still clinging to me. I admired her for her vigor, her authenticity, her delight in the landmarks we passed; and her frank disclosure of what was pertinent to her in this multifarious universe of New York City. There was so much she did not want to see and saw not. What she did see she had selected instinctively and made so her own that her impulsive sharing of it gave it a sort of halo of brightness.

Willa Cather's Fifth Avenue, as I look back to it, suspended in the perspectives and vistas of a comfortable world not yet at war, half way between the Age of Innocence and the Age of the Skyscraper, free of traffic jams, had at the lower end a goodly number, still, of fine old brick houses, with white trimmings, which stirred her sense of the Past. One couldn't pass such houses without thinking of Edith Wharton's Lily Bart—and Henry James's Catherine Sloper.

Then as the bus lumbered along the edge of Madison Square, still summer green, Admiral Farragut, on his pedestal—which then faced directly on Fifth Avenue—stared us right out of countenance in our high seats. Miss Cather burst into praise of our great American sculptor who had brought the French tradition to our squares. With Farragut below and Diana above in the blue, Madison Square affirmed its charm. She had been happy to publish Saint-Gaudens' *Familiar Letters* in *McClure's*. When she pulled off something like that, or like getting Ellen Terry's stage memories, she felt the job was worth all it cost her.

Now we were passing Brentano's with its tempting yellow-backs, and soon we were at Thirty-fourth Street, staring at the shabby splendor of the old Waldorf Hotel, which again made Willa Cather eager and enchanted. Had I ever been there, after the Opera, to watch the copper kings from Denver pouring their admiration and their jewels on the opulent knees of the stars? That was the place to go and eat oysters at midnight.

Did I, too, often see *Tristan* and *Traviata?* Not too well brought up on the Boston Symphony? I *did* think opera inferior to symphonic music, and was soon in full retreat, for her connection with *cantatrices*, rôles, scores was on the professional level. Her critical but burning enthusiasm for the voice and for the personality behind the voice, which she was later to register in *The Song of the Lark*, startled me. I had not known, till now, of those years from her teens to her thirties, when she so ardently studied the arts of the theatre and the opera and wrote musical critiques for

Lincoln and Pittsburgh newspapers. It had been a regret to
her that she had not been born into an inheritance of musical scholarship and linguistic gifts like the Viennese. There
were gaps, she said ironically, that youthful temerity and
native flair and assiduity could never fill. But at least she
could now go to the Metropolitan twice a week with no
thought but personal enjoyment; if she did this, the world
went right for her.

But now we had reached the Fifties, and I was again surprised by her delight in the false French château architec-
ture of the Smart Set; her comment on the Astors and
Vanderbilts with their French art collections and their
boxes in the Diamond Horseshoe. Since she was so really
simple herself I was unprepared to find her so respectful
of wealth and swagger—it was as if she turned to the drama
and the panoply of capitalism in spite of, or because of, her
daily association with reformers and muckrakers; who were,
after all, so grey and so boringly narrow.

When I asked her naïvely whether it wasn't better to
have written a good book or sung a fine rôle or painted a
fine canvas, than to have played the aesthetic or acquisitive
part of amateur or collector, she was wholly with me.
Novelists, opera singers, even doctors, she affirmed, have in
common the unique and marvelous experience of entering
into the very skin of another human being. What can
compare with it? she said, her eyes shining.

By now we were at Ninetieth Street and the reds and
russets of autumn leaves fairly blared over the walls of Central Park. She was down the bus steps in a second, laughing
and in clarion mood. She brimmed with physical life. You
could see that she was country-bred. Rapid motion was

essential to her. She had almost, she said bluntly, to dissolve into nature daily in order to be reborn to a task.

We took the path to the Reservoir, her favorite walk, and the red and gold of the trees, the vibrant air made us dash swiftly along the curving path that encircled the blue body of water held high in its stone embankments. I see her still, her wide-brimmed felt hat tilted over one eye, her red scarf streaming, and hear the cogent comments on French authors that flew over her shoulder:

Did I admire Mérimée—that caustic, that arrogant Frenchman from whose economical prose not one line could be cut? Of course—we agree about books! Did I value, as she did, that view of phantom towers to the south —the view that made New York unique, that made her endure living in the heart of urbanity?

But as we gazed I learned that, after a few months in the city, she got wildly homesick for the West. She would dash out to see her "family"—"my mother and father especially," and the wheat harvest, and then flee back to Pittsburgh to Isabelle McClung—for fear of dying in a cornfield.

Die in a cornfield? I was puzzled.

You could not understand. You have not seen those miles of fields. There is no place to hide in Nebraska. You can't hide under a windmill. She retreated obliquely.

But we had got into the subject of ties, human bondage. No region and no person one loved could really be left behind. She remarked with a certain curiosity that, like herself, I apparently accumulated people and places.

One was *captive*—that was all there was to it. We are what we love—that is all we are, she pleaded.

For her, London, London of all cities, and for me *Paris*,

Paris! For her, Pittsburgh, where ten years, almost, of journalism and high-school teaching had broken the ice of the East for her. One's twenties are an epoch; and a friend like Isabelle McClung—her voice rang sonorously as she said I must know Isabelle—tall, handsome, formally bred, yet so at home in the arts—such a lover of beautiful things and so terrified of do-gooders, she laughed, with a dig at this continued involvement of mine with "home-workers" and the contests between exploiters and social workers that raged around them.

"I understand your Chief S.S.—who is *not* scared of re-formers—" I got back at her, "considers the Bible 'the greatest piece of journalism ever written! Take the head-lines alone,' he said to a friend of mine. 'In six days God made Heaven and Earth!' "

Miss Cather seemed annoyed. It was unfortunate that in a magazine, cheap writing, patterns of popular success, forced even an honest editor to keep looking through dross for gold. Nobody in the publishing world could let an artist *be* an artist—some other motive seeped in.

With this she hailed a hansom cab; and we both felt so deliciously Londonish, as the horse whacked along to a favorite restaurant of hers—I remember it as Delmonico's—that she was soon telling me about an evening in a box at the new Irish players in London with William Butler Yeats and Lady Gregory. I could see how much at home she felt in such brilliant company, I could divine how these great literary figures enjoyed the fine, free discriminations of a cultivated American mind; which intrigued them the more because expressing itself in a very un-English accent.

A Bostonian was no treat to a Londoner, but a Nebraskan had the right "American" tang.

The elderly headwaiter at Delmonico's had his own ideas about my companion. While he divested her of her loose coat, at a table heavily draped in damask, with napkins big as door-mats, under the crystal chandeliers, where the discreet silence of the pre-jazz age reigned supreme, I imagined I heard a whistle of surprise. He had revealed, and dramatically, a very ornate, luxurious, conspicuous red-embroidered frock. Flirting his napkin, he bowed low, as for Emma Eames or Mary Garden.

Willa Cather took this gesture offishly, not with the smooth complacence of the prima donna. Bring tea that is hot, HOT, HOT, she ordered the table waiter. *Brioche, petits fours,* a *Napoléon,* two *babas au rhum.* And—with a prick of her porcupine quills that set him scuttling off— the *best* China tea, strong and delicate.

"You're not superior to the sense of taste, are you?" Willa Cather inquired gaily. Sharing a good meal with her remained from this day forth one of life's serious pleasures. Conversation must never divert one from the quality of the food on the plate and the wine in the glass.

Watching her tasting her China tea fastidiously in that Liberty gown it came to me that she was dressing the woman she felt inside, the woman one had already sensed was not to be obscure? But *who was she? Who would she be?*

Before I had gone to France in the spring, I had looked up old files of *McClure's* in the Boston Public Library, and discovered four short stories, written rather under the influence of James and Edith Wharton. I wanted to talk about them—she brushed them off as just magazine stuff. But how could I get hold of *The Troll Garden*, her first book of stories, and her book of verse, *April Twilights*?

With a grimace she said: "Out of print—all stray copies bought up and buried. I don't want you ever to see either book.

"I dragged you to Delmonico's to talk about Paris," she complained. "Take mercy on me. Tell me about that high-up walk you had under the gargoyles on the roof of Notre-Dame with the *vers libre* poet with the red beard. What made him give up regular metres?"

When I drew breath she looked at me reflectively and suddenly said: "You were dead right not to go to Germany —all this is for *Scribner's, The Century* or some other literary magazine. Do let me persuade you to be what you are and recount the France you know from the French standpoint. I'll help you all I can—read your manuscripts and advise you! Send the working girls to the *Atlantic Monthly!* Not to *McClure's*."

A long communicative silence set in. It seemed the fruit of a happy, rich afternoon. At last, tying her red scarf, sighing, she said there was something she wanted to say. And she looked away into that aloof world of her own I'd seen her search for in my *McClure's* interview.

I hung on her hesitancy. Now would I know? . . .

She was planning to give up her editorial job as soon as she could manage it.

Half smiling, she gave me a long look and I exclaimed: "You will write stories—novels?"

She assented.

One's powers do not last forever. One cannot eat one's cake and have it too. As the French and British writers know, money and success are unrelated to art. "But one must have simple tastes—to give up a good salary," she blurted out, and made for the restaurant door.

I followed, awed and lonely. But as we left she took my arm and said:

"Now it will always be easier to catch step."

She was on her way, swimming gallantly in full midstream. But her eyes besought me to jump into the river too, to come along, to be patient with her, to understand her complexities and her goal, without words.

CHAPTER II

Meetings Near Boston

To BECOME A PART of something entire, to possess psychic wholeness, is a lonely and usually unsatisfied need of Americans, especially the creative artists among them. Willa Cather suffered a truly gruelling inner pull between the opposites of East and West. Her restless doubling back and forth across our vast continent may have given her mental energy but did not assure integration and tranquillity until she turned the Nebraska of her childhood into a world of the imagination that she could share with her readers. Then she began to seem and be all of a piece. Sarah Orne Jewett and the New England literary tradition had something to do with it.

Sarah Orne Jewett and Willa Sibert Cather had met, oddly enough, as she told me, through Willa Cather's first assignment on *McClure's* as a staff member in 1906. Startling material relating to a leading religious leader and romantic personality of that time—Mary Baker G. Eddy—had been brought into *McClure's* by one Georgine Milmine. S. S. McClure was always interested in biography, from the hour that he discovered Ida Tarbell and she produced a life of Napoleon and one of Lincoln which immediately increased the circulation of *McClure's;* and he was always interested in novelty. Thus he saw in Mrs. Eddy a "natural" for *McClure's,* for her personal origins and idiosyncrasies, her marital history, the psychological and factual background of her ideas and her "message" in *Science and Health* had not then been publicized.

The material was touchy, and would attract a world of readers both of the faithful and the doubters. It must, however, be carefully verified, and Willa Sibert Cather, with four other members of *McClure's* staff, was chosen for this job. Since Mrs. Eddy was born and grew up on an ordinary New Hampshire farm, studied mental healing in Portland, Maine, and eventually erected her temple in Boston, the material for research lay in New England. Thither Miss Cather went, not very willingly.

The job seemed to her a little *infra dig,* not on the level where she cared to move. But she inspired confidence, had the mind of a judge and the nose of a detective when she needed it. Her path led her over many New England trails; to farms, fields and villages more bare of good material life than those she knew in Nebraska but with the old Puritan values, the old Anglo-Saxon pioneer legend still written large on the poetic land. She had found more than she went to get.

She was quickly fascinated by the psychological implications of her material, and made long stays in Boston to edit it. But the book that ensued was largely written in the *McClure's* office, and was a composite, not Willa Cather's personal work. It bears little mark of her own style, but it "stood up" as a dramatic and frank controversial biography, chiefly remarkable for the unique story it tells. With its serial publication *McClure's* announced that it was "as close to truth as history ever gets." The book that followed the magazine serial disappeared almost immediately from circulation—the Christian Scientists are said to have bought the copies. It is hard to find one nowadays, even in a big library, and the reader is likely to have to borrow the only copy from the chief librarian's safe, and be watched by a detective while reading it.

By this piquant route our most sober woman novelist gained her connections in Boston. There, under Beacon Hill, while doing her editing, the miracles that befall the greatly talented in their thirties, when life is moving along swiftly and imperiously, began to happen to her.

On Park Street, below the State House dome, Miss Cather caught the interest and confidence of a brilliant young literary editor, with classical tastes like her own. Ferris Greenslet had his hunches, like S. S. McClure, and the "fresh-faced, broad-browed, plain-speaking young woman, standing her ground with a singular solidity" took his fancy. Her approach to the high-keyed Eddy material seemed to him so sane and so subtle that he was soon wooing her for his publishing house, Houghton Mifflin.

On Charles Street under Beacon Hill, with its old brick houses and purple window panes, Willa was introduced by Mrs. Louis D. Brandeis—the sister of my friend and hers, Pauline Goldmark—to Mrs. James T. Fields and Miss Jewett. These elder great ladies seemed to have been just waiting in the long parlor on the Charles River for the vibrant author of *The Troll Garden;* for the editor who, in Miss

Jewett's phrase, "had important work to do." Her "low-down" on the odd Christian Science Temple that had burgeoned on Huntington Avenue—a socially ineligible region remote from the Hill and the Back Bay where the Boston Brahmins dwelt—enchanted them, and made them gay.

Miss Jewett belonged to the Brahmins by close association, but she was tied to her State of Maine roots, and had, for all her *Atlantic Monthly* connections, contributed stories to *McClure's* and even to the fiction syndicate S.S. had founded before he started the magazine. This gave the graceful authoress, with her high-piled brown hair and brown eyes, and her tinge of the fastidious and disdainful aristocrat, a special interest in this staunch young Western editor, with her effervescent enthusiasm, her sheer ability, and her rare grey-blue glance.

Mrs. Fields was all eagerness to adorn her young friend with sophistication. But Miss Jewett thirsted to revive in her a positive love of her own region, Nebraska. "The Sculptor's Funeral" was a powerful story but grim, bitter, vitriolic about the paucity and narrowness of the Midwest environment. E. W. Howe, the prairie philosopher, as he was called, the author of *The Story of a Country Town* had set that "Western" tone, in Willa's youth so Van Wyck Brooks reminds us. But in New England she met tradition —in Matthew Arnold's well-known phrase, the best that was known and thought in the world. The nature of the young editor was still malleable: half glimpsed, like some mysterious creature of the seas in a rock-pool, now expanding, now contracting, now clasping some treasure in its tentacles, now spewing it out, it had remarkable potentialities which Miss Jewett could help formulate. Already well-read in Flaubert: how many friends of Sarah Jewett understood, as did Willa Cather, the full import of those two sentences from the master pinned above the secretary in the great upper hall in South Berwick:

Écrire la vie ordinaire comme on écrit l'histoire. C'est ne pas de faire vivre, ni de faire pleurer, ni de vous mettre à fureur, mais d'agir à la façon de la nature, c'est à dire de faire rêver.

Rambles with her friend and mentor over gentle Maine hillsides where Dickens had never trod, drives back and forth from the Dover station, further drives to some Dunnet's Landing or other with one whose wit and dignity of character and gentle ways broke down fiercely careful barriers. The two ladies, Miss Mary and Miss Sarah Jewett, lived in the house that had come down to them from a grandfather, retired sea-captain and shipbuilder, who had bought it from the original owner. Willa loved the summer coolness, the sweet breath of the garden flowers in the shuttered lower hall where there were carved cornices, and wainscotting and panelling that were older than the American Revolution. The elegant worldly symmetry of the square formal rooms and bedchambers—there was even a "Breakfast Room" as in England—the "flock" wallpapers, the patina of the Chippendale and Hepplewhite, the old portraits and prints . . . the perfect service, in a Maine village, of two maids and a man.

Perhaps Miss Jewett wanted a literary heir: she described herself to a Boston friend in a flash of wit:

"I do not belong in this body. I come up only to my own shoulder."

Did she sense that though Willa Cather had so far not reached beyond her own waist, was squarish, middle-sized and Western, she would in her novels overtop her adviser in range and scope, if not in perfection of form and sympathy?

The creed Sarah Orne Jewett passed on, the harmony, simplicity and understatement of a mature prose style, was beginning to work like yeast in Willa's creative mind at just the period that I am recalling, 1911.

It was understood that when Willa could get away from her job she would run over to Boston to see Mrs. Fields whose sweet companion, almost daughter, had died in 1909. Miss Mary Jewett, left alone, claimed Willa too, and Mrs. Margaret Deland and lovely Miss Laura Hills, the delicate miniaturist—one of the two enchanting "Hills sisters" from Newburyport.

In the spring of 1911 I, also, was expecting Willa Cather as I worked on my French sketches in my little round study looking out on the Fenway in Brookline. When my younger sister's scales became too resonant, I would duck down into the laundry in the cellar where I had set up a table. The laundry had an outside door. I stole out to look for hawthorn buds and to search the sky for my friend, who would soon be here, like an early robin with red breast and swift wing.

It was indeed still windy March, when Willa summoned me to meet her on the Gloucester train. Days rather than hours shone ahead. Overjoyed by the prospect, I swung my suitcase through the dingy cars, and found her in one of the green velvet seats, looking morose. She had come from a

little visit to South Berwick. The old house had stirred
something up—she felt goaded. It was as if Miss Jewett's
spirit, which filled the place, had warned her that time was
flying. Miss Jewett's true powers as a writer of fiction
grew in part out of her leisurely life. Willa herself had no
leisure, none! She slouched her hat farther over her eyes,
and sat there like a stone.

Fog was blotting the outlines of sea and shore as we got
off the train. She lunged into it as into a narcotic—her dis-
consolate aura improving its tone with every stride. Gloucester, still devoted to fishing and salting the cod, as one's
nostrils told one, was empty of visitors and we borrowed
slickers and sou'westers to start for a vantage point of hers
above the harbor. There the sunset, if it broke through
would be especially fine.

"Fine" sang with meaning when Willa Cather used it for
values and estimations; it was the opposite of another favorite word—"cheap": which she pronounced with biting
frigidity.

Soon we were standing by great rocks, our throats
choked by the raw odors of kelp and jellyfish. Gulls spun
about us in the frothy mist, breakers roared below, I held
my friend's arm tight, for she had shed all signs of urbanity,
and was running with the breakers. Suddenly a flash of
ruddy crimson split the grey, and the anchored fishing
fleet, matchlike masts of sepia, furled rusty sails, danced on
the green quaking water of Gloucester Harbor against the
sunset.

"A Whistler etching," I said.

"You *do* like it?" Her voice told me she had set her
heart on my liking it.

She mentioned a young relative whom she was "sending through college." As a great treat she had brought her to Gloucester. But the prairie girl found nothing to admire. "Don't you even like the sunset?" "Where is it—I can't see it—too many masts in the way."

We exchanged comprehending looks, *la famille, la famille*, sounding out of the darkening skies.

Single women making their way to individual destinies—who in the home circle understands them? If they try to share what they have found in their further reach, who wants it?

Willa was a little dry and I felt callow beside her mature ability to give free-handedly out of her own earnings and yet make no sentimental bones of what it cost. Here was I, writing in the laundry, in the family cellar, with very little published work to show, as yet.

"What is so hard to find—though seemingly simple—as four walls within which one can write?" Willa Cather mourned gloomily. Her father in Red Cloud had wanted to build her a little "studio" in his backyard—but heaven knew she never could write there. . . . Many and better things to do in Nebraska—such as going up to the Divide to get the gossip of the year saved by old neighbors on their farms.

One had to be dull to write at all—one had to sleep. One needed to be alone, as in a hotel room in the country; or to work in a corner protected by someone who knew what it was all about—like Edith Lewis, her companion in New York, or Isabelle McClung in Pittsburgh.

But her New York apartment was too near to the office and too contracted; Isabelle lived more spaciously, and all the joys of youthful aspiration returned when she climbed Pittsburgh's Murray Hill. There she had—as she put it— written her book of callow verse, *April Twilights*, and her unfledged stories of *The Troll Garden*. She hoped she had left those effusions behind. When I insisted that I would not accept her harsh self-estimates and *must* see these works of hers, she declared tyrannically that I was to wait till she got on paper a story she was brooding over that might prove her first novel: it was about a bridge-builder, with a double nature. Of course she was talking of Bartley Alexander. I did not know yet that her next book was always the one that mattered.

That evening, in Gloucester, sitting in old-fashioned rocking chairs by a stove that heated our adjoining rooms, where sand seeped out of the musty carpets, she suddenly plunged into intimate talk of Miss Jewett—her gift for revealing in ordinary country people the treasure of life and feeling that lay below the pinched surfaces. Even now Miss Jewett's spirit separated her in a benign way from her worst temptations, she said. A shoot of orange flame burst through the broken isinglass of the stove door to heighten the ardor of her eager face.

What temptations? Well, the lure of big money rewards in the crude sense—for cheap work—magazine success— writing to pattern—letting all the people who wanted you steal your energy and time. Nobody who seconded a Chief like Mr. McClure could hoard in the office; he was the most high-keyed of men, always ill and bored unless he were rushing off to Europe to collect some new author; or to save some missionary abducted by bandits; or taking groups of his own staff abroad; exploding wrongs which would make headlines for his magazine. Not exactly, I perceived, one to calm the breast of a young woman tormented by the need to become a solitary. Not just a "writer" either— Willa's need was *to write life itself* as Miss Jewett had done at her best.

"But to do this paradoxical thing, one must have the power to refuse most of the rest of life. Could *you* do it— give yourself, dedicate yourself to your art, you who love life and find human beings so fascinating? Are you perchance thinking of getting married?" She hesitated and I think just avoided a warning that art was all.

What was she driving toward? This importunate urge in my friend that was insisting on being listened to had nothing to do with marriage and children. Art *was* all, to her, it seemed. Though obviously she enjoyed and cared for men, they did not pose the problem known to most unmarried women under forty.

Willa began, as the light from the stove faded, to tell me about the small green bedroom—the smallest and plainest of the four upstairs chambers where Miss Jewett wrote her stories. The room had a fireplace with Delft tiles, half-panelled walls, and a rather homely Victorian desk with sloping top and drawers at the sides. She made me see it so clearly that I had a shock of recognition when Miss Laura Hills, remembering Sarah Orne Jewett for me, in her rose-leaf mood of the nineties in Newburyport, quoted her:

"I was born here and I know the room I want to die in, leaving the lilac bushes green and growing, and all the chairs in their place."

A day or two later Willa and I were making our way along Charles Street, to the old brick house where Mrs. Fields still lived in a now noisy business street. Willa was eager to show me this rare person, preserved in a medium of a past far more fine than our rough-riding age of the trust-busters. One got along with her by asking a tactful question that would lead her to one of her yesterdays. Just try the theme of Charles Dickens and his American lectures. He had often stayed at the Fields'. We should probably find Mrs. Fields, dressed in lavender, lying under the portrait of Dickens as a young man.

It was reported on Beacon Hill that Mrs. Fields was in love with Dickens, I hazarded. Willa laughed and said it was more likely the other way around. The unique, fascinating old lady I was about to meet did have, still had, a weakness for English lions. But she had been ever so bound up as a publisher's wife with the rôle of creating a native American literature. Ticknor and Fields had boldly taken the lead with American authors. There were not many American publishing houses, and nobody else had Mrs. Fields' gift and grace of bringing these Bostonians, full of foibles, into her personal circle. Mrs. Fields had the power to turn a peccadillo into a peacock feather.

Could I induce her to talk about James Russell Lowell? I nervously inquired, and what about Amy Lowell? Willa shuddered—new poetic forms were not welcome where we were bound—nor would Willa want them to be! And she rang the bell and stepped into the hall, speaking warmly to the maid who took our wraps and showed us upstairs.

Since Willa Cather in a memorable essay—which first appeared as a book review of M. A. De Wolfe Howe's *Memories of a Hostess*—has said her final say about the great lady, I recall my single moment of literary immersion with her at 148 Charles Street only for the special gleam of light it threw on herself. What struck me was how the delicious, fragile, faded hostess, spare, slim, hollow-breasted as Whistler's Mother, her hair framed in black lace, like George Eliot's, received my friend as a sort of Midwest grandchild, a creature of zestful surprises who still needed a little toning down.

Willa's way of chiming in with all this—with the gently superior manner of the hostess, the old, old Boston flavor, the Smoky Souchong tea, imported, Mrs. Fields let fall, by "a cousin of Professor Barrett Wendell of Harvard"— was one of tender homage. That queer phrase of Willa's in her essay on 148 Charles Street about her own "Boeotian ignorance" (because she had not read the poetry of John Donne) was quite sincere. Willa could at any time feel impatient with the limitations of her prairie education. Now, on the day of our visit, she stepped right out of her dominant personality and melted into the warm light of our hostess' coal fire.

Mrs. Fields, I thought, revealed, with her flitting, piquant touch, a real curiosity about the contemporaneous in English literary circles—Galsworthy, Wells, Hardy, May Sinclair—the "great" Willa had met in London on her missions for *McClure's*. But my friend was refractory—turned the talk to the manuscripts, the portraits and photographs that crowded the walls and tables. When the atmosphere thickened with ghostly presences, murmuring their wit and wisdom, Willa was happy and things were as they should be.

I must add a coda to this memory of an hour with two prime donne who resembled one another in no way save in their love of great books and their interest in genius. I learned rather recently from Mr. Mark Howe, the last survivor almost of Mrs. Fields' salon, and her literary executor, that when he asked Miss Cather's permission to retain a number of her letters to Mrs. Fields in the large collection of papers which provided the substance of *Memories of a Hostess*, she refused peremptorily. When he made the same request again, just before the papers were acquired by the Huntington Library, and urged:

> Some day this material bearing upon your thoughts and feelings at an important time in the establishment of the position you now occupy will be of great interest to some critical historian of the period,

Miss Cather again requested that her letters be destroyed, and for special reasons.

Her letters to Mrs. Fields were not at all characteristic. She was completely at ease with Mrs. Fields when they were together and she was drawing her hostess into reminiscence. But when she took up her pen, the image of a very special and fragile old lady, opening a letter at the breakfast-table, froze her words into careful formality. After all, she came from the plains where the high winds blew, and she did not feel sure they would not cause havoc on Charles Street.

Later in the spring of 1911 I procured at last a secondhand copy of *The Troll Garden*—all this time I had not read it. I devoured it and found three of the stories as brilliant as I hoped my remarkable friend's work would be —these three were "The Sculptor's Funeral," "Paul's Case" and "A Wagner Matinée."

Passion inspired them—passion for the free expressive

life, especially the life of the arts, hatred for the limitations
of a mediocre setting, a culture still young and unshaped,
imposed on sensitive human beings. The theme of the three
stories was the same: the struggle of the individual of
unique gifts with an unfavorable environment.

Paul was not a Midwest boy, he was any high school boy,
hungry for luxury and self-expression, who lost his sense of
proportion and came to a tragic end. Miss Cather's use of
the word "case" was a sling at the social workers. By no
means was Paul described in the lingo of today as "para-
noid." He was some real boy for whom the author felt
compassion and insight: the first of the young men whom
she was to draw with a special sympathy.

I wrote her something of my joy and critical estimate,
and the answer came straight back from the little green
bedroom in South Berwick, from the very desk where Miss
Jewett wrote her Maine stories.

Willa told me bluntly that she was happy I'd discovered
something to enjoy in *The Troll Garden* stories—written
so many years ago that they now hardly seemed to belong
to her. She herself had outgrown the harsh mood that had
inspired the Western ones. The starvation of a girl avid
for a richer environment seemed to stick out, to deform,
to make the picture one-sided, especially in the composed
and quiet atmosphere of the old Jewett house, where the
spirit of another very young woman author, who grew up
at peace with her environment, still haunted house and
garden.

Since Willa Cather's death, I have come upon a letter
from Henry James, the god of her young literary life,

which bears precisely, if a bit remotely, to be sure, on this very first book of stories, *The Troll Garden*, which she so fiercely repudiated to me in 1911, and nine years later drew on, in part, in her second short story collection, *Youth and the Bright Medusa*. Possibly James's letter shot the first barb at Willa's young and shining armor. It takes us back to the year 1906, the year after the publication of the book —when, already seasoned in dealing with words, and thirty-two years old, Willa Cather became a member of the *McClure's* staff.

A cub member of the same staff, a young poet just out of Harvard, Witter Bynner, although he had heard from James comments on "lady novelists who victimize the supine public," had hopefully sent *The Troll Garden* as well as his own first book of poems, *An Ode to Harvard* to the famous literary exile at Lamb House, with whom he had spent some time when James was in New York in 1904. Here is James's answer from Lamb House, Rye, Sussex, England:

DEAR WITTER BYNNER:

I have your graceful letter about 'The Troll Garden'; which duly reached me some time ago (as many appealing works of fiction duly reach me); and if I brazenly confess that I not only haven't yet read it, but haven't even been meaning to (till your words about it thus arrive), I do no more than register the sacred truth. That sacred truth is that, being now almost in my 100th year, with a long and weary experience of such matters behind me, promiscuous fiction has become abhorrent to me, and I find it the hardest thing in the world to read almost *any* new novel. Any is hard enough, but the hardest from the innocent hands of young females, young American females perhaps above all. This is a subject—my battered, cynical, all-too-expert outliving of such possibilities—on which I could be eloquent; but I haven't time, and I will be more vivid and complete some other day. I've only time now to say that I *will* then (in spite of these professions) do my best for Miss Cather—so as not to be shamed by your so doing yours.

Believe me,
Yours ever,
HENRY JAMES

This drew from Willa Cather, to whom it was sent by Bynner, a reply both humorous and awed for she, at that time, considered Henry James the commanding figure in American letters and as she later said, in *Not Under Forty*, the keenest mind any American ever devoted to the art of fiction.

Henry James had answered in just the spirit she might have hoped for. If he and a few others did not feel that way about promiscuous fiction, the moral effect of his words would be lost. But she frankly admitted trepidation as to his verdict. She asked Bynner to sympathize with her plight and let her know the worst, with all dispatch.

But, characteristically, no second letter came. Possibly James had glanced at the opening story, "Flavia and Her Artists" (which is in truth a callow experiment, later discarded, with a Jamesian theme) and did not move on to the mature and powerful second story, "The Sculptor's Funeral."

In the light of today, it is surprising that Willa was so humble and penitent about her first book of stories. She had discarded even "Paul's Case," even "The Sculptor's Funeral." Instead, she shyly proffered "The Enchanted

Bluff," published in *Harper's Monthly* in 1909, the year of Sarah Jewett's death. It was simple, had no pretensions. She sent it along.

The story—never reprinted as it stands, but appearing as a "recurrence" in a chapter of *My Ántonia* and evoked in a final way in Tom Outland's story in *The Professor's House* —was, indeed, a sketch, plotless, atmospheric and tentative like some of Miss Jewett's early work. It was written in the mood of autobiographical reminiscence. For "Willie" Cather was surely one of the raggedy, freckled Sandtown boys, who made their own retreat of the loops of a shallow prairie river, bordered by bluffs, box elders, and willows, where sand islands good for camping and night fires had formed. Delicately, unobtrusively, through the boys' conversation, it led one into a beyond, into the spirit of a land to which the Spanish explorers had come in search of gold, led one to "The Enchanted Bluff," where in prehistoric times an Indian tribe had been isolated by a landslide.

"The Sculptor's Funeral," much more final and objective, had brought the reader up against a stone wall. But "The Enchanted Bluff" seemed to come from her heart. It suggests a perhaps unconscious experiment with the story within the story, later more perfected in certain of her novels. And it was written before she had ever travelled Southwest and seen the Mesa Encantada with her own eyes.

Again I turned to the Boston Public Library and re-read the four Jamesian stories published in *McClure's*—and never republished—while she was on the staff but before she assumed the managing editorship in 1908. One could not quite imagine James saying of them as he did of Katharine Fullerton Gerould's first short story: *"Am I as like that as that?*" For some passages are authentic Cather, others, as in "The Profile," reveal characteristic temperamental twists—in this case the author's strange abhorrence for physical defect. "Lop away so much as a finger and you have wounded the creature beyond reparation." Is it because she grew up in the prairie world where physical prowess is so revered that she had this morbid detestation for a blemish?

"The Namesake," a Paris artist story, proved of interest to me because it reflected something from her roots. (A poem of the same name in the 1903 edition of *April Twilights* was later suppressed.) The best of the four stories, I thought, was "On the Gull's Road," where for the first time in Willa Cather's fiction one gets a favorite theme of hers, the image of a beautiful woman in a young man's heart and senses. Mrs. Ebbling, the Scandinavian, had red braids and other romantic attributes that led straight to frustration.

In the autumn of 1911 I read Miss Jewett's letters edited by Mrs. James T. Fields. Most of them, addressed to dear Annie Fields, disappointed me not a little.

But there was one big exception: Miss Jewett's letter to her young friend, Willa Cather. Here one caught the voice of the knower, the insider, something prophetic, some compulsion to pass on wisdom, instinctive or acquired.

Do not hurry too fast in these early winter days—a quiet hour is worth more to you than anything you can do in it.

In *The Troll Garden*, "The Sculptor's Funeral" stands alone, a head higher than the rest, and it is to that level you must hold. . . . You are older now than that book in general,—but if you don't keep and guard and mature your force, and above all, have time and quiet to perfect your work, you will be writing things not much better than you did five years ago. . . . Your vivid, exciting companionship in the office must not be your audience, you must find your own quiet centre of life, and write from that to . . . the human heart. . . . Otherwise what might be strength in a writer is only crudeness, and what might be insight is only observation; sentiment falls to sentimentality—you can write about life, but never write life itself— To work in silence and with all one's heart, that is the writer's lot; he is the only artist who must be solitary, and yet needs the widest outlook on the world.

This much-quoted and now so familiar letter lay before me like new-minted gold. I saw that it had been written not long before Miss Jewett's death. Yet Willa Cather never yet had found a way to give up her managing editorship!

Just then the telephone rang and I heard her voice inviting me to come in to the Parker House for lunch. Bring my French sketches along; she wouldn't after this be seeing me for some time. She was—and what buoyance flowed through the receiver into my ear—going to take leave of absence from *McClure's*—going with Isabelle to lovely Cherry Valley, west of Albany, New York, where the McClungs had old connections, to write a couple of stories that had been bothering her for some time.

Was it Miss Jewett's counsels, seen in cold print, that had given her the courage to cut loose from the magazine for a while?

Over our steak we talked of Edith Wharton's new book *Ethan Frome*, a story of stark frustration which challenged

Sarah Orne Jewett's New England, her spirit of mercy and compassion. We recalled "Poor Joanna" in *The Country of the Pointed Firs*—the woman who had a misadventure in love and to expiate went to live alone on an island. The fishermen would tack back and forth, keeping an eye on her and throwing her parcels of food; and nobody was allowed to laugh at her or hinder her queer way of life. Mrs. Wharton could never have written "Poor Joanna," nor Miss Jewett *Ethan Frome*.

The brilliant outsider, a New York summer visitor for a mere six years, had levelled her cold lorgnette relentlessly and with a kind of bang, snapped up New England curtains that William Dean Howells had been nervous about raising, even as much as an inch.

CHAPTER III

The Golden Year
1912

GALLOPING GROWTH, sure forward movement, are fine things to observe and share. In 1912, after a long period of submission to a daily job hard for a creative writer to carry, Willa Cather's own literary life began to burgeon and bear fruit. She had been working joyously at Cherry Valley—all through the autumn and early winter of 1911 with a release from *McClure's* to do her own writing. After the turn of the New Year she began to make occasional lively reappearances in New York and Boston. The first sign of new work was her novel (the one which she many years later described as her "first first novel"). It began to appear in *McClure's* in February, 1912, under the title, later discarded, *Alexander's Masquerade.* In the book published by Houghton Mifflin in June of this year the magazine title was changed to *Alexander's Bridge,* and in the simultaneous English edition to *Alexander's Bridges.*

Naturally, I turned to the first number with avidity, and saw at once that it had a Jamesian touch as to backgrounds

(Boston and London). As I remember it, Willa intervened, when she heard that I was reading the serial, and begged me, instead, to read the book proofs, in which she had made changes. We did this, I remember, in Boston. I took the galleys to Brookline, brooded over them, returned them to Willa, with timid suggestions that she surprised me by honoring. I had never before seen a galley and it was an exciting business but to my discomfiture the story seemed conventional. (This feeling was enhanced by the frontispiece both to the serial and the book. Two lovers in evening dress in one another's arms and the actress saying: "Are you going to let me love you a little, Bartley?")

Bartley Alexander, the hero, a Westerner and a bridge-builder with a correct Boston wife, was in the midst of a personal predicament of an insoluble kind. He wanted, even under Beacon Hill, to eat his cake and have it too. He wanted marriage, success in his work, but he also wanted Hilda Burgoyne, a warm, gay little Irish actress in London who led him to a rediscovery of self and youth. So the intemperate Bartley recklessly plied back and forth across the Atlantic. There was a fourth character, a pale, wise, observant professorial friend, the first of a line of Cather observers,—though I could not know this in 1912—who was a bit squeamish about the whole business.

A vital theme and delicate writing; but somehow spun out into finesse. I could not find in the story the author of strength and latent power I valued in life. When Bartley's bridge went down, and he with it, in a sort of cosmic if not moralistic splash, sending Bartley back to the "element" that in himself seemed unredeemed and of the wilds, the death was minor, the great chorus of tragedy failed to sound.

Willa, rather depressed, pulled my uncomfortable disappointment out of me—and more or less agreed with it. She said that though Mrs. Fields was all praise and delight, she was through with Bartley. In his book she had for the first time in her life tried to be literary and she feared that she had come a cropper. But in Cherry Valley she had been working on two little Western stories. One was a Swedish thing: chill and grey, not ready to show. The other was a Bohemian story she would like me to see. It was different from anything she'd ever written, in an entirely new vein. She was convinced that no magazine would consider it. But she somehow liked it herself.

That I was responsive to the more fertile process that was now established in Willa's mind led her to send me, before long, the manuscript of "The Bohemian Girl." It had exactly the potential I had divined in her and had not found in the bridge-builder's story, where her pen had been guided by a fashionable pattern. Here, at last, was a Willa Cather story that was true to the person. To the woman of essential vision—generous, sure, writing of a region she knew and the public didn't—about those Swedes and Bohemians who cropped up in her talk of her youth. I was so excited that I rushed over to see Willa in New York. She remained incredulous at my certainty that *this was it*. We spent the better part of two days arguing about it at the Brevoort, on the bus, and in the Park, though the season was March. As I took my Boston train I hoped she had ceased her self-queries, and was offering the piece to Cameron Mackenzie, S. S. McClure's son-in-law, then business manager of the magazine.

All the way along the reaches of Connecticut and Massachusetts on the railroad, I thought about the return to Nebraska of Nils Ericson, the wanderer in a big family of brothers, the rest of whom had stuck to the farm. The wind had whispered to Nils names out of the geography books, they had suggested the sea, or something "trying to tear loose." Off he had gone and done well for himself. But his favorite Bohemian girl, Clara Vavrika, who had meanwhile married the dumbest of his brothers, "teased him like a wild tune." Clara was at odds with her environment and "pulled Nils out of his boots." He persuaded her to run off with him. These European Midwesterners, so lacking in guilt, so equal in maturity—not always true of lovers in Cather novels—were welcome after Ethan Frome and his girl and Bartley and his doubts. Then I found a fine quality of conviction in the relationship of the people to the country, and a great beauty of sensuous style in describing it.

> The moonlight flooded that great, silent land. The reaped fields lay yellow in it. The straw stacks and poplar wind-breaks threw sharp black shadows. The roads were white rivers of dust. Everything seemed to have succumbed, to have sunk to sleep, under the great, golden, tender, midsummer moon. . . . The senses were too feeble to take it in, and every time one looked up to the sky, one felt unequal to it, as if one were sitting deaf under the waves of a great river of melody.

Next day came a letter from Willa. Mackenzie had lunched her and taken possession of the manuscript, then asked her to tea at the Brevoort, and simply floored her by offering $750 for "The Bohemian Girl." To which she had briskly replied that, as she knew far better than he, no story was worth more than $500 to *McClure's*. He told her she was a goose and made her promise to take more for the next story. Everybody in the office, even those she did not expect to please, spoke up about it. That was puzzling. What did they see in it? And how could she ever resign from this devoted *McClure's?*

But the big news was that she was on the edge of her first trip Southwest—to visit her brother Douglass in Winslow, Arizona. Now that her hero, Alexander, was on his way and Clara Vavrika on hers, she could go with a clear conscience. Life was splendid. It had been splendid to have those days together.

So at last I saw my friend at the jumping-off place for the writer's life. "The Bohemian Girl" was the springboard. But where with her abounding vitality, and her royal gifts, would she dive to? She refused to say. She was off to rest and travel, not to write.

The first news of her came from 1180 Murray Hill Avenue, Pittsburgh. The McClungs stood for "family" in Willa's Eastern life and she struck a serious family event when she arrived there. Mrs. McClung had had a sudden critical illness, and Willa must, for a bit, stay on, in the stilled household.

She was keeping normal by long walks in the damp, smoky air and reading the third volume of Michelet's *History of France*. She urged upon me Wagner's autobiography: he didn't stop to plead his own cause, or pause to meditate—just recorded action, and this she admired.

Then I heard from Red Cloud, where she had stopped to see her father and mother. She had written a new scene into "The Bohemian Girl" in Pittsburgh, and, to be frank, the story seemed right when she again made human connection with the region. It was like the people and had taken the shape of the land. Again, she thanked me warmly for backing her in this story.

But the general effect of the West had been overpowering—she had run into the same old shock she used to suffer at the mere size of it. When she was in the East, she forgot everything but the sharp, specific flavor. Once there, an unreasoning fear of being swallowed by the distances between herself and anything else jumped out at her—as in childhood, again. On the plains the wind is a soporific. She was afraid to drowse and to dream. Why did she have such feelings if she were to write about the country—unsuitable, wasn't it?

In North Carolina, where I was recovering from flu and riding horseback, I pondered this comment. So Willa preferred detachment and discontent, as far as Red Cloud was concerned? Maybe she needed them, to keep her contented in New York? Or just to enable her to write of her childhood world?

Soon came vivid, uncensored descriptions of Winslow, Arizona, where she was feeling fit, if baffled. The little house where her brother hoped she would write was a shell, and the town an ugly little railroad and trading settlement surrounded by vast spaces of rubbish. But beyond—ah beyond!—began the red sand of the desert, with its dull green rabbit brush and sage. Across the tracks was a most alluring little foreign settlement—Spanish Mexican—which redeemed the boredom of the desert and the crassness of the frontier by its whole gentle, homely, free-handed atmosphere.

As Willa's brother went off for several days at a time with a railroad construction gang, she would be left alone in the *casa*—quite in line with the *mores* of Winslow—with an irreproachable brakeman, who had mined and prospected in Mexico and looked just like Henry Miller in William Vaughn Moody's *The Great Divide*. He was a devotee of Ralph Waldo Emerson, and bought a magazine at every station—so he was replete with useless information which he expressed in bi-syllabic Latin words. If he, too, was off on a "run," she always had the companionship of an English Cockney housekeeper-and-cook her brother had rescued from starvation. The Londoner spoke queer French and, when drunk, which was most of the time, sang sentimental ditties about "them fair, deceivin' eyes." So she had had to fall back on the Mexican village.

She had found there a string trio of Mexicans, who often came to play for her delight: two section hands and a bartender. Also, a young Antinous of a singer from Vera Cruz, with a mellifluous name and a few simple thoughts and feelings. His golden skin, his ancient race, his eyes with their tragic gleam—well, he reminded Willa of some antique sculpture in the Naples Museum. Being with him was like living in a classic age.

Here she interrupted herself to apologize. Nothing bored *her* more than to hear ecstatic accounts from friends about the charm of Venetian gondoliers and Sicilian donkey boys. But this one was different. His words seemed to come from the Breviary, they were so full of simple piety and directness. He would go anywhere to find wild flowers, or hunt a spring of water, as she would do as a child in Nebraska. But when asked to visit cliff dwellers he was indifferent—"*por qué los muertos, pobrecitos?*" Mrs. Bell, Mrs. Fields' witty Bostonian friend, used to say that after the motor-car came, there were only the quick and the dead. The Mexican singer saw things similarly—you say Masses for the dead and forget them. Only the living matter.

Besides, he had told her a story of an Aztec Cleopatra, called "The Forty Lovers of the Queen." (This sounded like a Rider Haggard story.) Willa would write it down when she could go to the place where it happened—she did not work from an imaginary base. (Nevertheless, the rather sadistic story was told to the heroine of "Coming, Aphrodite!" by her artist lover.)

Will you go to *Madre Mexicana* with me sometime?

In fact, she was suggesting now that I come to Albuquerque where she was sure I could work—not Winslow: I was over-civilized for Winslow. (Did she mean too finicky?) Albuquerque had a Spanish feel, and was set in the most beautiful country she'd ever seen—something like the country between Marseilles and Nice but more luminous. Even finer than the Rhône Valley. She would come over to see me; a night on the train was nothing in the West. She described Indian villages set around Spanish Mission churches built in Queen Elizabeth's time; talked of a priest who had driven her about to them. In this Rio Grande region the grandiose and historical scale of things seemed to forecast some great spiritual event—something like a Crusade, perhaps; something certainly that had nothing to do with the appalling mediocrity and vulgarity of the industrial civilization.

Having thrown off a prophetic idea, which was, in a sense, to flower in one of her greater books, Willa moved on to the Grand Canyon, which she described by understatement as the most alluring and let-alone Wonder in these United States. But geology cannot long be endured without human beings: one had to come to the desert to know how fascinating they are. Douglass, declaring that his sister was wearing him to the bones, was a fine companion—always had been. The well-read brakeman, too, in the upper canyons where they camped, shed his Emersonian altitude—became the kind of resourceful Westerner formed by the sheep camps, who could tell you a story or companion you down a cliff one hundred and fifty feet high, at an angle of forty-five degrees.

One more trip was planned with Douglass before she left Arizona: to hunt cliff dwellings along the Little Colorado. (It was as if they were again tomboy kids inventing prehistoric adventures along the muddy Republican River.) Then she had promised the Spanish trio and the troubadour (she enclosed a Serenata of his, for *vox contralto*, which must be sung only by a married woman, either to her husband or her lover) to attend a Mexican *baile* (ball) in Winslow. All those gentle, dark-skinned people who lived south of the railroad tracks would be there. . . . There would be fine folk dancing and she would be the only white. . . .

I am willing to wager that the staid editor of *McClure's*

never, in her most bohemian hour, attended an artist ball in Greenwich Village, but it was not hard to imagine Willa's Western self, her youthful, resilient, tough, gay-hearted prairie self, now set free and moving with the current, whirling around a whitewashed dance hall, with small-waisted, red-sashed Mexican partners, who took their pleasures from their roots. Such men, whose hearts knew well what reason knoweth not, respected and loved her because in a frontier town, where "Mexicans" were misprized, she put the joys and the music they gave her above the prejudices of the white ruling class. Naturally they spun Willa Cather around and around, like a top, and then seated her by their lean angular wives and their dolorous *madres*, shawled and patient as Goyas, on the long adobe benches, while they displayed, on the floor, the intricacies of a native dance. They gave her a new Spanish world to think of—and eventually to write of—and added their share to the golden elixir distilled by the Arizona desert in two months' time.

Two months was all she wanted, apparently. She told me how, suddenly, after she went on to New Mexico, she was hit by a cold gloom. It happened at the pueblo of Santo Domingo, a large, old-style village west of Santa Fe, where the law of the white man is scarcely accepted and a white lady sitting by the sluggish, ruddy Rio Grande, *reflecting*, is an object of suspicion.

There, however, Willa sat, and suddenly a bitter wind seemed to arise from the peaks and she saw, written before her in the dust, a sentence from Balzac she had long forgotten:

Dans le désert, voyez-vous, il y a tout et il n'y a rien—
Dieu, sans les hommes.

Everything and nothing—God without men!

So that was what was wrong! Not even her brother, not all the brakemen and troubadours of the desert, certainly not the Indians, could replace a civilization—her civilization. *Her own.* Panic seized her—it said the West is consuming you, make tracks for home.

She did, and by mid-June was back in Nebraska seeing the wheat harvest in the Bohemian country for the first time in many years. There was a great sound of cymbals in the air, for all at once—as if her journey had been taken for no other purpose—she had a new story in mind.

It would be called "The White Mulberry Tree," and would, she feared, terrify Mr. Greenslet. In two weeks she would be in Pittsburgh and start working. Meanwhile she enclosed the carbon of a poem which showed how the wheat country had seemed when she returned from the Southwest.

> Evening and the flat land,
> Rich and sombre and always silent;
> The miles of fresh-plowed soil,
> Heavy and black, full of strength and harshness;
> The growing wheat, the growing weeds,
> The toiling horses, the tired men;
> The long empty roads,
> Sullen fires of sunset, fading,
> The eternal, unresponsive sky.
> Against all this, Youth,
> Flaming like the wild roses,
> Singing like the larks over the plowed fields,
> Flashing like a star out of the twilight;

Youth with its insupportable sweetness,
Its fierce necessity,
Its sharp desire,
Singing and singing,
Out of the lips of silence,
Out of the earthy dusk.

This is the poem—entitled "Prairie Spring"—that stands at the beginning of *O Pioneers!* It suggests that Willa Cather was suddenly in control of inner creative forces which had tended to swamp her and make her dismal so long as she could not use them. The vast solitude of the Southwest, its bald magnificence, brilliant light and physical impact, too, had the effect of toning up her spirit, and made available a path in which a new artistic method could evolve from familiar Nebraska subject matter.

After all, it had been in the little undistinguished prairie town, which she had left at twenty-two in a cloud of dust, that she had had the appointment to meet the rest of herself, and the literary fate she harbored, which she still knew very little about.

Willa was deeply involved with her book when I next heard from her in August, from the McClungs' in Pittsburgh, a shut-in place where, established in emotional security with a sympathetic woman friend, the spirit of her inner music could imperceptibly change from the *crescendo, crescendo* of the Southwest to the *molto moderato* of Pittsburgh's wet and somber skies.

She was working three hours a day—for her a normal day's work. She was getting a lot of sleep. She and Isabelle were reading aloud the ninth volume of Michelet—six vol-

umes further on than in March. They also read my French
sketch "Standards of a Bourgeois Family" in the August
Scribner's, and had good things to say of it. "The Bohemian
Girl" had come out in the August *McClure's.* One reader
wrote in to the effect that Willa Sibert Cather was Pro-
curess to the Lords of Hell (quoting Tennyson). But on
the whole the letters to the magazine about this story, and
the serial also, were so warm, and the new work went so
amazingly well that she was freed from her editorial servitude, this time for six months—which, in fact, proved suf-
ficient for the completion of *O Pioneers!*

I had gone to England by autumn and then to Paris,
where I lived on the rue de Sèvres, *chez* Madame Gaston
Paris, the widow of a great mediaevalist, who had been
succeeded by Joseph Bedier at the Collège de France. In
this intellectual and aesthetic environment, huddled over a
boulet fire, looking out on a closed garden where roses still
hung and chrysanthemums scattered their petals, I heard
from Willa that she was on the last lap of her novel. The
cold Swedish story she had written in the autumn of 1911,
Alexandra's story, had entwined itself with the Bohemian
story, "The White Mulberry Tree," and somehow she had
on her hands a two-part pastoral: the most foolish endeavor
imaginable, she mourned. She now thought of calling the
book by Whitman's line: *"O Pioneers!"*

She knew, as she proceeded, that it was much better
than "The Bohemian Girl." She spoke of a murder—she
was three days killing off the lovers, she mentioned rather
lightly. The reference was to that moment under the mulberry trees, when the wild Bohemian farmer, Frank Sha-
bata, shoots his wife Marie in the arms of the tender,

frustrated young Swede Emil, favorite young brother of Alexandra—a scene that by its passion and its tragic restraint has taken its place as a lasting passage in American literature.

So 1912 ended for Willa with the knowledge of an inner achievement. Once this was reached, she had made the turn, as if unconsciously, and found herself at a new level of the spiral of work and living.

CHAPTER IV

O Pioneers!

1913

As 1913 OPENED, Willa settled herself, for many years, as it proved, into an apartment at Number Five Bank Street; so she always wrote it, in her firm, level, succinct, small longhand. A letter from her was a personal thing, and with its even margins and fine script, a pleasure to the eye, as well as to the mind. She never typed personal letters. Her handwriting looked open as her face, at first sight. When one hit an obscure spot, it was worth puzzling over.

At this time, Bank Street was in a quiet demure almost soundless corner of Greenwich Village. No big arteries brought traffic coursing by, no movie houses intruded. Willa was fanatical about noise; but in 1913, peace and security reigned.

Miss Edith Lewis, now Willa Cather's literary executor, who companioned a genius through many books and years, had made the happy "find" of the apartment. It had good woodwork and good windows and fireplaces and a number of pleasant rooms. Her last stay in Pittsburgh had been shadowed by Mrs. McClung's illness; she looked forward to a home of her own that satisfied her. Miss Lewis had a magazine job that took her out early in the morning. Willa did the marketing (Jefferson Market was close by), and then, in perfect solitude, her stint of work before the maid came to get the lunch. She was, indeed, "all set," in more ways than one. The Society Library was only across Fifth Avenue, the Metropolitan Opera just up Broadway. Her book was nearly done, and it had started her on the way of no return.

Though *Alexander's Bridge* was doing well enough, Willa Cather's lady-like Jamesian days of writing about the best people in merely sophisticated settings were over. Gone was her bitterness about the Anglo-Saxons of Red Cloud and their limitations—at least for the present. "You must know the world before you can know the village," Miss Jewett had said. Well, now she did know the world and her pen, of its own volition, started unwinding the Swedish, Bohemian and French lives of the Divide, as memory presented them from pristine childhood fortunes. Inspiration, says Santayana, comes from the heart and is, at the outset, as blameless and courageous as life itself.

Willa did not tell me that she had written of these foreign neighbors for college periodicals. She was, when interrogated about early work, transformed into a wooden image. Her beginnings just did not count. We know that her little room in "The Rose Bower" in her parents' home was locked when she went to college—something hard to enforce in a large family in a town where everybody was interested in everybody else's business. The Cather parents had unusual insight into a rebel daughter. Willa's great friendliness, her contrasting susceptibility, her drive, her perplexing secretiveness and detachment made her no easy girl to raise. Surely they suspected that their eldest child had a special destiny waiting for her.

Some time before I went abroad I had seen my friend during a moment of convalescence and consequent gloom and self-disparagement. Indeed, I had shepherded her back from Boston on a Pullman in this typical down-hearted state of mind in which, through physical illness, she had, in a way that was baffling to me, lost her own self-respect. With our chairs turned toward the moving landscape, we watched the flying fields and blue bays, till at last sentiency took over in her, she cast her mood like an old skin, and accepted the world as good again.

Suddenly she remarked: "Now *you* must write a novel."

I said timidly that I lacked the imagination. But, she replied in her positive, assured, blunt way, *imagination is not necessary*—all you need is the insight and the style you give evidence of in your French sketches. But, I said, those were *French* people—if I wrote about neighbors, friends, or New England family I should hurt their feelings—what does one do about that?

Willa said she did not like hurting people's feelings either—we all want to be liked. She implied that her characters were largely composites. How "close to life" the characters in *O Pioneers!* were I was never to know with exactitude from herself, in spite of our many talks about the book.

Though Willa had apparently not conceived "The White

Mulberry Tree" when she started for the Southwest in March, 1912, she did have, in first draft as I have said, Alexandra Bergson's story—the story of the vital young Swedish pioneer woman who took on the master work of producing a successful farm out of land largely untilled and with stupid brothers who could not see or feel the future in the untamed prairie. The Swedish manuscript ended, Miss Lewis has told me, with Alexandra's dream which came to her when she was overtired: the fantasy of being lifted and carried bodily, like a sheaf of wheat, by a man she never saw, great in stature, yellow as the sunlight, with the smell of ripe cornfields about him. This man relieved Alexandra of all weariness.

Since the Alexandra of the story married that rather weak, sensitive man who, in the pioneer world—and even in these United States in general—does often marry the strong matriarchal woman, we may divine, if we please, that the man of the cornfields was simply a psychological figure that gave a writer the lifting courage to become a great novelist—no matter what Red Cloud thought of it or how many feelings were hurt.

Willa sent to me in Paris early in 1913, shortly after New Year's, the typescript of her new story. The book was more than twice as long as *Alexander's Bridge*. She noted, too, some hasty writing in it—and a lot about crops and farming. But it was either a fair success or an utter calamity. Maybe it had too much the tempo of *The Swiss Family Robinson?*

Anyhow, she had done what she cared to do without concern for consequences or critics, submitted herself

humbly to her own creative impulse, dismissing all precon-
ceived ideas as to what a novel "ought" to be. She had let
the story run along at its own pace and length, without
trimming it to pattern. The country insisted on being the
Hero and she did not interfere, for the story came out of
the long grasses, she felt, like Dvořak's *New World Symphony* which program notes always said was based on
Negro melodies. She knew better. Dvořak had actually
spent several weeks in Nebraska, in the early eighties. Yes,
her themes were all there, but something had to happen to
herself before they could rise up and reach her ear, and
take form in her mind.

But, she quickly recanted, she was just boasting, because
she really felt low and tense, as always when she finished
something and got separated from it. Exposed to a cold,
windy world. Not more than half a dozen people in the
United States would be concerned. Yet it was the story
that had teased her for years and she could not bear to fail.

Since, she said, there were just three people whose judgment she valued (naturally, this went to my head), she
begged me to hand her the unvarnished truth. She was
given to emotional writing—if I found any, come down on
it hard. She was not one who took offense—she could be
detached from something she had created. Should "The
Bohemian Girl" be published in the same volume or did
this stand best alone?

I was to pass the story on to an agent in Paris who might
get a translation for it.

Since *O Pioneers!* had to me the sobriety, force, and
freshness of a literary discovery, I decided to try it out on
the French cultivated mind. After *déjeuner, chez* Madame

Gaston Paris, the family gathered about the salon fire for an hour of fine needlework and conversation. So it was that the old mother of ninety, Madame Paris in her sixties, a young daughter in her early twenties, listened with poised attention to the reading of *O Pioneers!* They had all read *Piers Plowman*, Chaucer, and Walt Whitman in English, and were genuinely thrilled by the emergence of an indigenous American novelist.

Très original! Alexandra interested them. No Frenchwoman for centuries had seen virgin soil. Alexandra's return from the river farms singing a Swedish song, sure of the future of the wheat on the Divide, was poetry and legend. For the first time, Willa Cather wrote, since the land emerged from the waters of a geologic age, a human face was set toward it with love and yearning. "The history of every country begins in the heart of a man or a woman." The French listeners thought the history of Nebraska had now found the right heart to come to birth in.

"We French who love the land, have it in our bones, can see the quality of her writing. . . ." They thought the American agent who had refused *O Pioneers!* for French translation asinine; they prophesied that this American friend of mine, with her acute poetic sensibility, would be known to the cultivated French reader in the end. . . .

In the grey, wet months that follow Christmas in Paris, I arranged to go to the South of France with a friend who came from London to join me—Mrs. James F. Muirhead, wife of the Scotch editor of the Baedeker for the United States, and author of *The Land of Contrasts*. Helen Quincy Muirhead was an "old" Bostonian with a difference.

Whether one stayed with her near Hampstead Heath, or was drawn into her circle in Cambridge, Massachusetts, one was offered the varied fruits of a rare intellectual curiosity and detachment. H.Q.M. had a generous and eclectic literary taste, a compassionate, searching interest in many kinds of human beings.

My first knowledge of the works of Henry Adams had appropriately come from this Quincy. She loaned me, soon after I left Bryn Mawr, his *Mont-Saint-Michel and Chartres* in some privately printed form, and later his autobiography. Since we were both Jamesians, H.Q.M. had taken me with her to the stately home of Miss Grace Norton, the Queen Victoria of Irving Street, opposite neighbor of William James and Josiah Royce, and sister of Professor Charles Eliot Norton of Shady Hill.

It delighted H.Q.M. that Henry James had chosen as a confidante for some of the early inner questionings he lived through in deciding to become an expatriate, this now dumpy, scholarly, old Cambridge lady who was a good friend of his. Miss Norton had worn caps since she was thirty, learned Greek at seventy, and even now rose at six to carry on her literary correspondence before breakfast, in order to devote the morning to her work on Montaigne.

Max Beerbohm's cartoon of Lord Tennyson reading *In Memoriam* to His Sovereign suggests the tiny, plump, authoritative figure we gazed at across her Victorian carpet. In this instance it was the Sovereign who benignantly read to her subjects, H.Q.M. and me. In spite of Miss Norton's maternal excisions of revelatory subjective passages, the matter we heard made clear to us just why the first fiction

writer of his American time had had to leave the land
where an *Atlantic Monthly* editor, W. D. Howells himself,
urged the "happy ending." In Europe, Turgenev and
George Eliot were still there, to sanction H.J. if in a story,
as in life, Fate showed a dark wing.

Willa had inquired eagerly about these early James letters. She had met H.Q.M.'s witty sister Fanny (Mrs. Mark
Howe) at Mrs. Fields' and I divined that I might venture
to show Mrs. Muirhead the manuscript of *O Pioneers!* on
our Riviera trip. Willa was still in need of reassurance
about her new story—wasn't it heavy and earthbound? She
said she had written it only for herself—then I had unac-
countably liked it, and Ferris Greenslet had too, against all
her expectations—he was rushing it to publication in June.
But somehow she was down about it now, and would welcome more comment from me while there was yet time.

H.Q.M. reacted to Willa Cather's spontaneous unpat-
terned novel as Justice Holmes, much later on, did to *My
Ántonia*. It made her sense the core of her own Americanism, and feel prouder of her country that these people of
European stock, who brought their *mores* and their hopes
to the Nebraska Divide, so quickly blended their lives with
its deep red stains.

The story of the pioneer Puritans, "our over-rated pro-
genitors" (after all they were middle-class malcontents,
chock-full of narrow prejudice) had been a hundred times
told, H.Q.M. said, like the story of the covered-wagon
days. But this fiercely untamed, untrammelled, sweeping
natural world of the Divide, of which the author gave such
rare and measured visual images, had new, almost cosmic

vistas, overtones and undertones. Though the story unfolded with deceptive simplicity, it had majesty, even terror. The author seemed to be looking through objective lenses at something new God had made.

After H.Q.M. went back to London, I journeyed north up the Rhône, still with *O Pioneers!* in a bag I kept under my eye, and settled myself for the spring in Avignon, which happened to be one of Willa's favorite towns in all the world. Springtime really is merry, sensuous, expansive in Provence; one has to give in to it and merge with it— harsh one day with bitter biting cold mistral, warm rioting and expanding the next, like the speech of the Provençaux who always "languish" for everything, as I wrote Willa. *Je languis de te revoir, je languis de me promener avec toi, dans les Alpilles.*

Willa replied, mourning that she was not with me drinking a *petit verre* in the Place de la République and catching the jolly come-on-with-you gleam in a French soldier's eye. . . . If I wrote her of the yellow irises flaming in the ditches, and the tall black cypresses piercing the blue like arrows, she matched me with the yellow mustard in the tragic theatre at Arles and the little willows of Avignon resting their elbows in the flooded Rhône. Her most splendid memory was of the Rocher des Doms and its Virgin, golden above the great river, finest in the world, maybe. Did the same swirling mighty current rush past the old Pont d'Avignon?

How Willa loved all that was potent, mighty in nature! My first view of her at *McClure's* had brought that vision of red earth. Her future might prove as broad as the

windy spaces of her state which, thanks to her gifts of
memory and description, now lived in my mind as a concrete backdrop for her Eastern life.

When I let her know that the only flaw I could find in
O Pioneers! was that it had no sharp skeleton, she swiftly
replied, true enough I had named a weakness. But the land
has no sculptured lines or features. The soil is soft, light,
fluent, black, for the grass of the plains creates this type of
soil as it decays. This influences the mind and memory of
the author and so the composition of the story. Some time,
Willa promised, there would be a story with sharp clear
definite lines like the country in which I then was. . . .

More, more, tell her *more* about Provence. Like the
Southwest it was a land that made one mad with delight.
There *was* plenty more, especially about the Provençal
poets, artists and writers whom I met through my French
literary friends in Paris; or through my Scotch hosts at the
Avignon pension. Through staying with the Soeurs Gardes
Malades in Arles I had also fallen into a little nest of Catholic clergy, red-cheeked, devoted, hearty men in black
soutanes who loved good living and shot quail and grouse
in the Camargue. It was in company of two curés and a
Sister Superior that I went to Maillane, that green village
on a dusty plain where the old poet Mistral, with his goatee,
and his sombrero on the back of his head, was drinking
eau sucrée in his garden. He did so closely resemble "Boo-
falo," as he called Buffalo Bill, that the two of them had
once bowed low and exchanged hats in a Paris café.

The curés presented me as an Arlésienne, taking much
pleasure in this innocent deception. The Sisters had made

me into a perfect counterfeit of the native article, headdress, fichu, black bodice, full skirt and Roman nose included. Mistral was so pleased that he promptly invited me to attend the forthcoming fêtes of his literary group, the Félibrige, who wrote in the native dialect.

I must have written Willa about all this light-hearted initiation into the poetry and legend of the land; about my walks with Provençal artists and writers in the dry Alpilles; and how my portrait was painted by a Cubist from a vineyard—*un sauvage*, a wild man, he called himself, a *"Fauve,"* who had already exhibited in New York.

Willa was intrigued, especially by the Cubist. She determined I should expound modern art to her. She had been urging me to stop with her at Number Five Bank Street when I landed in late June and this was now arranged.

She hoped I would like her new home . . . I would find that she had had to become separated from *O Pioneers!;* get it out of her system by seeing it through proofs and into press, before she could be clear enough to admit to herself that she really wanted to do a very different kind of story!

This surprising remark undermined all my ideas about Willa's treading in the footsteps of Sarah Jewett, and writing of a region. What next then? She talked more and more of a new enthusiasm of hers, the Metropolitan Opera star Olive Fremstad. I had certainly heard Fremstad sing Kundry, Isolde and other Wagnerian rôles? Fremstad, born in Sweden, grew up in Minnesota, but she had the rebellious dubious eyes, far-scanning and keen, of the pioneer woman on the Divide—and an intelligence that challenged you and put you sharply and brusquely on your mettle. Willa wanted to tell me more about Fremstad when I got to Bank Street.

She ended by thanking me for caring for her book, for wanting to care for it, but even more for caring about the whole thing—that is, the art of creative writing.

Part Two

---◦⊰{ }⊱◦---

I was the first to bring the Muse into my country.
—Virgil's *Georgics* III, as paraphrased in *My Antonia*

---◦⊰{ }⊱◦---

I Was the First

IN THE GUISE of Jim Burden, the narrator of *My Ántonia*, Willa Cather meditated on this line of Virgil, and by implication brought its meaning to bear on her own attachment to Nebraska:

Primus ego in patriam mecum . . . deducam Musas.

She was the first! Her own "firstness" as a writer of Nebraska stories was one of the luckiest hazards of her human fate. It filled her with transcendent happiness. Her pilgrimage toward a deeper, richer Eastern culture had been at heavy inner cost. But Sarah Orne Jewett had comforted her: she had used all her example, all her urgency to temper the wound, and lead her disciple back to native Nebraskan fields in a Virgilian spirit.

"The measure springs subconsciously out of the poetic mood." Goethe was speaking of a folk-song. In *O Pioneers!* and *My Ántonia* the main characters are certain folk of Europe, seen in the midst of an American transformation process. The author had been witness to the pattern taking shape under the hands of the folk, as southwest Nebraska moved into the modern state of the Union.

The pioneer vision of those two books was unique. The folk-song quality never later repeated itself. By the time the so-called "novel of the soil" became a commodity in the book market—it was often written by native sons and daughters as Willa Cather's Nebraska novels were not—she had turned away from her early childhood memories. To be sure the first part of *The Song of the Lark*—written between *O Pioneers!* and *My Ántonia*—derives from adolescent, small-town memories. They also were precious, pristine, "not over twenty," but they were cultural not bucolic; and at the end of the book, at the Metropolitan Opera House, the novel became urban, middle-aged and fortyish, like the author.

One of Ours, published shortly after the First World War, and concerned with it, leads us back to the prairie sequence—which of course was not a sequence in intent. No family followed from one generation to another; no historical background consciously outlined; no social significance pointed up; no geography really mapped. Mrs. Bennett in *The World of Willa Cather* particularizes Willa Cather's "Divide" as "a broad plateau, with little water, lying between the Little Blue and the Republican Rivers." Willa Cather, evoking it imaginatively and sensuously in *O Pioneers!* makes its symbolic image live for us unforgettably, as in a poem:

> . . . the furrows of a single field often lie a mile in length, and the brown earth, with such a strong, clean smell, and such a power of growth and fertility in it, yields itself eagerly to the plow; rolls away from the shear, not even

dimming the brightness of the metal, with a soft, deep sigh of happiness. . . . The grain is so heavy that it bends toward the blade and cuts like velvet.

There is something frank and joyous and young in the open face of the country. It gives itself ungrudgingly to the moods of the season, holding nothing back. Like the plains of Lombardy, it seems to rise a little to meet the sun. The air and the earth are curiously mated and intermingled, as if the one were the breath of the other. You feel in the atmosphere the same tonic, puissant quality that is in the tilth, the same strength and resoluteness.

Yet the Nebraska novels give also essential facts on which our minds can feed. We learn, almost incidentally, how not only the Anglo-Saxon families of genteel tradition, like the Cathers of Virginia, but the Scandinavian families like the Bergsons, and the Czech families, like the Shimerdas of *My Ántonia*, rooted themselves into a particular section of the future cornbelt; how the generations grew, flourished, interacted, amalgamated into groups bound by blood kinship, finally Nebraskanized themselves and the land they had rescued from the wild.

One of Ours related, in an unexpectedly contemporaneous form, the Nebraskanization process. Willa Cather, too, wrote "a novel of protest" though in theory she disliked such novels. The Midwest farm family of Anglo-Saxon stock (the Burdens are now the Wheelers), dignified in the frontier period by courage in the face of hardship, was now reliant on mechanical farm instruments and cars. The young farmer had at least a share in a car, but his father and mother permitted him only a meagre education at a narrow denominational college. Claude Wheeler, the hero, a misfit on a farm where money was poured out for gadgets and denied to cultural effort, joined the great adventure of his time, by volunteering in the A.E.F., and lost his life.

This act of Claude's made him one of "hers," one of Willa's: Claude was a spiritual and probably biological descendant of the Virginia Grandfather and Grandmother Burden of *My Ántonia*, who had built the original homestead on the Divide.

Claude, the failure, the family fool, is contrasted with his successful brothers, sellers and promoters, who did not volunteer and take ship for France. From these scions of progress Willa Cather turns her face away after she has starkly revealed them. None of hers, none of hers . . .

The archetypal pull to be a soldier went back to the American Revolution in the Cather family. When Claude spills his blood we recall, too, that, even as a youngster, the author had allied herself with Southern Confederate emotion; her uncle William Lee Boak, who died at nineteen in a Virginia regiment, had been the object of an impassioned early poem, "The Namesake."

Claude could not lose his illusions; he was held to them; he died to save them. But Willa Cather—and this is where she grew—did discard illusion when she published *Youth and the Bright Medusa* and *A Lost Lady*. The subjective arc traced from Alexandra and Ántonia to Kitty Ayrshire —who "wished to believe that everything for sale in Vanity Fair is worth the advertised price"—and from her to the romantic figure of Mrs. Forrester, lost by her defects of moral and spiritual grace, cannot be neglected by the psychologist and the literary critic.

Thea's life story, like that of Alexandra and Ántonia, is

told with admiration, a passion of admiration. The grim enough details of the climb to fame of a prima donna, who started from the grassroots, are all suffused with a golden haze of Promise. Someone off-stage seems to be singing a great aria all the while. But in Claude's story the light is that of a rainy day; the warmth, the heat are in the boy only. Something is changing in the writer herself. Her first Knopf book, *Youth and the Bright Medusa* (1920) again included the stark Midwest stories which she had thought so little of; and the career singers are unsparingly observed.

Finally, on the verge of fifty, worldly-wise and complete. Miss Cather looked back on the most fascinating woman of her Red Cloud youth, Mrs. Silas Garber, and no longer hesitated to deal with the treachery of sex and beauty in womankind. No doubt, even at twenty Willa had really *seen* her, if only in hearing a dangerous woman just laugh. But it took her thirty years to reduce her to a quintessence; to turn her into a paradox. Guy de Maupassant's sharp tools now moved freely in her hands, and the brilliantly etched portrait of Mrs. Forrester was not only a literary masterpiece, it was a psychic milestone.

"Life began for me," Willa Cather said, "when I ceased to admire and began to remember."

My personal impression of Willa Cather, during this great decade, was that she so lived and swam in the high seas of memory that she could not in any way reach dry land. One book followed another as one wave his brother in a rising tide. The new one, the pursuing wave, the next book, always pushed and shouldered the one that was rolling its crest triumphantly on the upper sands.

Like Claude, Willa Cather at this period demanded of life that it have "splendor." The word recurred so often in her talk, her books, and her letters of those years, that I think of her as living it out. As, for example, when her own university gave her her first honorary degree, in 1917.

From the period of retreat—*recueillement*—in which the books were written flowed the journeys, discoveries, and re-discoveries of Midwest persons and places. Major chords of human passion, heard dimly in youth, now understood with maturity, sounded once more and she was so sensitive to their harmonies that they rose magnificently from her pages. William James asked amusingly once, what would happen if the general, the surgeon, the presiding chairman let their nerve currents run down into their viscera instead of "keeping up among the convolutions"? Willa Cather's great virtue in these years was that she did have nerve currents from brain to viscera and that her writing arm recorded life in a way to touch the vitals of her reader; even as she had hit S. S. McClure's solar plexus when she sent him her first stories. His judgment of fiction (he said) did not come from the brain.

Willa Cather fascinated me because she carried with her a creative force of which she was aware, yet largely uninformed. As in an iceberg, the greater part of her load was submerged. That of course made her masterful, and somewhat alarming. She moved in her own powerful, inflexible direction, impervious to many aspects of life that to others might be significant. She knew when she was in motion, at least, and when she was jostled and churned up from below by meeting, usually through memory, a figure she could not deny. Then she paused, gazed, apprehended her fullest inwardly and communicated in a story what she saw and felt.

I have seen her many times, in this state of mental-emotional passion about a new character. But never more excitingly—to go back, far back again—than when I landed in New York in late June of 1913, from my pilgrimage to France, and paid her a little visit in her home at Number Five Bank Street.

CHAPTER II

The Song of the Lark
1913 – 1915

THE LATE JUNE DAY I am recalling some forty years back, was as hot and dense as New York's summer days can well be. *O Pioneers!* had been out but a few weeks. As the boat eased into her slip, and we passengers, packed along the rail on the lower deck, looked down on a sea of waiting faces, blobs of white, crimson or brown, like patches of paint on a Pissaro canvas, one blob came to life for me. It was oval, rosy-cheeked, and so vernal and joyous under a hat nodding with red poppies and blue cornflowers that my heart already alight, burst into speech:

"How are the reviews?" I called.

Willa heard me, searched for my face along the row, flushed, waved and answered:

"Splendid, splendid!"

Next I see her in her green linen and myself in my new Paris clothes sitting on my trunks, surrounded by the multifarious luggage one carried in those old days, waiting for the customs inspector.

Willa, in her sweeping exhilarated way, was discussing her reviews—how they in the West said she had been right about the *country;* and that was what she cared about. She had not wanted her readers to think about her, the author, she'd wanted the writing to stand alone. Did it? Still needing reassurance? I countered, unbelieving.

But she was irked by the Inspector, scattering on the dirty dock gloves, frocks, scarves, from Paris and Avignon, books of Provençal poetry inscribed with many flourishes in purple ink, canvases and drawings by the *Fauve*—which she began at once to study with interest, since they represented a new way of *seeing.*

Willa could interpose a marble-hard wall between herself and whomever or whatever she wanted to ignore—in this case the Inspector. As I have a more passive and adaptable attitude in my dealings with the world, I was soon trying to placate them both. How we got to Number Five Bank Street, along the burning dirty waterside, clanging with trucks, I don't know. Letters, those deceptive strands of connection between friends, had moved quietly back and forth for some nine months—now the provocative living woman jogged my elbow. How close may one come to the throbbing, smoking flanks of Pegasus, without danger from a flying hoof?

I heard the word "Fremstad" which had already appeared in her letters. Fremstad, Fremstad, wonderful Fremstad . . . Nothing, nothing, Willa murmured in the cab—still quite unaware of my Provençal daze, my whirling head—could equal the bliss of entering into the very skin of another human being. Did I not agree? And if this skin were Scandinavian—then what?

But now the taxi had drawn up to a plain brick house with white trimmings in a quiet corner of Greenwich Village. Willa put her hand on my arm.

I must have noticed, she said, how reluctant she had been to have me come to the halfway houses she had enforcedly occupied so far. Place meant so much to her. She so hoped I'd like her home behind that row of windows on the second floor above the street, facing south—she wanted to live there the rest of her life!

Here is a sanctuary, here is a temple, her voice implied: should I take off my shoes at the front door? When it was opened by an exuberant maid out poured a heavy-spicy perfume of summer flowers. My first impression of Bank Street was a sensuous one. Rightly so, for Willa's work was carried on, at any season, within a fragile screen of hovering flower-scents, and gay petals.

Later, I was to know her apartment in winter, by the smell of orange blossoms, camellias, violets, freesias. I was to see it in spring, when jonquils and narcissus stood on the table, and lilac and dogwood branched on the mantel. Now, as I told her, it was as if the waxy syringa, and the purple iris of the South Berwick garden had migrated to Bank Street.

Willa stood reticent, confident, as I gazed about me. Everything in the rooms but the flowers was simple, plain, all but Spartan. There was space, and the good windows and marble fireplace asserted their lines. In this walled stronghold of her very self, a plain desk, a small writing table with a typewriter, and a tidy sheaf of manuscript were central.

There was no piano—I had imagined one. Bookcases

nicely filled, but not overflowing. There were no heir-
looms to entangle the Muse's attention, no armchairs so
comfortable that she would pause to sink into one, no
magazines, no "causes" hidden in the corners. Willa had
cleared the decks and sanded them down.

She just stood there watching my face, and we did not
need to exchange a word. Then I was pushed along, still
in my own daze of Provençal sunshine, to a bedroom.
Miss Lewis, whom I barely knew at this time, was away;
there was room for a guest.

The next two or three days were a blend of excellent
meals, little neighborhood walks and above all—talk!
About the Southwest, about Provence, about her last and
her next book, and how books came to pass at all.

When a friend cares to offer hospitality in the spirit of
Ceres, one does not forget the meals, especially the first
ones. I still see the bounteous gesture of Willa's arm, well-
rounded, white, pouring a dry Burgundy she had found
for me. She had also hunted through the Jefferson Market
for perfect leaf lettuce—la salade classique as a French
friend called it. Willa's dressing, mixed at the table, was
compounded of light French olive oil and of the richest
wine vinegar, with a dash of tarragon. She insisted on the
tarragon.

We were (or I was) drinking to O Pioneers! and Willa
rose suddenly in her resolute way and laid at my place a
little brown book. It had a half-tone frontispiece of a
handsome Swedish girl, and on the flyleaf an inscription I
still cherish.

"To Elsie Sergeant, the first friend of this book."

A little later I was reading it again, and also a sheaf

of reviews she had laid on my pillow. I had not been wrong about *O Pioneers!* She also retired to rest with the yellow novels I'd brought her—*La Porte Étroite,* for instance—who was this fellow Gide?

China tea, hot and smoky, the kind used by Mrs. Fields, at four; and dinner at six-thirty for the sake of the maid. Dinner with Willa always had an aspect of formality. She wore that night one of her Liberty dresses of thin silk from London, to which some Czech embroiderer had added charming patterns. As for my Avignon dress with its lace fichu and sprigs of flowers, she said she would put it in a story.

She asked me many questions about the wild man from a Provençal vineyard, a *petit bourgeois* by birth, who had got to painting in this new and startling way. In later life, nothing interested her less than what the French call *le mouvement,* in poetry or novels. The *avant-garde* . . . But in 1913, the story of *le sauvage,* as his mother called him, and above all, his new way of painting, piqued her interest.

I had told Willa that the artist's parents had opposed his study of painting until he ran away and shipped as a sailor. That act of rebellion had made his family allow him to study at the Beaux Arts, but soon he had military service to do, and he had begun to paint in his head, for lack of any other chance. When he got out of the Army he found he was a Cubist, *malgré lui*—he'd never heard of Cubism before he started practising it. But the Cubists had a formula and that had alienated him.

So he threw away Cubism, and started hunting for his own style. You can't paint la Provence as if it were la

Touraine—at bottom it's harsh, desert, has etched lines, nothing fluid or vague—spatial. . . . I showed Willa the abstract drawings mostly on the back of menus . . . and she mused.

"You'd better write a book on Cubism," Willa joked. "But what if you have to marry the Cubist?"

I reminded her that she had not married any of her Southwest characters, not even the one who seemed a replica of a statue in the Naples Museum.

Willa looked reflective, and rather pleased with me.

As for the *sauvage*, she said—

She had wanted my understanding of her turning to the wrong side of the railroad tracks in Winslow, to discover those singing Mexicans who had come up from the South, from *Madre Mexicana*, from Spain before that, bringing to the desert that old courtesy, and that equally old folk music that binds the human race together.

Is it the fate of the creative writer, I asked (and here we were getting to the crux of our talk) to use the stuff of intense personal human experience for art only? Must a novelist—especially a female—go around saying I'm only a mirror? And never crossing the street without seeing herself do it? In living itself—even with a high objective like hers, didn't one get entangled—even in full professional swing—have human duties to perform, faiths and ties to fulfill? Could one let all private and personal experience be burned in the fires of *art?*

Then Willa got up and wandered about the room. To be free, to work at her table—that *was* all in all. What could be more beautiful, if you had it in you, than to be the wife of a farmer and raise a big family in Nebraska?

There were fates and fates but one could not live them all. Some would call hers servitude but she called it liberation! Miss Jewett, too, had turned away from marriage.

I had been waiting to ask Willa how, in *O Pioneers!* the two-part pastoral, as she had first discussed it, grew out of those two separate stories: the Swedish story she'd had on her desk for some time, and the fiery Bohemian story which had come to her on the edge of a wheatfield in Red Cloud on her return from the Southwest trip a year ago— and which she thought of at first as a complete narrative.

She said she could only describe this coming together of the two elements that made the book as a sudden inner explosion and enlightenment. She had experienced it before only in the conception of a poem. Now she would hope always for similar experience in creating a novel, for the explosion seemed to bring with it the inevitable shape that is not plotted but designs itself. She now believed that the least possible tinkering with the form—*revealed* from within, the better.

Next morning after breakfast with red raspberries in their prime, Willa invited me to share the little meander through the Village streets she took for domestic ends before settling down for her two-hour stint of work.

It was fun to market with her, for she enjoyed turning countrywoman, and frowning over a housekeeper's list; selecting items of her predilection, like fresh plump chickens and mellow fruits, and ripe French Camembert, and using her brisk, reliable humor with tradespeople. She found them more real and interesting than conventional people with smooth surfaces and punctilious manners. We paused to buy from a great crony of hers, an old Italian in a blue cotton cap, with stubbled chin and obtrusive tooth. Willa compared him to a correct young man who happened to pass, wearing a hard straw hat with a black band. Surely that one sold bonds on Wall Street, and no doubt his mother had had his teeth straightened! Mouths should be left as nature made them—mouths were individual as ears, or eyes, (her Western brothers, she said parenthetically, wore to her annoyance, only Arrow collars and Stetson hats) but the dentists insisted on deadly conformity.

Since *O Pioneers!* had come out, letters inviting her to join this or that group were arriving just in this little space of time. Perish all social clubs for women! Perish all these altruistic organizations!

When Willa talked of what she hated, her whole personality changed. Her chin hardened, her shoulders pushed forward, and one felt that the rigors of her life had made her tough or touchy. Her emotional nature was disciplined on the surface; but not far below burned a fiery furance. When the wrong kind of person—for her—approached her with seeming kindness, an uncontrollable antagonism flashed out.

When I stole in to Number Five at noon, Willa was sitting at the typewriter, dressed in a childlike costume, a middy blouse with navy bands and tie and a duck skirt.

Certainly she had a face of bliss, like a child's, as she jumped up to greet me. She said she felt about writing as her brother felt about poker and golf—it was sport, recreation to her! She never sat down with a sense of duty, even when doing a pot-boiler magazine article for *McClure's*— as for example, this one on opera singers.

Homer, Farrar and Fremstad were her subjects. Louise Homer, known as a good family woman in her private life, lived in Pittsburgh, so that part was easy. Farrar was fun, in lighter vein. But the great reward was this Fremstad, mezzo-soprano in the grand manner, peer of Melba and Caruso, who sang the great Wagnerian rôles. Fremstad was a legendary creature herself—one could imagine her coming out of the dark German forests of old instead of from a small town in Minnesota.

Fremstad had somehow ignited Willa Cather's inner fires and projected her toward a story that would take a lot longer than *O Pioneers!* to write—a story about a great voice, and a woman impelled to discover and develop it, though her meagre home background sanctioned no such effort.

Willa looked essentially young and ardent and candid as she stood there, arranging fresh flowers on the mantelpiece, and talking about her next book. It made me happy that she had not assumed the rôle of "celebrity." But she was deeply an individuality, even more than when I sailed for France—and more than ever likely to arouse intense devotion or an equal enmity. There were so many people and things she ignored or disdained, and she was so armored against them.

She gave me a lonely feeling, somehow; she said she would feel very isolated when I went on to Brookline and New Hampshire and left her stranded in the desert of the city.

Luckily I perceived already that a novelist, once launched, always had a character to turn to. With Willa it was usually a heroine. Willa loved her friends most loyally—but her heroines! From now on they were the very stuff and core of her being.

Soon I was recommending *O Pioneers!* to my neighbor, Helen Thomas Flexner, at Chocorua, under the shadow of the White Mountains. Mrs. Flexner had been my teacher of descriptive writing at Bryn Mawr, and unlike some others among my teachers, showed quick interest in the Nebraska story. I recall that she made a little objection to Willa Cather's use of the word "globule" for dewdrop, and that Willa defended it stoutly. Dewdrops could be of several shapes but only globule described the firm round drop that formed on prairie grass.

It was not easy to bring the Muse to my unplastered bedroom in a house full of young people. At last I found a deserted farmhouse, furnished one room with a kitchen chair and table and some mosquito netting and set forth every morning through cathedral pines, taking my lunch in a basket. The French sketches I had discussed with Willa were on the way and I wanted to consult her. But she had now moved off into a poetic distance. She had half promised me to come to Chocorua for a visit, though she avowed that she never "visited"—at the McClungs' she belonged, and she never stayed more than a day or two with Mrs. Fields or Mary Jewett. Fremstad had summoned her to her camp in Maine—but after all, the diva cared only for music—why risk boring her?

Hurry your sketches to me, Willa said. The need to travel was upon her. Neither Red Cloud nor the Southwest would see her that year—she would go to Pittsburgh, to Lake Erie, at last in September with Isabelle to Gore, Virginia, her birthplace.

She got there to find Gore dismal, ghostly and a bit sentimental. But a driving trip with Isabelle in the North Mountains, with six-mile daily walks in the rain, lifted her spirits again: the woods being especially rare in the rain. Any thoroughly untamed aspect of nature refreshed her. She said that the air was totally different where fields had never been cleared and harvested nor virgin forest cut. When I thought about this, I saw that her intimacy with nature lay at the very root of her relation to *O Pioneers!*— and indeed of her power to work at all.

Once refreshed and renewed, however, she was as impatient to be through with Virginia and back at a desk as she had been to reach Pittsburgh a year ago, after her Southwest immersion. Soon she was, in her sheltered, companionable corner at 1180 Murray Hill Avenue, moving so fast with her singer story that she could hardly keep up with it. There were interruptions like a visit from S. S. McClure and a wedding in the McClung family. But in six perfect weeks she wrote twenty-eight thousand words and wrote them twice.

Then she went back to Bank Street, all but barred her front door, disconnected her telephone, leaving even Fremstad to ring Chelsea 2036 in vain. The period of unprecedented creative activity which had set in had followed her to New York. She felt as if she could keep it up indefinitely and wanted nothing better. She had no personal problems when she was writing.

But the year 1914 started tragic repercussions in American hearts, especially those attuned to Europe, fed by European culture, or descended directly from European stock. As a Nebraskan Willa Cather was slower than most Easterners to fall under the doom of the First World War. She knew how divided loyalties split the Midwestern soul. The conflict loosed in 1914 soon tore her apart, nevertheless, and loomed to her historic sense as the most important event since the French Revolution.

From then on—though at first it was spoken below her breath—she was to utter a sad little refrain which her friends dreaded to hear her repeat: "Our present is ruined—but we had a beautiful past." She said it in letters and she said it in conversation, mournfully.

In the spring of 1914, when the world was still in ignorance that the Germans would be marching into Belgium in August, Willa had a piece of personal bad luck: her scalp became infected by a minor hat-pin scratch and she had to spend many sick and feverish weeks at the Roosevelt Hospital.

Declaring that there was no place in her philosophy for the unlucky, Willa raged at the foolish kind of illness that separated her from her book. She made sardonic comments on the price of wearing a new hat. A glance at a somewhat contemporary photograph is suggestive. *Encore jeune*, attired in velvet, with a long chain and a brooch, Willa allowed her top-piece almost to extinguish her simple, smiling hearty face. The hat is a Pasha-like turreted turban, so heavy with gold lace, velvet, and aigrettes that it might have come right off the opera stage.

Miss Lewis, of course, stood by, for this serious illness. Miss McClung moved down for a month. A head tied up in bandages and fiery pain brought a cloud over Willa's spirits. Her comments on her illness sounded the note of "The Profile." A physical blemish is so abnormal it creates a mental deformity. Willa went so far as to say she deserved derision, such as was given to lunatics in Dickens' time!

Yet Fremstad, wonderful Fremstad, had only to arrive at her bedside, laden with spring flowers, offering a scarf which could be draped about her poor head like Elizabeth's in *Tannhäuser*, to bring her to herself! Fremstad, at the peak of her powers, and only forty-two, made a dramatic official retirement from the Metropolitan Opera on April 23, 1914. The public registered its sorrow and enchantment by calling Elsa of *Lohengrin* before the curtain nineteen times, an ovation of forty minutes, unheard of in the annals of any prima donna.

After her recovery, which brought with it a drowsy contentment, Willa was remarking that she could not be sure of where her new heroine was headed—she must get away to Pittsburgh, and points west, before she did more work. She needed change.

When I decided to go over to New York to see her before she left, she urged me to visit with her some cliff-dweller finds that archaeologists had set up in the Natural History Museum.

New York was becoming my professional center. I was hoping to be able to live there the following winter, and to do some work with a new liberal weekly—still in the making—that had sought me out for French literary articles and criticism. So I found myself again in Central Park with Willa on a fine afternoon in May. We sat on a bench

near bushes laden with spicy hawthorn bloom, before walking across to the Museum.

Willa seemed tense and low-spirited. Writing, she said,
is the result of a surplus of vitality. One must feel light on
one's feet, light as air. But when we got to those glass
cases, where were displayed tan pots with ridged designs
in relief, and great black and red pots with complex geo-
metrical patterns, she was rapturously unaware of her physical depletion.

Willa reminded me of the potsherds she had rather
shamefacedly shown me after her first visit to the Southwest. It had seemed a sacrilege to take anything for oneself
from those cliff dwellings that hung along Walnut Canyon,
on "streets" that were hewn from the chalky rock. Hard-
boiled archaeologists, however, had dug up the pots in the
glass cases—some were whole, others artfully pieced together. You were able to conjure up the women who,
under conditions of incredible difficulty and fear of enemies, had still designed and molded them, "dreamed" the
fine geometry of the designs, and made beautiful objects
for daily use out of river-bottom clay.

Willa's lyrical gift of speech brought me the burning sun
of Arizona; the cry of the cicada in the great silence of a
cliff city; the aromatic odor of yellow flowers growing in
rocky crevices. Willa said that nobody could just "sit and
look" in such a place—the rock walls challenged one to
climb and one might end by hanging on by one's finger-
tips, measuring oneself with that ancient image, Death,
which so easily overpowered a white man in this environment.

Next day I went to Bank Street to tea. Willa was again

downcast and in a mood to talk of certain problems in her heroine's life that were alien to her. When a book did not write itself, she knew enough to leave her manuscript and do something that was germane to the story, in another way —for instance, she had been going to singing lessons, hearing voices tested, getting into a behind-the-scenes opera row—instructive though unpleasant enough.

She was far from feeling "in the vein." Madame Sand, over the mantelpiece, whatever her love affairs, was quite able to complete one novel at three A.M. and start the next at four!

We talked of Madame Sand and Chopin, the man who said of "new" music in his day: *"Rien ne me choque!"* But Madame Sand managed to go on looking down at us coldly contemplative, like a home-keeping grandmother in a daguerreotype.

I put off as long as I could telling her that I had agreed to write French literary criticism and articles for *The New Republic,* which was to start that fall. Willa did not want to dampen my enthusiasm but why desert the novels she knew I could write? I tried to rouse her interest by telling her about the brilliant group of editors—Herbert Croly, author of *The Promise of American Life;* Walter Lippmann, a prodigy among young political thinkers; Francis Hackett, with his fiery Irish literary touch, and Philip Littell, a sensitive New England eclectic.

These people, she supposed, were rivals of *The Nation?* They were doubtless Wilsonians, Bull Moosers and such? Indeed they were! After all, said I, you yourself worked on a new kind of magazine created out of exactly nothing but brilliant hunches by a man, who like these editors-to-be regarded our America as an unfinished affair, which needs constant remaking to help its growth.

Willa abruptly changed the subject, asking me if I had been reading the *Autobiography* of S. S. McClure in the magazine. She admitted to having a hand in it. She could, she laughed, write better and truer McClure than McClure himself—and that was just the result of listening to him attentively. Having an ear—

What had most struck me in the *Autobiography* was the story of the boy's arrival at Knox College with eighteen cents a week to live on. He had to meet real hardship, yet dared to propose to the beautiful daughter of the leading professor: "Will you marry me in seven years?" and got yes for an answer. So the most important thing in life was settled for him.

And the continuing story of S.S.'s arriving in Boston after his graduation, with just four dollars in his pocket. He had resolved to go to Colonel Pope, the manufacturer of the high Columbia bicycle, to ask for a job, and the whole passage might have come out of a novel by the creator of Paul or of Emil in *O Pioneers!*

The thin boy, his face worn with loneliness and longing for things he could not get; the idealistic boy who had always lived in the country and in the future, walked up the Colonel's steps—and right there was abruptly left behind by S. S. McClure, who had decided to live in the present. S.S. had hardly given him a farewell look—the boy went back to the woods, and S.S. went into business.

Now that is your style and no mistake, I said to Willa, who looked pensive as we finished our tea. When *My Autobiography* was published by Stokes that same year, I found that the Managing Editor who reigned from 1906 to 1912 was not even referred to. But the Foreword said—along with full acknowledgments to the girl who had waited seven years:

> I am indebted to the cooperation of Miss Willa Sibert Cather for the very existence of this book.

The summer of 1914 began very quietly for Willa in Pittsburgh, where she went on with her novel so easily that she could go to two dinners a week—and doubtless meet the kind of conventional Pittsburgher whom she satirized in her short story "A Gold Slipper" in 1917—as well as the German-musical kind of Pittsburgher and his friends among the elite, described in "Double Birthday" in 1929. The McClungs' substantial mansion on a hill was approached by a steep paved street, lined with poplars and the rose-gardens of other substantial mansions of brick and stone, where people did not concern themselves too much with the fate of the steel workers. It used to surprise me that with all her talk of Pittsburgh and for all her connections with *Mc-Clure's*, Willa never once mentioned to me those Pittsburgh steel mills which, during the age of reform, came in for so much social criticism from people like Jane Addams.

She and Isabelle were reading Henry James's *Notes of a Son and Brother*—the sentences were so full of afterthoughts and parentheses and recoil that he ended with everything cancelled out. Knut Hamsun's *Shallow Soil* was more rewarding.

Before long, jacking up her courage, Willa went, after all, to visit Fremstad (now retired) in her Maine camp. To accompany Bruennhilde-Isolde as she fished, cleaned fish, cooked fish, rowed, tramped and cut down pines was an exhilarating adventure.

By August Willa had gone to Red Cloud, and by the fourth, when the Germans marched into Belgium, she was in the French and Bohemian country, with the temperature at ninety degrees—among country people dear to her from childhood. They were to Willa like characters in a story that rolled on like *War and Peace*, always more dramatic and interesting than anything she could have made up in her head.

The shock of the European war had at first been absorbed by space and the vast "wideness" of the West that Willa was always talking about. In Keene Valley in the Adirondacks, where I was spending the summer near my friends the Goldmark sisters, the shock was inescapable. At a gathering of New York intellectuals we heard the Germans' march into Belgium interpreted by Dr. Felix Adler, who did not mince his words. Europe had crumbled, France was in mortal peril, war and with it the tragic sense of life had come to abide with us. The Germans were fifty miles from Paris. . . .

I cancelled a sailing for October, and a contract for a Provençal book. But Willa went on to New Mexico in restless, hopeful mood. When war cut into her joyous travels, even in the Sangre de Cristo Mountains, and suddenly, all the European values seemed threatened, she rushed back to Pittsburgh, with a hostage from Red Cloud, her youngest brother Jack, whom she had entered at the Carnegie Institute of Technology. She described him affectionately as a six-footer just off the farm, aged twenty.

She would play with him and write at the McClungs' till January.

I felt impatient with her for being so detached—quite wrongly, certainly, since *One of Ours* was storing up in her all the time. When *The New Republic* appeared on November 7, 1914, for the first time, I called her attention to a leading editorial—"The End of American Isolation":

> Independence in the sense of isolation, has proved to be a delusion.

Willa did not know that yet. She was deep in *The Song of the Lark* again, which was hard to keep pace with; it went so fast. It was to be completed and published in 1915.

In early February, 1915, Mrs. James T. Fields died in Boston. Willa Cather lost in her not only an affectionate elder friend and a distinguished New England retreat and background, where she was ever welcome and wanted, but a whole series of values that she would never meet again, nor try to put into final words for another twenty years. She was no sentimental worshipper of the Golden Age of New England; indeed in private talk, could be funny about the moral lesson of "The Chambered Nautilus," or of "The Barefoot Boy," which were taken very solemnly in her Nebraska schoolroom. But all change was distressing, and in Mrs. Fields she had again lost Sarah Orne Jewett.

Perhaps a month later, I met some Bostonians, some Pittsburghers and some New Yorkers at a tea-party at Number Five Bank Street. All were talking about Mrs. Fields and her captivating spell. Whether Willa and Miss Lewis had as yet begun their Friday tea-parties, their "at homes," I am not sure. This was a similar occasion: a mélange of various kinds of friends from various past or present lives.

Handsome, vivacious Isabelle McClung always cast a glow which was reflected in Willa's shining face and quick stumbling rushes of talk and color. Ida Tarbell brought something of feminism and something of the old *McClure's* in her benign, searching look. Ferris Greenslet, Willa Cather's high-strung, sensitive Boston publisher, who so clearly was no born Bostonian even if he did "belong," made little witty asides down his chin—annoyingly hard to catch. He took obvious pride in his discovery from Nebraska—understandable pride. Willa Cather was important and she was new.

Mr. Greenslet, as a young *Atlantic Monthly* editor with Latinist tastes, had known Mrs. Fields and Miss Jewett well. He called them "great ladies with childlike hearts," and was ready to start an argument with anyone who denied that a childlike heart must be a part of the equipment of all "great ladies." Alice Hoyt and her husband Henry, Elinor Wylie's brother, a painter, dark-skinned, black-browed, with a dash of red or orange in his ties and his nature, here joined in, because Alice had Boston relatives in Mrs. Fields' literary circle. Where now would Mrs. Bell display her wit?—the Mrs. Bell whom Wendell Holmes adored and who could laugh even at the Jameses!

"A conundrum. 'Why is Henry James's novel called *The Wings of the Dove?*' 'Because you can not make head or tail out of it.'"

Or this: "I do not believe Henry James is so silly as to pompously announce that he is no longer an American. He probably said it was a pleasant day in such a roundabout way that no one knew what he was driving at."

But a dozen quotations from Mrs. Bell, though they might set us all laughing, did not turn Willa herself into a wit, or give her a "light touch" in conversation. Unquestioned in her primacy, eager as a countrywoman to feed and warm her guests, she had no gift for changing a collective conversational mood or amalgamating disparate human elements. Edith Lewis gracefully helped and seconded, Willa just prevailed. Genuinely, bluffly, almost awkwardly she cared, come hell or high water, for the loyal friends who gathered about her—with no underground motives of self-interest or social esteem.

One learned much about her—as one learns much about the heroine of a Cather novel—by the way her guests looked at her, spoke to her, felt about her. One met few writers at her teas. She seemed to have no "circle" of intimates, whose vibrations and exchanges arose from propinquity and mutual converse in a given social or literary milieu.

Willa never in the world sought to use her growing success and reputation to dip into the realm of "Society" or "Important People." Important to whom? She cared about musicians, actors, singers, and sometimes painters and writers—*if she admired them individually.* Not otherwise. What she was accumulating without came from within, so to speak: and that made her tea worth drinking and the talk at Number Five generous and human.

Willa avoided discussion of her own work in any general group. She was, however, now finishing *The Song of the Lark,* going through the last throes of revision. Randolph Bourne, the young illumined liberal with the sad hump on his back, whom I had met at *The New Republic's* Round Table lunches, was eager to read it, and as he was musical, might review it. He had enormously admired *O Pioneers!* In the psychic stress that prevailed in this group of intellectuals who were trying to forge group feeling and a policy that would fit our national and world dilemma, War in Europe, Bourne spoke up for literary values against war madness; and pitted the younger against the older generation in a way to make one stop and take notice.

Alvin Johnson also, with his Western bluffness, his mind of genial breadth, was ready to go all out for Willa Cather as a true novelist of Nebraska.

O Pioneers! was being translated into the Scandinavian languages. Johnson, he said, had been to visit Willa Cather in Bank Street. But all they managed to talk about was— food!

By spring of 1915 Willa was dealing with her voluminous proof-sheets. She had promised to give me some page proof to read but decided to make me wait for the book. The person who could help her, she let me know, was a very discriminating newspaper music critic. His enthusiasm helped her out of the down-hearted moment that always, always, came with proof-sheets.

She had consulted nobody, no musician anyhow, about the musical problems of a technical nature she had inevitably run into. She had had to work them out in her own fashion. So it was reassuring to find that the critic could forecast the nature and quality of Thea's voice (nowhere described) from her early lessons. She had jumped this hurdle without a sprawl, it seemed. Best of all, Fremstad said it was the only book about an artist where there was "something doing" in the artist, and that she did not know where Willa ended and she began!

There was good British weather, in New York, that June. Jack, Willa's young brother, had eased her mind by going to "Morris Dance" in Maine with Cecil Sharpe. She spoke warmly of my article in *The Century* on Frédéric Mistral, which again recalled to her the sun and breath of Provence; and brought back to her Mrs. Fields' and Miss Jewett's visit to the poet in his native Maillane, as well as my own. Her next trip to Europe would not be toward Provence; it might be toward Germany. S. S. McClure wanted her to carry out a mission for him and if so, Isabelle would go along.

This war journey did not take place because Judge McClung forbade his daughter to go. So Willa, ready for a major holiday, threw herself into selecting khakis that she and Edith Lewis would wear at the Mesa Verde. She fancied some that she thought resembled those worn by Kurt in *Fidelio*. I still have a jolly, faded snapshot of her in a cowboy hat, on the side of a Colorado cliff, where she now looks to me not like Kurt but like Tom Outland, who was not definitely born in her mind at that date.

Although visitors to the Mesa Verde had to ride or walk with guides, Willa Cather and Miss Lewis had a rugged, scary, but magnificent experience of getting lost afoot by night in a canyon. But both of them enjoyed it; awesome though it was, Willa was back on her horse in four days, asking again to be taken in hand by Mother Nature.

When this was all over, Willa happened, by luck, to meet Fremstad in Lincoln, just after the singer received and read an advance copy of *The Song of the Lark*. Willa felt the burden of the author roll off her shoulders when the diva declared she was infatuated with it, and said that even the end had the right tone. Willa could imitate Fremstad's slang to perfection.

"You might think it would be old hat to me, but I knew what Thea was up against, and wanted her to make the grade."

My summer had been quietly spent in Medfield, Massachusetts, with my own people, writing in a study in the garden. Henry James's splendid essay on Mr. and Mrs. James T. Fields came out in the July *Atlantic Monthly*. And in August, Mr. Ellery Sedgwick introduced a new American poet to his readers: Robert Frost. "Birches," "A Tuft of Flowers," and "The Road Not Taken," were at length published where many another early poem had been refused. In the same issue a discriminating English critic, Edward Garnett, whom Willa Cather had known in London, forecast Frost's future fame.

Willa had probably noticed "The Death of the Hired Man" in *The New Republic* in January, selected by Ridgely Torrence, the perceptive poetry editor. It was much discussed at the Round Table lunches, and the *N.R.*'s public, at least, was waiting for *North of Boston* and *A Boy's Will* to be published by Holt; the two volumes had found a publisher in England, and high critical recognition, and now the New York critics were hot on the trail.

Willa's mature judgments were final and never revoked. She chose Frost for her own at once. Disliking heartily, as she was free to state, in her colloquial, daily diction, the free-verse bunch from the Middle West, she rejoiced in

Frost's tight, tenacious, regular metres. This poet had a voice, a song, cadences, speech echoes of his own, original, that caught her sensitive ear. And he brought a new mental climate, almost a twilight climate, to New England. Wasn't it something like Chekhov's? His verse was important, though it lacked splendor.

Back in Brookline, in the autumn of 1915, I received *The Song of the Lark*, a thick blue book of 490 pages—small type, too—three times as long as *O Pioneers!*

Naturalistic rather than suggestive or allusive, it related in detail and in full how Thea Kronborg, a tense, prickly, fair-haired, fair-skinned girl, with high cheekbones, yellow eyebrows, and greenish hazel eyes—the daughter of a Norwegian minister in Moonstone, Colorado—was impelled toward an artistic fate. This fate Thea Kronborg but slowly comprehended, yet struggled for and finally brought to conscious birth through her intelligence, her rugged will, and through her singing voice, a wild thing, on which her inner tension and her outer achievement rested. This great organ, imprisoned at first in her beautiful strong body, and in a world of uncomprehending provincial human beings, finally created her adjustment to the whole of life.

The story, as I read it, bore out much of what Willa had said to me about the desire, the passion which takes a woman of exceptional gifts away from the usual instinctive woman's lot of marriage and children to fulfil a directive that is altogether impersonal. Willa had experienced something of the sort, and where the imprint of her own passion fell, I was enthralled and convinced.

It fell with utmost intensity in the first part of the book:

"Friends of Childhood": the section begun and almost finished in Pittsburgh in 1915, after Willa's trip to her roots in Virginia. This very beautiful and complete story of a young genius is also almost a poem. Yet the lyricism is not overstressed, and the sensuous detail and description exist to make real to us the spiritual awakening of a girl of twelve in a little bedroom with flowery wallpaper divided off from a cold loft. There Thea came to realize what was "different" in herself from family, day school, Sunday school. There she met her personal daemon. It was

> more like a friendly spirit than like anything that was a part of herself. She brought everything to it, and it answered her; her happiness consisted of that backward and forward movement of herself . . . —a kind of warm sureness.

At the piano—which was not to prove her instrument—she met difficulties like enemies she must subdue. One day old German Wunsch, her teacher, a tramp musician, showed her the score of Gluck's *Orpheus*—the first great music she had seen—and induced her to sing Orpheus's lament:

> *Ach, ich habe sie verloren,*
> *. . . Euridice, Euridice!*

Soon after, Wunsch brought his pupil a lyric of Heine and impatiently, angrily tried to enlarge her maturing insight to accept a mystery:

> What make the rose to red, the sky to blue, the man to love—*in der Brust, in der Brust* it is . . .

Had the novel ended here, Thea's story might be accounted one of the perfect works of Willa Cather, rather than the imperfect, paradoxical thing it became when she tried to join the finality of her own childhood experience to the more vicariously apprehended life of a mature artist in the great field of singing. Much of the later part, especially the Chicago student chapters, was very fine; but the author dreaded (she told me) from the first page of the book that she must push Thea right out onto the Metropolitan Opera stage, where even a small-town intelligence would recognize her success.

When Thea goes to the Canyon of the ancient people, and meets the brewer's son—a more mature admirer than the brakeman, Ray, whose dying bequest paid for her early study—we hope she will experience love deeply. But it was the cliff city, the canyon with its brooding presences and powers, that awakened her deep passion and her inner nature. The rich, blond young male was rather incidental. Romantic Doctor Archie, the home-town doctor who loved her as a child and glimpsed her "difference" not as "queerness" but as human promise, loaned her money to go to Germany to study with Lilli Lehmann.

It was, then, naturally enough, Doctor Archie who dragged the truth about her personal life out of Kronborg, the prima donna, in a moment of high triumph at the Metropolitan Opera. He was anxiously questioning her about it:

"My dear Doctor, I don't have any. Your work becomes your personal life. You are not much good until it does. It's like being woven into a big web. You can't pull away, because all your little tendrils are woven into the picture. It takes you up and uses you, and spins you out; and that is your life. Not much else can happen to you."

This theme was again taken up by Willa Cather, in the Preface to the revised edition (1932). She regretted having written Thea's life in full—for what she cared about was the struggle and not the success: the awakening of the girl's spirit, not its worldly triumph.

But even in her Preface the author still maintains that a great opera singer must sacrifice the woman in her to her fame. The something final, dry and ruthless that happened to the mature diva far removed her from the intense, passionate, richly endowed child and girl, and reduced the male figures on whose admiration she depended, to understructure for a stage figure.

The author herself seemed hardly conscious of the split, and at the time I could speak to Willa only of what I admired in the book, for she was deeply—by her own account —identified with her character, who had many of her traits and had undergone many of her own experiences. She, however, said that it was as if Thea lived in her own right, objectively, and was not a creation of hers: she depended on Thea to such an extent that when the book came out and the close inner tie was severed, she felt the pang and emptiness of one deserted.

---⊰ CHAPTER III ⊱---

My Ántonia
1916 – 1919

IN THE SPRING of 1916, I had the first inkling that Willa had a new story in mind. I never asked questions—she was the initiator of any communication about an unborn or unfinished work.

She had not been able to forget that, in these war days, the youth of Europe, its finest flower, was dying. Perhaps our American youth had also been designed for sacrifice—by now we feared so. But a growing vital work, with Willa, usually took precedence, even in her thoughts, over the life around her.

She had come in for tea at a small apartment facing south on a garden, in the East Sixties where I was living. As it was not far from Central Park, she arrived flushed and alert from one of her swift wintry walks. I think of her as always wearing red-brown fur in winter in those years; it made her hair shine, and she had the warmth, charm, assurance, and fullness of being that allied her, despite her individual direction, with *the* American woman in her forties. She said more than once to me that nobody under forty could ever really believe in either death or degeneration. She herself carried that physical nonchalance right on through her fifties.

While I boiled the kettle Willa sat down with Henry James's *Notes on Novelists* which lay on my writing table; turned to the passage where he says that the originator has one law and the reporter, however philosophic, another. "So that the two laws can with no sort of harmony and congruity make one household."

Willa was amused by James's elaborate, subtle phrases— a bit impatiently amused by now. But with this comment she fully agreed: she had not altogether banished the reporter in her last book. Now she aimed at a more frugal, parsimonious form and technique.

She then suddenly leaned over—and this is something I remembered clearly when *My Ántonia* came into my hands, at last, in 1918—and set an old Sicilian apothecary jar of mine, filled with orange-brown flowers of scented stock, in the middle of a bare, round, antique table.

"I want my new heroine to be like this—like a rare object in the middle of a table, which one may examine from all sides."

She moved the lamp so that light streamed brightly down on my Taormina jar, with its glazed orange and blue design.

"I want her to stand out—like this—like this—because she *is* the story."

Saying this her fervent, enthusiastic voice faltered and her eyes filled with tears.

Someone you knew in your childhood, I ventured.

She nodded, but did not say more.

So I sometimes wondered, later, whether she was thinking of Ántonia or Mrs. Forrester. Often she thought about her heroines for years before they appeared in a book.

Another day, of the same period, when we were walking in the Park together, past skaters on the icy pond, under brilliant blue skies, she told me of a major change in her personal life—this rather drily, rather bluntly.

Her friend, Isabelle McClung, whom I knew to be an animating force, was getting married. This, after first youth, one did not expect or foresee. But it had happened. Judge McClung, by then an old man, had died in the fall; 1180 Murray Hill Avenue would cease to be—and of course I knew that, even since she'd had a home in Bank Street, she had spent some months of every year writing in Pittsburgh, where Isabelle had always protected and quickened her work in her perfect way.

Isabelle was a musical amateur, and she had married music too: Jan Hambourg was a gifted and scholarly violinist, known on two continents for his concerts with two musician brothers, a violinist and a cellist. The three brothers had an old Russian father who was also a musical scholar, and a family home in Toronto. Isabelle and Jan would not desert American shores during the war. But Willa felt they might end up in Europe.

Her face—I saw how bleak it was, how vacant her eyes. All her natural exuberance had drained away.

"So you will have to find a new remote place to work," I said, grasping at the aspect of the situation most easy to talk about. It could not be South Berwick: Miss Mary

Jewett sat on at the front window, but now it was her nephew, Dr. Eastman, whom she really watched for.

Red Cloud? She said no to that. Her father was always fancying she might write there but she never did or could. No, she would have to be quite on her own.

The person she now longed to see was her brother Roscoe. Douglass, the brother she had visited in Winslow, Arizona, the one whose shoe-leather she had worn out in 1913, had not married. But Roscoe had a wife and three fine youngsters; lived near the Wind River range of the Rockies in Wyoming. She would visit him in the summer to come and get further acquainted with the younger members of the Cather family for whom she had a passion. She, Douglass and Roscoe had formed a group of three, had always stuck together and had a special feeling for one another. She hoped to see more of them now. Anyhow the West was restorative.

Willa and I had a sort of plan, recurring from time to time, to meet in the Southwest. I had decided to take my first trip West in the summer of 1916, after completing the proofs of my first book *French Perspectives*. Her publishers, Houghton Mifflin, now also mine, were bringing it out in the fall. Willa told me Wyoming was tame compared to New Mexico—so why didn't I try New Mexico, though it was not too easy to travel alone there? She would keep in touch with me. Maybe we would meet somewhere. But she never made exact plans far ahead.

It turned out that I had got only as far as my galleys when she tore out to Taos with Edith Lewis and let me hear of its charms. This was before Mabel Dodge, Maurice

Sterne, D. H. Lawrence and other celebrities brought Taos into the news. What Willa described to me was a small "Mexican" village, reached by a tiny station on the Denver and Rio Grande Railroad, Taos Junction. Thence one proceeded by a horse-drawn stage (John Dunn's) some thirty miles to a small "native" hotel on the Plaza. It had a courtyard with the closet and the well side by side. Wonderful cantaloupes and no "Gringos" (now they are called "Anglos"); saddle horses cheap; lovely villages, Spanish and Indian, within riding distance.

I had not been on a horse since my rides in the North Carolina mountains in 1912. I decided—tamely—to go first to a "dude ranch" in Wyoming, where I learned trail riding from a cowboy.

Willa had departed for Red Cloud, before I reached Sheridan. She had had a glorious visit with her brother Roscoe, in Lander: two rivers met in his backyard and there had been trout fishing and camping trips in the Rockies. Now, while I was taking my fill of the faded-green undulating cattle country—it was patched here and there with blue-green alfalfa in scented purple bloom—and of the sailing peaks, Willa had trekked back to the flat plains of the cornland, settled down in Red Cloud for several late summer and autumn months, to bring her mother out of a serious illness.

She wrote me—and I was astonished—that she had taken over the cooking—for eight—and was devoting herself to learning the mysteries of a kitchen range and the know-how of good pastry.

She was always pleased when restored to those who called her "Willie," and remembered her as her mother's eldest daughter. But having five books to her credit now, the finest of them almost an epic of Nebraska, must have helped that blind terror that sometimes seized her: the fear that she was but a cell in the family blood stream. Her roots and her destiny were now one, and it was a blessed moment of reconciliation. One never saw Willa, in an intimate moment, without realizing how deeply she desired to be of use to her blood-kin, in simple human ways. She, too, was a "plain family woman."

Willa drove busily about to visit old country neighbors when she spent time at her childhood home. The isolated families saved stories of the year for her—offered her their Bohemian delicacies, like *kolaches,* as Sarah Orne Jewett was offered a plate of lobster stew or a slice of mince pie on the coast of Maine.

Willa used to tell me about her Christmas boxes to these long loved and remembered Nebraska farm families. After the translations of her books into the Scandinavian and Czech languages her gifts sometimes included offerings she had herself received from admirers in the old countries of Europe: color prints from Prague, fine shawls and the like. But in case of crop failures on the Divide, seed corn was not forgotten. Her presents were always directed to an individual, whose subjective or economic needs she knew. She was a specialist in Nebraska farming, because she had grown up with it.

The detail of it never stands out obtrusively in the Nebraska novels, but it is there, like her authentic knowledge of flowers and trees. Weather, too, she knew like a farmer. The great consolation of the bleakness in her childhood had been the ravishing wild flowers which she had gathered in heaps and wept over because nobody seemed to notice them. Later she knew them botanically—and never failed to make clear to the specialists among her readers exactly what she was describing, whether it were in Nebraska, New Mexico or the Province of Quebec.

My lone first experience of the West—Wyoming and California, and finally the Southwest—kept my mind galloping madly to keep up with what my eyes feasted upon. Willa, though so deeply engaged in Red Cloud, declared herself homesick for California when I wrote her my impressions. Our Pacific-American civilization seemed in many ways like the Mediterranean. But some letters from the French Army reached the Italianate Berkeley garden where I was visiting, and my trip to Taos dissolved—for another five years.

I stopped but twice on my stirring journey over the Santa Fe Railroad, both times in Arizona. At the Grand Canyon and at Willa's "Panther Canyon"—in reality Walnut Canyon, near Flagstaff—whither I drove with a taciturn Westerner concerned about rattlesnakes. In that strange cliff city Thea and her lover were not to be seen. But the ancient voices spoke, and the austere and planetary Southwest gripped my soul in such fashion that I knew I should return. Willa was glad I'd had even that much of it.

When I reached Brookline, the first copies of *French Perspectives* came to my hands and I despatched one to Red Cloud. Willa was now driving out with her mother and would not be back till Thanksgiving; she planned that meal with Miss Lewis in Bank Street.

But for the fear that the little volume should not prove

worthy I should have dedicated it to Willa who had done much to project the sketches in this form. Perhaps she knew this: anyhow she wrote me and told me later, that she had spent a long day of snowstorm with my book, and had found it more than a collection of sketches of French life and character: all the pieces were part of a whole, they derived from a base of deep feeling, and presented a moral revelation of the French spirit. These French people have values, aims, a point of view, and have acquired wisdom from the enduring verities. One did not find anything of the sort in the Middle West.

In the October *McClure's* I found a brilliant sketch by Willa of a singer: "The Diamond Mine"—a forerunner of *Youth and The Bright Medusa* and an indication that Thea's long book had not exhausted her creator's interest in women singers. But it was Annie Pavelka, the future Ántonia, whom she brought back to New York, from those renewed farm visits, on the Divide.

Our American declaration of war came in April, 1917. Of course, not unexpectedly, for President Wilson's speeches had been preparing the country gradually for what lay ahead. Willa had no patience with this aloof, stiff, intellectual leader of ours, who did not hesitate to borrow his phrases from *The New Republic*: for instance, that one about Making the World Safe for Democracy; and that other which in our time sounds still more deluded, about Fighting the War to End War. But, in truth, that is what we the American people thought we were doing at the time. Our quest in Europe was one of ideal mercy and helpfulness.

By September, the underground currents that had been almost compulsively pulling at me since 1914 had swept me across the Atlantic to wartime Paris, which became my base for correspondence for *The New Republic*. In due course I was summoned to American General Headquarters by the Commander-in-Chief.

Then it was, when eating at the G-2 mess; or with that more worldly mess, reputed for its French cook, where one found Colonel Frank McCoy and Colonel Douglas MacArthur and others later known to fame and generalship, that I was able to compare the bluff, full-fashioned "C.-in-C.," as his staff called him, and as I saw him, with an earlier image Willa had left with me when I decided to go to France.

She had known General Pershing as young cadet, with a slim waist and yellow moustaches, stationed at the University of Nebraska when she was there. He was very gay, reputed a crack shot; had founded an organization called The Pershing Rifles which took prizes everywhere it went. You will find a passage in *One of Ours* to the same effect.

Randolph Bourne had reproached me sharply for not retiring to write a novel in some Western or New England retreat where war could be forgotten. Willa clearly realized that I had to go. She was herself, however, in no wise drawn to do anything but get on with her new story. Before I sailed, I had the comfort of knowing that she had made her first connection with Jaffrey, New Hampshire, which was to prove, in a final sense, a new writing centre; a replacement of her Pittsburgh refuge.

Two women friends of Pittsburgh days had a hand in it. They had rented from Mrs. James Harvey Robinson, for the summer of 1917 and again in 1918, a charming house called High Mowing which has a sweeping view of Mount Monadnock.

Below High Mowing to the west, on the thickly wooded fern-green road from Jaffrey to Dublin, stood the quiet Shattuck Inn, a hostelry of good repute known to Bostonians. There, Willa found bed and board for the first time in 1917. Her newly married friends, the Hambourgs, were with her. But her engrossing work claimed her mornings and the kind ladies of High Mowing offered to pitch her a tent on their lower slopes of field and meadow, backed by a thick fringe of woods.

The tent was pegged to Mother Earth, furnished with table and camp chair. Willa, ever an early riser, found a path near the inn through this wood where lady's-slippers and Hooker's orchids grew.

Over a stone wall next: she was carrying her pens and paper, and the manuscript of *My Ántonia*—and to her tent for two good hours of work. Most of Book Two, "The Hired Girls," was written in this hideout.

This information came to me through the kindness of the present owner of High Mowing, whose son, a young Marine, fell in the Pacific in the Second World War. He had written Willa Cather a letter (now lost) about his joy in *My Ántonia*. He had read the book in his North Carolina camp, and wrote from there. Willa replied to many outpourings of young American hearts about her books.

Her intimate letter to the young Marine, which he sent to his parents for safekeeping before going overseas, had the ring of memory. It derived, she told him, from their mutual love of High Mowing, and from the fact that *My*

Ántonia had a real connection with the place where it was
—in part—written. Jaffrey people, by the way, have noted
a number of their local proper names applied to Black
Hawk characters.

Willa made the point that in general she never talked of
her writing as she was doing it; her young correspondent
was, then, the *"first"* to know what pages were written in
the tent.

Was *My Ántonia* then (I asked myself in 1950 when I
read this comment) a real turning point of literary maturity, when encouragement or criticism from without became
irrelevant? Certainly I had received many disclosures about
the writing of her first three novels. I was separated geo-
graphically from her during the writing of *My Ántonia*,
which she completed in New York in the winter of 1917-
1918, my first winter in beleaguered Paris (air raids driving
us into the wine cellar of the Hôtel de France et Choiseul;
the American Army on the Boulevards, making the cocottes
cry and throw red roses; the Big Bertha dropping pot shots
into streets and a famous sanctuary).

Certainly I was to know much less, as time passed, of
what Willa had "in the works." But she did when I saw
her, sometimes suddenly, unburden herself.

In the following as it were, suspended, summer of 1918,
the Boches swept over the Marne again and dug in fifty
miles from Paris, where I continued to live and write: during the uncertain and bloody fortunes of the Meuse-Ar-
gonne battle, when our A.E.F. gave all for victory, Willa
was engrossed at last in her new story, *One of Ours*. The

proof sheets of *My Ántonia* were hardly dry but she was working again.

In Paris I was waiting longingly for a copy of *My Ántonia*. Ferris Greenslet, my editor at Houghton Mifflin, sent me an early one to the American Hospital of Paris, where I found myself bedded down for seven months of care, infection and recuperation after a critical war accident that brought my correspondence for *The New Republic* to an abrupt conclusion.

With what eagerness I held this incomparable book in my hands, as Dakin's solution dripped into my war fractures! Just to skim a page or two, to get the American measure and flow, the candor and newness, was better than a sedative to calm my pain.

When I was able to *read* rather than just *apprehend*, I was absorbed in the autobiographical elements of the book. Willa would never write a novel of her early life in the first person and, in talk, did not say much about her childhood and youth. As I read *My Ántonia*, I learned far more than she had ever recounted; from the point where, for her, Virginia ended, with an interminable railroad journey "across the great midland plain of North America." The platform where a boy alighted in the dark of night, was obviously the same on which the embalmed corpse of the sculptor was set down, in that early story. The Bohemian Shimerdas with their four children were huddled there too, ready to fare forth to the sod hut in which they were destined to suffer severe hardships and such sorrows as the suicide of a father. Jim (or Willie, his symbolic twin-sister) riding in his Grandfather Burden's wagon box in the cold dark night looked for creeks, rivers, fences, a mountain ridge against the sky. All he made out was "land not a country at all but the material out of which countries are made . . . the dome of heaven all there was of it. . . ."

I looked sharply to find Ántonia, (the "My" in the title indicated that she belonged to somebody) as I felt Willa had forecast her to me; as a beautiful object in the middle of a table, which could be viewed from all sides and in varying lights. At first the story did not seem at all like that. The background was full and rich. There were other farm girls who became hired girls in Black Hawk besides Ántonia, the oldest Shimerda. All were described in terms of character and individual experience, through interweaving themes and detailed scenes in genre painting.

Willa had told me that the story "wrote itself" and that it had no plot. But if it had no plot it had a framework and—in itself a contrivance—a narrator. Jim Burden was presented informally to the reader in this rôle, in an introduction where he is seen to be intellectual and urban, a railroad lawyer with an unhappy personal life. (This story was wisely cut short in a later edition.) The memories of a pioneering experience at his grandmother's homestead, that came to him by an accident of fate at an age of acute sensibility, and lasted until he went East to study law, are the stuff of the story. Like Ántonia, Jim Burden's observations and perceptions had been sharpened and pointed by his migration from a more mellow region to the vast, inchoate land of Nebraska.

Jim would not have fallen in love with a woman like Alexandra Bergson, with her masculine vision and her power to "dominise," as the South Carolinians say, the land of her inheriting and increasing. Alexandra was as strong as the Virginian pioneers: could rival or surpass them. But Ántonia was simply and lustily contained in the country of her Bohemian parents' choosing. Her rôle was so primeval, and so much woman's, whether she plowed for her brother or cooked for Mrs. Harling in Black Hawk, that a detached lonely boy could think of her in the confused terms of a youthful projection of love and nature blended.

The first time Jim returned to the prairie after he went East he found Ántonia, slaving on her brother's farm, with a baby by a railroad conductor who had betrayed her. She was thin from farm work and still but twenty-four.

> "Do you know, Ántonia, since I've been away, I think of you more often than of anyone else in this part of the world. I'd have liked to have you for a sweetheart, or a wife, or my mother or my sister—anything that a woman can be to a man. The idea of you is part of my mind; you influence my likes and dislikes, all my tastes, hundreds of times when I don't realize it. You really are a part of me."

Anything a woman can be to a man? That the reader doubts. If so why had not Jim and Ántonia loved and married, why did not this happen now? Both were young and free. No, Ántonia was a big sister, or a kind of great earth mother, a symbol so central to Jim's heart that he cherished her within himself, and surrounded her figure with a gentle clarity like the early morning or sunset light on prairie and cornfields.

Twenty years later he came back to discover that "his" Ántonia had married a kind negligible husband who had given her a nestful of happy children.

She was a battered woman now, not a lovely girl; but she still had that something which fires the imagination, could still stop one's breath for a moment by a look or a gesture that somehow revealed the meaning in common things.

Ántonia's passionate involvement with her surroundings is here contrasted with the tender compassionate and semi-detached mood of the observer, the oblique reflector of the *femme éternelle.*

The story, I saw, was dedicated to Carrie and Irene Miner, childhood friends of Willa's in Red Cloud: "In memory of affections old and true." The Miners were neighbors of the Cathers. It was no secret that she had in "Mrs. Harling" drawn an exact portrait—her only exact fictional portrait she said later—of Mrs. Miner, the musical wife of the local grain merchant and storekeeper, who was born in Christiania, and had taken Ántonia as a hired girl. Mrs. Miner had died during the writing of the novel and Willa resolved to keep her in life:

> Mrs. Harling was short and square and sturdy-looking, like her house. Every inch of her was charged with an energy that made itself felt the moment she entered a room. Her face was rosy and solid, with bright, twinkling eyes and a stubborn little chin. She was quick to anger, quick to laughter, and jolly from the depths of her soul. . . . Her rapid footsteps shook her own floors, and she routed lassitude and indifference wherever she came. . . .

The "recurrences" in this story are striking and rendered in final terms. Old Mr. Shimerda, with his homesickness for the musical life and the cafés of the old world, his subjection by his hard son, Anton, his burial at the barren crossroads, is a piercing portrait of an American immigrant in whom the will to live did not persist against intolerable odds. I was happy when I found the substance of that delicate sketch of boyhood, "The Enchanted Bluff" distilled into the finer essence of the hired girls' picnic on the river bluff—a noonday dream full of fascination.

Later Willa would say delightedly after a trip to Red Cloud: "I saw Ántonia—she . . ." A story had not detracted from a friendship—rather added to it.

It was during the joyous period following the Armistice, when Allied hopes for a future world redeemed and purged by war ran so high, that I had read *My Ántonia*. When I wrote Willa about it, I included some account of my accident, which had taken place a month before the war ended, on a journey to a supposedly safe devastated region and the then "old" battlefields of the Marne. The official woman guide of the Maison de la Presse had picked up a souvenir—which promptly exploded, killing her beside me, blowing off the arm of the French officer who was with us, and filling my legs and ankles with steel fragments. I had never even tried to go to the Front; yet I was unable to complete my work.

Just before Christmas I had, in the Neuilly hospital, a shocked and very compassionate letter from Willa. She had been in the West when my accident was reported in the newspapers and believed I had escaped with minor injuries. She had returned to New York just before the Armistice.

She went back to her own scalp poisoning which had

brought her so much pain and psychic revolt: it helped her now to understand my plight. She said she thought this war was fated to register in my flesh and bone, as it had in my heart and mind. She was happy that *My Ántonia* had reached me from Ferris Greenslet. She had meant to send me a copy, herself, but—as usual—when she corrected proofs the novel had seemed to her but a grey and chilly thing.

Then her letter sprang forward, every word so alive that it jumped from the page, describing the returned troops. The *Mauretania* had brought the first five thousand in December. Now one met "Ours" everywhere—in hotels, restaurants, on Broadway where a new form of French seemed to be taking root, as in England after the Norman Conquest. *Vive le* France, for instance! The newspapers and the Tammany mayor put on a lot of side about the soldiers, and how America had won the war. But the doughboys were not like that themselves—they were sure they did *not* win the war; and they hid their decorations—for instance a Croix de Guerre—under their greatcoats.

They were so surprisingly endearing, vital! Her rapturous sentences gave me the final assurance that Willa's new novel concerned our soldiers.

In May, 1919, I walked off the gangplank of the old *Rochambeau,* on two sticks, into the arms of friends and relatives. My sister Katharine, who had lived in Cleveland before the war, was by then established in New York with her husband and her little girl. A day or two later Katharine and I were having tea with Willa Cather in Central Park.

"The wistaria is in bloom at the Casino!" she had exclaimed. So our reunion took place at a skimpy little iron table outside the rambling old trellised building long since disappeared, where the hanging violet-blue wistaria clusters seemed part of the Victorian age.

There is a photograph of Willa, taken in 1924 by Nicholas Muray that matches my memory of how she looked that sweet spring day: a standing picture in an embroidered coat, with her two hands resting on her hips and her eager, happy, dedicated head thrust forward. Her way of delivering herself completely to the situation of a little party she was giving and of making a friend feel welcomed was most charming. The warm, assertive, direct outgoing side of her nature still came up from the depths of her distance to meet an occasion.

But it was soon evident that she was greatly involved in her soldier book, so greatly that one cup of tea had scarce been drunk before her questions started. She "wanted to know," with that eye-in-every-pore quality that took possession of her, when she was bent on her own ends.

I "wanted to tell," of course, but like all returned soldiers —and I felt like one—I did not know how to bridge the gap between her idealized war vision that was to be apparent in *One of Ours*—and my own stark impressions of war as *lived*; of France as overrun, not just by the Boches but by the boisterous trans-Atlantics and trans-Pacifics.

Then there was the fact that I had been very ill and was facing a lot of more trouble with the orthopoedic doctors; and that I had myself started a book in the American Hospital of Paris. It was the journal of a wounded woman, who sees the Armistice and the Peace Conference vicariously through her visitors at the hospital.

Could I speak of it? I just did, perhaps vociferously, for my sister with light irony has recalled that afternoon as one in which two writers insisted on talking of their own books.

One of the matters Willa wanted information about was "shell shock." I was able to describe a nervous case who was otherwise quite well but had lost his memory and his hearing. I had seen him at Savenay, a dismal American base hospital near a muddy little French village. And there also I met Alexander Woollcott, the former drama critic of *The New York Times,* and future wit, in the hideously unbecoming garb of a hospital orderly. Woollcott had asked me to have dinner with him in the village and what did we have? A wonderful wine, and Crêpes Suzette . . .

Willa was delighted to hear of good cookery but asked more about shell shock.

I tried to tell her of the great contribution to the subject of nervous war-cases—which I had heard of at the American Hospital of Paris—made by Dr. Thomas Salmon, chief consultant in psychiatry of the A.E.F.—the first psychiatrist honored in any army. He would hold sessions with soldiers who had retreated out of fear—sit up all night with any one individual soldier, three people being present—himself, the devil, and the soldier—and win out over the devil. Dr. Salmon and Dr. Alfred E. Cohn of the Rockefeller Institute for Medical Research, had noticed a nervous heart disease, which proved curable as it was not organic. All this was long ago, you see. I did not yet know Dr. Salmon but his reputation proved him one of our great war leaders. . . . I told Willa.

I had also brought her a couple of volumes of a "new"

French writer of whom I'd first heard in Paris, from Jean Giraudoux. He was named Marcel Proust: *À la recherche du temps perdu: Du côté de chez Swann* was a rare thing, a new kind of French psychological novel—more than Jamesian. Giraudoux had told me that Proust lived in a padded room, frequented the salons of the *haute bourgeoisie*, and was surely the original of the little boy who became the eye and the ear recording the story.

Willa knew that I had translated a book of Giraudoux', *Lectures pour une Ombre*, when he was in Cambridge with General Joffre, teaching the military art to Harvard students. A career diplomat, he had been more than once severely wounded. So he was in Paris in 1917, when I got there: used to take me for walks in the *vieux quartiers* and for an occasional lunch in perfect little unfashionable restaurants, remote from the *quartiers américains*.

Willa was always happy to know of new French authors, whom she preferred to new American authors. There was Proust and also one André Maurois, whom my friend Daniel Halévy had recommended. Maurois had written one or two novels of his province—he came of a family of manufacturers—and as he spoke English was, like Halévy, attached to the English Army as liaison officer. Result: *Les Silences du Colonel Bramble*, a delicious little book that dared to be satirical about the British, even in wartime.

But Willa, crumbling her brioche, was back with her own book, over our last cup of tea. No story she had ever written drove her so hard as this one, she let me know, and she was, as always at this season, eager to escape from New York. It seems to me that she was going to Jaffrey and had arranged for rooms on the third floor of the Shattuck Inn outside the old village. The owners were thoughtful and understanding about her mornings; no foot would trample overhead. This was a great consideration with her by now. The Hambourgs were going to live near Paris, but she would feel at home in Jaffrey.

I was again bound for Chocorua, much closer to the White Mountains and far from her. I hoped to stay late into the fall, for those last lingering days of northern New England beauty—when the boarders went back to the city; and the maples flamed; and the birds suddenly stopped singing; and the air was frosty; and one saw a flash of tawny deer-color under the pines.

Willa and I shared the passion for such days. She had no sympathy with my new enthusiasm, The League of Nations. But landscape and weather, books and writing made us cling together.

CHAPTER IV

End and Beginning
1920 – 1923

WILLA CATHER has been widely quoted as saying of 1922 that the world broke in two, in this year, and she belonged to the earlier half. The statement seemed paradoxical, for Willa was full of creative ardor, very well, very productive, and steadily gaining in literary reputation.

In the year 1920 she had taken a step certainly leading to the future and professionally speaking, a major one. She transferred from Houghton Mifflin, the old Boston firm that had, between 1912 and 1918, published her first four novels, to Alfred Knopf who was still young in the publishing world. I gathered that Willa's decision had something to do with her going less and less to Boston. The neighborhood of Beacon Hill, with both Miss Jewett and Mrs. Fields lost from Charles Street, brought up nostalgic memories. Moreover, Ferris Greenslet, her admirer, editor, "discoverer" on Park Street had been away frequently in Europe in the war years and the aftermath. It was—so he told me—during one of these absences that the "divorce" took place. Houghton Mifflin retained the rights to the early novels, and from time to time new editions were published; sometimes with important prefaces.

Willa was frank about her shift and spoke of Alfred Knopf and his wife Blanche with enthusiasm. These "young people," not long out of Columbia University, had started a publishing house and had built up a reputation and a success in which the values she most cherished—the literary values, not the wide-sale values—were supreme. She respected their taste. The House of Knopf grew in fame with her own fame; Willa never, I am sure, regretted her decision. It was a final commitment on both sides, and that fact, in itself, made for success for both author and publisher.

Before long there appeared three brief pages, printed in *The Borzoi*, the broadside of her new publishing house: "The Art of Fiction." This pregnant little essay is now included in the posthumous *On Writing*.

The quintessential point made was that art should simplify:

> That, indeed, is very nearly the whole of the higher artistic process; finding what conventions of form and what detail one can do without and yet preserve the spirit of the whole—so that all that one has suppressed and cut away is there to the reader's consciousness as much as if it were in type on the page.

A first-rate picture or a first-rate novel, equally, must have in it the strength of many sketches, many stories that have been sacrificed to it. Writing may be the manufacture of stories as a commodity for the market, or it may be an art:

which is always a search for something for which there is
no market, something new and untried, where the values
are intrinsic and have nothing to do with standardized
values. The courage to go on without compromise does
not come to a writer all at once—nor, for that matter, does
the ability. Both are phases of natural development. In
the beginning, the artist, like his public, is wedded to old
forms, old ideals, and his vision is blurred by the memory
of old delights he would like to recapture.

Her own strongest early influences had been Henry
James, Edith Wharton, Sarah Orne Jewett. Were they to
be wholly discarded? I did not believe it. But what was
the new and untried path to be?

The noticeable change in Willa's first Knopf book,
Youth and the Bright Medusa, published in the autumn of
1920, was one of tone. *My Ántonia* had been notably warm
and glowing. The new book was dry, almost sardonic at
times. Not quite satirical.

Willa had seen too much of singers to idealize them. The
first singer story (my own favorite) had, to be sure, a romantic tinge left over from the good old artist days in
Washington Square, when horses drew the buses and a
handsome young *cantatrice*, her name not yet on the bill-
boards, could have her love affair with a painter not yet
known to fame either. But the story of Cressida Garnett
disenchantedly revealed a woman with a voice but no musical intelligence, pushed from behind by a designing Sven-
gali-like accompanist, and devoured by a train of family
leeches. And "A Gold Slipper" lightly derided the rich,
stuffy, dense Pittsburgh business man in relation to music
and a fascinating singer.

These stories were chosen from a considerable number of magazine stories that Willa had published since she left *McClure's*. She did not hold all she wrote worth preserving. Her selection of the four angry early stories from *The Troll Garden* to complete a collection dealing in general with artists and the artistic impulse was sagacious. At present "Paul's Case" (one of the four) is the only story of hers that may be printed in anthologies.

About Christmas time in 1920, I moved to New York to stay, and settled for two years with a friend at 56 West Tenth Street, only a few zigzag blocks away from Number Five Bank Street.

In Katharine Ludington's little Victorian front parlor, there were bright coals in the grate, as there were at Number Five Bank Street. Willa had sometimes "trundled her own" in a wheel-barrow, during the war. She still complained of food substitutes—think of carrot marmalade, for instance!—but was now able to enjoy, by a red glow with a blue halo, the brioches, crumpets, and the little French pastries that required butter in abundance. The twenties at least offered physical sustenance. Prohibition cut sadly into our veterans' growing knowledge of good wine, but they returned with appetites whetted by international delicacies which now began to appear on New York City menus.

Willa's letters had for ten years preserved a continuity in our friendship. Casual, frank, gay, affectionate, often more confidential than meetings, they were treasure-trove. But unless letters are closely spaced, as love letters are for instance, or constant intellectual exchanges, like the famous

Holmes-Pollock letters, they slide deceptively over human, mental and philosophic differences which develop when human beings are face to face and talk.

Willa did seem not to enjoy talk as *difference;* as argument and ferment. When she had made her mind up, she wanted to prevail. I had been young in experience, and very much a learner and tyro in writing when I first met her. Now I was at least on my own, and at least must stand my ground—or be silent.

First, about the war. In the summer and fall of 1920 Willa, in France with Miss Lewis, saw for herself how the last reach of her Western pioneer dream had registered in the American graveyards lifting their stark crosses to the soft French skies. My "war-book," *Shadow-Shapes,* came out in her absence; she read it on her return. She cared less for it, I believed, than for my first book *French Perspectives,* though she never quite said so. My best readers were my comrades in a shared experience, a sort of mystery, an atmosphere, at least hinted at, in my pages, but not fully communicated to those who had not participated; who could not register, in Melville's now trite phrase, "the shock of discovery."

War was a *story* to Willa. It had been a story from the moment when she first heard of it in 1914—in the French and Bohemian country of Nebraska. No soldier she had met on Broadway had told her the truth of it. He couldn't. He wouldn't. Neither would, nor could I.

Her intolerance began to trouble me. She was truly skeptical about the post-war world. Take this Viennese Freud: why was everybody reading him? Tolstoy knew as much about psychology—with no isms attached—as any fiction writer needed. I didn't agree. Freud was *here*: I had to try to read him, because I lived in today's world. But Willa, like the Pueblo Indians who—I had been told in New Mexico—had no word for "future," looked backward with regret. Our present lay about us in ruins but we had, she wistfully remarked, a beautiful past.

Awkwardly limping beside her in the Park as winter came on, I was aware that my brisk friend had to curb her impatience. She was greatly sympathetic that I'd had bad luck—but she did easily shun the actual perception that an ankle or a leg had been filled full of steel: a human body should remain intact and as God made it. I was not yet forty; yet here I was with a cane. She rejoiced over my trip to New Mexico in the beginning of this year. Dr. R. W. Lovett of Boston, my orthopoedic doctor, had insisted that my power to walk would come back if I stretched my ankles in the stirrup. To quit industrialized urbanity, to explore on horseback ancient America where primitive pioneering conditions still prevailed, and the overwhelming drama of nature still ruled men's minds and thought, must have been, Willa said, an immense release from wounds and world problems.

But, I retorted, world problems exist in the Southwest in microcosmic form. Primitive man, in New Mexico, a state three fifths the size of France, is living in a stratified society. The few whites—"Anglos"—on top, the native Mexicans, on the next layer, and the Indians at the bottom of the heap. The classes and the masses, as in Europe or in a French or British colony. What is the Pueblo Indian's relation to American democracy?

Willa did not ask herself such questions. I told her I'd

tried to find out how the Pueblo felt about the war. There were only a few Pueblos among the eighteen thousand Indians who volunteered. The treaty agreements still held; Indians were not conscripted. But some of them felt guilty. A man I'd met out there had told me that once on a hunting trip in the mountains two or three leaders from a large village which had resisted white education stopped him in his wagon and indicated that they intended to kill him.

He argued with them. "What's the matter? You know me. You know I am a friend to the Indian."

"Maybe. But you German, we think?"

"Yes, I have German blood. What of it?"

"But Washington U.S.A. fight the Germans. We not go. But we say, if we kill *one* German, everything O.K."

The German-American had been able to talk them out of it.

Willa laughed and moved on to her major interests: landscape, the perspectives of history, the cliff dwellings.

These involve one, I remarked, in new fields of scholarship. American archaeology alone—what a "literature" there is . . . and anthropology—I had had to work at that. Botany—all the flowers of the dry plains are different.

Willa had done very little reading in anthropology—some archaeology, of course. But if there was one book in the world she would have liked to write, it was Clements and Clements *Rocky Mountain Flowers.*

I told her about some of the wild flowers that grew on the rocky knoll that rose sheer from our adobe, our "mud house" (Gertrude Ely's and mine) in the Tesuque Valley. I had yielded to Gertrude's suggestion that we buy an old New Mexican house on a ridge, with fine beams and a flat roof; a couple of spectacular acres, an orchard, big cottonwoods and poplars, a ditch that ran around it like a moat (The Acequia Madre) all for five hundred dollars!

Willa envied me the cottonwoods and wanted to hear about the views; the sandhills; the canyons; the Mexican neighbors who sang their mournful folk songs along the Acequia. . . . I told her about Salomé, of brigand appearance, who, for ten dollars a year, engaged himself to be our guardian, and keep the wandering burros away from the apple trees. The house was in disrepair. Next summer we would go out and put it in order.

Willa and I could not talk of Wilson, nor of the Allies' feeding of the Germans. The social and political values carried over from pre-war times were, after all, the social and sociological values of the Theodore Roosevelt era, established in part by *McClure's Magazine*. She did not esteem them. She saw or divined more clearly than I how finally the Victorian age had, when the peace was signed, retreated into the past. But we could, as ever, talk about books.

Main Street appeared in 1920, and the next year came *Three Soldiers* by the still unknown Dos Passos. Willa had no patience with these precursors of the "novel of protest," and the sociological fiction of the twenties. What did I think of Sinclair Lewis? Before I could say a word she hotly asserted that he had been satisfied to get an external view of the small prairie centre. She explained, defensively, that in every town like Gopher Prairie there existed at least one family, probably several, where, at least in one field, standards of world culture, music, the arts, the languages were preserved. She had brought in such a family—that of the storekeeper and grain merchant—in *My Ántonia*.

But, she said, when Sinclair Lewis looked at his small town, he found nothing of the sort—only commonness, cheapness, ignorance. He had the point of view of the drummer who stops in the businessman's hotel; gossips with the loungers at the drug counter!

Sinclair Lewis, even in 1920, admired Willa Cather's Nebraska novels. He said, lecturing in Omaha in this year:

> Miss Cather is Nebraska's foremost citizen. The United States knows Nebraska because of Willa Cather's books.

Later, in the days of Willa Cather's and Sinclair Lewis' fame, the two became fast friends. It may well be that Willa came to estimate the whole reach of Lewis' work differently. We never talked of it after *Main Street* appeared, and then she placed *Sister Carrie* and *Jennie Gerhardt* as superior in this mode. She had recommended them to me when I first knew her, saying that though one could not call Dreiser an artist, he had the stuff and power of the novelist. Lewis was a herald of a changed world, and so were social-minded, free-verse poets like Carl Sandburg and Edgar Lee Masters, whom she demolished with a word. (Masters' work, of course, was rather close to the spirit of "The Sculptor's Funeral," and as for free verse, Willa Cather wrote some herself.) At this time the Imagists were active and vocal. She dismissed them severally and en masse.

Amy Lowell, their leader on this side of the ocean, was a friend of mine, as she knew—a very amusing character she called her, who sat up all night and worked and ate at the wrong hours. If one did not admire old Boston, traditional Boston, she said, one might enjoy Amy Lowell. Willa herself did not. Miss Lowell had regular metres in her very blood stream—yet she was a rebel in poetry and played the tyrant in her public and private life.

Here Willa began to sputter and I was moved to inquire into a story, already apocryphal in literary Boston, about a visit she had made a few years earlier with Professor George Edward Woodberry of Columbia University to Amy Lowell's Victorian mansion in Brookline. The distinguished elderly English professor and Willa Cather—so she began her story—were guests at Mrs. Fields' on Charles Street and it was arranged that Miss Lowell should send her limousine to fetch them.

By the time they reached Sevenels, with its mansard roofs, lawns, shrubberies, and gardens Professor Woodberry had told Willa Cather about the Keats manuscripts, letters and books that Miss Lowell was indefatigable in collecting: Miss Lowell had discovered, she claimed, a good deal that was fresh. He itched to see for himself.

But after they were introduced into the waxed, baronial spaces that one might well expect of a Boston Lowell, a considerable delay set in. Miss Lowell was still dictating—in bed, of course—to her secretary aloft. Mrs. Ada Russell, her devoted ex-actress friend and lady-in-waiting, offered them tea and a dozen amenities and explanations. But currents of impatience had set in, and the bulky, dynamic Poetess-Imagist rushing upon them, at last—full of casual bonhommie and friendliness, in her long, plain, rich silk, buttoned, Quaker-like, from collar to toes—perhaps found them a bit stiff: if Amy Lowell wanted the esteem and sought the friendship of a noted scholar, this was hardly the way to behave, Willa thought.

Of course, her opinion was not important to Amy. Willa Sibert Cather was just a Houghton Mifflin author whom the Imagist *might* get around to reading in due course. Though, she preferred detective stories to novels of the prairie!

Well, they were eventually led, as I recall, fairly fuming, to the Sacred Precinct; the safe where Amy kept her treasures; or else, perhaps, the Keats material was unlocked and brought by the Priestess-Imagist to her library table. In any event, the Professor, so modest and so learned, eventually extended his eager right hand.

But the owner stepped forward touchily, seized the "item," set her thumbs and fists firmly on the two edges like a monk with a missal and held it herself under the Professor's nose. He must not *touch* it—nobody might *touch* her rarities. It was clear that they were so much a part of her person that a violation would occur if the most revered scholar so much as turned a page. She, Amy, would do the turning.

Willa, at this point in her story, stifled with fury, just blew up. Her sentences, always broken, emphatic, and colloquial but ordered, exploded like fireworks. Woodberry, the great Woodberry, revered of students and scholars was at Sevenels but a slum child with dirty hands!

In the winter of 1921-1922 I was back again in Tenth Street, after a long stay in Tesuque Valley and in Santa Fe. Willa was warm-hearted about four articles I had written

for *Harper's Magazine*, "The Journal of a Mud House,"
by which I'd paid my way. She was concentrating her own
attention on the novel as a literary form; in spite of her
resistance to the opinions of *The New Republic*, I noticed
that she did not scorn it as an organ for her own ideas.
"The Novel Démeublé" appeared there on April 12, 1922.
One of her most provocative and artfully condensed critical essays—later reprinted in *Not Under Forty* and the posthumous collection *On Writing*—it pleads, like her Borzoi
essay, for the novel as imaginative art, divested of journalism, free of literal material descriptions except as emotional
penumbra—as in Tolstoy—to the characters themselves.

In these eight pages of print she deals succinctly with
Balzac, Tolstoy, D. H. Lawrence, Mérimée and Hawthorne. And writes several passages as good as the following:

> Whatever is felt upon the page without being specifi-
> cally named there—that, one might say, is created. It is the
> inexplicable presence of the thing not named, of the over-
> tone divined by the ear but not heard by it, the verbal
> mood, the emotional aura of the fact or the thing or the
> deed, that gives high quality to the novel or the drama, as
> well as to poetry itself.

This essay seemed to account for the method used both
in *O Pioneers!* and *My Ántonia;* it stirred up plenty of
highbrow talk and critical concurrence.

But when *One of Ours* came out, at last, in September,
1922, it did not seem "unfurnished." Indeed I was troubled
by the chorus of critical dismay that arose from the intellectual periodicals. The evocative style of the earlier Nebraska novels had been scrapped, they said, for a lot of

pedestrian detail about Midwest farm life. Was Miss Cather deserting to the mass audience? Even Mencken and Nathan, her most ardent admirers, were in a state of shock and dismay.

One of Ours reached me in Tesuque when the aspens had turned to glorious patches of pale gold on the dark-forested flanks of the Sangre de Cristos and my own poplars and cottonwoods were aflame. I was by then embarked on a fiery, contemporary and, at first, local venture: fighting, with the artists and writers of Santa Fe, the Pueblos' battles against Senators Fall and Bursum, who tried to capture their lands; and against Indian Commissioner Burke, who wanted to suppress their rituals. The long crusade had started under John Collier's leadership.

One of Ours seemed out of key. Like the critics I missed the evocative glow of passionate young memory. The novel seemed at first, middle-aged, cold-hearted, almost querulous about the faults and miseries that a boy with a finer grain than his brothers had had to endure in the contemporaneous Midwest. But before I had read it through I received a hot-foot, high-spirited comment on her critics from Willa, dated, I noticed, from Central Park.

She had been seeing our mutual friends, the William Allen Whites of Emporia, Kansas, and had been gaily twitted in biblical terms by Will White: "If thy Mencken and thy Nathan desert thee then the Lord will take thee by." White, who had contributed to *McClure's* and joined the band which bought *The American Magazine* before Willa took on her *McClure's* editorship was an emphatic low-brow. It was important to her, he felt, that Claude, Willa's fellow Nebraskan, should win the big audience.

The book was selling, Willa told me, ahead of *Babbitt* in some Midwest cities. (That was the first time she had ever mentioned sales.) She really felt pleased with her story; she had been able to carry out her own intention. In fact she was (critics or not), just discovering how to write; intended (belligerently) to go on learning. Occasionally through the long autumn I would receive an envelope with clippings about the controversy that continued to rage over *One of Ours*.

Willa was always fearful of the New York reporters but rather free to talk when she got to Nebraska, where people remembered her and were proud and envious of her achievements. One of the matters that she disclosed to the press on this occasion was that the character of her hero, Claude Wheeler, was inspired by that of a near relative, a first cousin, G. P. Cather, who had been killed in 1918 at Cantigny. Her aunt—whom everyone promptly thought of as Mrs. Wheeler and remembered as resembling "Aunt Georgiana" in "A Wagner Matinée"—had given her the boy's letters. He was her own flesh and blood.

The hero [she told a reporter of *The Omaha World Herald*] is just a red-headed prairie boy. I always felt it was presumptuous and silly for a woman to write about a male character but by a chain of circumstances I came to know that boy better than I know myself. I have cut out all picture-making because that boy does not see pictures. It was hard to cease to do the thing that I do best, but we all have to pay a price for everything we accomplish and because I was willing to pay so much to write about this boy I felt that I had a right to do so.

This was not a portrait like that of Thea Kronborg but a story of youth, struggle and defeat. The young inarticu-

late man, "butting his way through the world," was painfully thwarted, he twisted his chin over his collar when he
talked, as if he had on a bridle-bit, and said things about
life that echoed Willa on her dark days.

"I don't believe I can ever settle down to anything [he
says to a friend]. Don't you feel that at this rate there isn't
much in it?"
"In what?"
"In living at all, going on as we do. What do we get
out of it? Take a day like this: you waken up in the morning and you're glad to be alive; it's a good enough day for
anything, and you feel sure something will happen. Well,
whether it's a workday or a holiday, it's all the same in the
end. At night you go to bed—nothing has happened."
"But what do you expect?" [asks the friend] . . .
". . . Well, if we've only got once to live, it seems like
there ought to be something—well, something splendid
about life, sometimes."

Claude's personal good fortune in the A.E.F. was a fellow officer, who in private life was a violinist: David Gerhardt the kind of chap his German friends the Ehrlichs, in
Lincoln, would have appreciated; the kind of comrade in
his billets who could interpret France, the old France, for
which the Americans were fighting; who could introduce
him to it, in a way to bring him many human and cultural
pleasures and realizations.

After her character, Gerhardt, had been recognized by
fellow musicians in New York as almost surely deriving
from a distinguished young violinist, David Hochstein, a
nephew of Emma Goldman, who had been killed in the
Argonne in 1918, Willa gave a long interview which appeared in the book section of *The New York Herald* on

December 24, 1922. She avowed that Hochstein had been the model for Gerhardt, though she had met the violinist but three times in New York, before he went to the war.

The interview resembles in emotional tone, observation and enthusiasm the letters Willa wrote her friends.

"Yes," Miss Cather said, "I think that character must have been done from David Hochstein. It's not a portrait, it's not even an impressionistic sketch of him!" . . .

"You say you didn't know Hochstein well?"

"Not at all. But he was the sort of person to whom you gave your whole attention. One knew him as well as one could under the circumstances. The first time I met him was at Harold Bauer's apartment in the Wellington Hotel, one afternoon in the winter of 1916. A group of musicians had met together to play things they liked. Hochstein was among them. I had not heard him before. . . . They played a lot of chamber music that afternoon. . . . What I particularly remember was their beautiful playing of Schubert's *Die Forelle* (The Trout), a quintet not often played in public because it requires two cellos. That afternoon Boris Hambourg took one cello part, Maurice Dambois the other. Thibaud played first violin, Hochstein second and I think Monteux, now conductor of the Boston Symphony Orchestra, was at the piano. I was very much interested in Hochstein from the moment they began to play and in that quintet I thought his playing simply splendid. I had the feeling that he was playing at the top of his form and that he cared particularly for that composition. . . .

"I felt that he was a very poetic violinist and that he had the *stimmung* of that particular composition on that occasion more than any of the other players. He was enjoying himself thoroughly. To this day I cannot be sure whether his eyes were really yellow-brown or whether that color simply stays in my mind as a connotation—the yellow brown of trout streams in sunlight. He was sitting by a window in a strong glow of afternoon sun that made his hair distinctly auburn. He looked very handsome—very young and fresh among the older men; he was then, I believe, about 24. His face and the shape of his head were distinctly intellectual. There is a certain drawing of Father Damien, one that used to hang in the rooms of college girls, which might stand as a portrait of Hochstein. The resemblance was quite remarkable. . . .

"After the music was over the musicians settled down to talk. Hochstein didn't care to talk apparently. He said he must be going, and put on his hat and overcoat. We went down in the elevator together and up to Carnegie Hall, where I took my bus. We were talking about the Schubert things they had been playing. I found that, as I had suspected, he was a very thoughtful young man; that he had a great many ideas and opinions and rather kept them to himself. He was reticent, but what he had to say was extremely interesting; and you didn't feel that he had said it all before to a great many people. He hadn't, in short, yet acquired the professional manner which an artist must have to save his soul, but which is, after all, more attractive in the breach than in the observance. His manner in conversation with a stranger, even with his friends, was cordial but not effusive—distinctly not effusive.

"I did not meet Hochstein again until after America had gone into the war and his number had been drawn for military service. There was, of course, warm discussion among his friends and fellow artists as to whether he ought not to get exemption from military duty. He was very low in mind about the matter. He hated the idea of giving up his work and going into the service; and he hated the idea of being a quitter. From the beginning of the war his sympathies had not been entirely pro-Ally. He had got his musical training in Germany and admired many things about German civilization. Moreover, he hadn't the kind of mind that easily takes sides, that adopts opinions and says, 'These opinions are right, and are the only right ones, because they are mine.' He was a Socialist and had read and thought a great deal about economics and systems of government. His father, I believe, was a student. I got the impression that Hochstein himself had given a good deal of time to the study of philosophy. He knew too much about history to draw rash and comforting conclusions. He didn't believe that any war could end war; he didn't believe that this one was going to make the world safe for democracy, or that it had much to do with democracy whatever. He couldn't see any Utopia ahead. He didn't believe that the war was going to get the world anywhere, no matter how it came out. But he didn't like to see himself getting exemption. That picture didn't attract him. That role looked undignified to him. However, he applied for exemption. The Local Board looked into his case, found he was the only support of his widowed mother, and granted his discharge. After he got his discharge he was unhappy. He presented himself again before the Board, told them he had made arrangements for his mother during his absence and wished to enter the service. The chairman of the Board wrote that they were 'struck by his manly bearing and fine appearance.' . . .

"I met Hochstein again after he had been in camp a few weeks and he was a much discouraged young man. The drill, the wooden discipline, the apparent waste of time, the boredom, were very hard for him to bear. He terribly missed the companionship of men with his own interests. He said his mind felt heavy, as if it were going to sleep, as if he were drugged. And, he couldn't but feel it was all for nothing. He was giving up everything to adopt a course of action which was mostly the deadliest kind of inaction and which led nowhere. He didn't talk about it a great deal, but he looked much older; his face seemed frozen in a kind of bitter resignation. I couldn't believe it was the same countenance, so full of romantic feeling and delicate humor, that I had watched that afternoon when he was playing the Trout quintet. It was soldiers of his kind, who hadn't any simple, joyful faith, or any feeling of being out for a lark, who gave up most, certainly.

"About three months after this I saw Hochstein for the third and last time. I had in the meantime heard from some of his friends that David was feeling very differently about everything that pertained to his military duties; that he had become quite reconciled to his life in camp. He looked, indeed, very different. He was not dejected, he bore himself as if he liked his uniform. Something keen and penetrating and confident had come back into his face. When he talked there was a glow of enthusiasm in his eyes. When I came upon the scene he was talking. Yes, he was saying, he wouldn't have missed it. The life at camp was a deadly grind at first, but now he wouldn't have missed it. He had found something there that he had vaguely felt the lack of all his life.

"Someone asked him if it was the exercise, the regularity, the lack of any personal responsibility. 'Oh, it's everything,' he said. 'It's difficult to explain.' He went on a little further. I don't remember just what he said; but those of us who were with him understood clearly that what he liked, what he got something out of, was his relation to other young men. He didn't mention the war, didn't seem to be dwelling on the larger issues of it. His whole attention now seemed fixed upon his company and what was going on at Camp Upton. We asked him if he wasn't bored. No, not at all now; the men were splendid.

"Splendid, no doubt, but not very stimulating, probably, and all a good deal alike. Hochstein laughed and shook his head. 'No, they're not alike. The men are all right, fine fellows. I'm learning a great deal.' Didn't he miss the kind of food and comfort and personal freedom he had always been used to, we asked him, and the company of other artists? 'At first,' he said, 'but not now. For me there's something in that life, just as it is; something I've always wanted.' . . .

"He didn't say what that something was, perhaps he couldn't have said. He was not loquacious, but by a few words he could indicate a great deal. His friends felt absolutely reassured about him. He had never looked handsomer, never seemed easier in his mind or more easily pleased and amused. . . .

"The next autumn the news came that Hochstein had been blown to pieces by a shell in the Argonne Forest. On the night of the 14th of October, Hochstein and a fellow officer had brought a small wagon train of hot food over almost impassable roads, under shell fire, up to men who were to make an important attack in the morning. The next day, Hochstein, in command of the headquarters runners, was killed during the action.

"Letters to his mother, some of which were published, show how seriously he took his military duties. Soon after he got his commission he wrote her:

" 'You don't know (I don't yet) what it means to be a platoon commander. It means having the lives of fifty-eight others in your control. And they must be cared for. It isn't just commanding. I never before (even after ten months in the army) realized what it did mean. I have no military ambition, but I know how few can lead; and I know that I would rather lead than be led.' . . .

"Again he writes his mother:

" 'When you have seen and met men who have been through the inferno many times, every belief you ever held is either destroyed or tempered more strongly, and I have had many to destroy—in whose place I find newer, better and stronger ones. Everyone finds his belief, his religion—here I have found mine. I adhere to no creed, no more than my father did, nor to any particular kind of God, but dear mother, I *believe*. I have faith. I know that for all these heroic souls gone to the beyond there is some future. But those who die, be it recklessly or by the most unexpected exploding shell, have a compensation more than a mere title of hero or a posthumous service cross. You don't try to explain it—but you know it in France.' . . .

"From a very thoughtful young man, critical by habit, a doubter of governments and religions and schools of thought, such statements mean something. They mean that something very revolutionary had happened in Hochstein's mind; I would give a good deal to know what it was!

"In the days when I met David Hochstein I was not writing *One of Ours*. I was busy writing *My Ántonia*, and this latest book of mine was no more in my thoughts than it is in yours. An event which touched my own life rather closely, and which came later, produced the book. Afterward in 1920, when I was deep in this story, I wanted my red-headed soldier from a prairie farm to 'get some of his back,' as the phrase is, through a fine friendship; so many splendid friendships grew up between young men during the war. I wanted him, in daily life, at last to have to do with someone he could admire. I had the good fortune to know a great many fine young soldiers, some of them very well, so I had a wide latitude of choice.

"But when I came to that part of the story, it was the figure of Hochstein, whom I had known so little, that walked into my study and stood beside my desk. I had not known him well, but neither would Claude Wheeler know him very well; the farmer boy hadn't the background, the sophistication to get very far with a man like Hochstein. But there was a common ground on which they could know and respect each the other—the ground on which Hochstein had met and admired his fellow soldiers at Camp Upton. And Claude would sense the other side of David and respect it."

Compare these extremely moving thumbnail sketches of a gifted musician who had a fundamental disbelief in war and nevertheless became a greater American when he gave himself to it, with the rather pale and insubstantial David Gerhardt of the novel. The latter was recognizable as Hochstein, but not "created," even as a secondary character, in the sense that Claude's quivering mother, tied to a crass, hectoring husband, whose humor ever put Claude in the wrong, was created; or, above all, Mahailey, the muted, the wily old family servant who divined so much and knew so little. (For interest in a "recurrence," compare Mahailey with "Poor Marty," a poem that is to be found in the 1933 and 1937 editions of *April Twilights*.

It seems that the true creative process with Miss Cather was a slow and inward thing, and that her deepest compassion was aroused by voiceless human beings whom she felt to be at the mercy of life and fate—like an old poor-white servant, or an old grandmother—whom we shall meet later—people who never talked and so never thought, but did feel.

"It wasn't American to explain yourself; . . . [Claude says.] you didn't have to! On the farm you said you would or you wouldn't: that Roosevelt was all right, or that he was crazy . . . if you tried to say more, it was because you liked to hear yourself talk."

Hochstein, of course, did not belong to the voiceless. The war climax, in which the disappointed farm boy found his transfiguration, is unconvincing to the war hero of today, the veteran of World War Two, whose typical experience leads him to find himself a helpless unit among millions from other nations. This veteran has expressed his own sense of his tragic fate in raw books like *The Naked and the Dead* —a title from which Willa would have cringed. The title she gave to the A.E.F. section of *One of Ours* is: "Bidding the Eagles of the West Fly On."

In her story there are a few smelly corpses, but no profanity, no sex, no rebellion, no chaos are even hinted at. Avaricious French peasants, whom we used to hear of during the First World War, as exploiting our doughboys, are absent. Instead, we meet comprehending French people of the upper and lower bourgeoisie. The sense of order, veracity, and *politesse* are such that the army as an institution is fully upheld, and Claude's fulfilment in a heroic death suffers no disillusion, till the last pages and sentences of the book.

This is, no doubt, why Willa Cather received the Pulitzer Prize for *One of Ours*. Thousands of American parents and many American veterans, too, saw the rewards of their sacrifices here displayed gloriously. The intellectual and more humanly or philosophically conscious, veteran found the war narrative "off the beam."

Willa was visiting her friends the Hambourgs at their villa in Ville d'Avray, outside Paris, when a reporter found her and delivered the news of the Pulitzer Prize in May of 1923.

Her surprise was great: she had had nothing of the sort in mind; had written to please herself; had no expectations for the book.

Whatever prizes or degrees came to her were nothing

she aimed for; she was too stalwart, self-directed and honest for that. But she liked this prize and never ceased to say, in print and out of print, that Claude was her favorite of all her heroes. Was it because he was almost a piece of herself, left behind in Red Cloud? Claude is the only young hero she had, except Paul and Tom Outland, and all three died young. There are a number of other young men in the novels who serve as reflectors for her heroines. Her older heroes, like Bartley Alexander and Professor St. Peter, subtle and complex characters, strike far deeper into her mature estimates of life. For she had, of course, realized that it is in middle life that the complex man cannot evade his psychological fate.

In 1923, Knopf brought out *April Twilights and Other Poems*, a new edition of her first book. The dedication reads: "To my Father, for a Valentine." Some of the early poems, which had made the author blush in 1911—and, as she said to me then, had led her to buy up and secrete the copies, were suppressed. Others, published in magazines in the *McClure's* period and later, were added.

Willa's poetry, if not taken just affectionately or autobiographically, as a youthful notebook on life—if taken critically, reveals echoes of Housman, of William Butler Yeats, and other masters. I regretted that she reissued the early book, at just the point when she had become a master of original prose. For her poetry could not rank with that of modern American poets she admired, like Robert Frost. Nevertheless, a good case could be made for the reissue of *April Twilights*, if only because Willa herself had the poet's response to life, including the typical sense of the lyric poet that youth and the emotions of youth, because of their great intensity and simplicity, surpass all other emotions. Dorothy Canfield Fisher has suggested how unusual this mood and belief is in a novelist, who commonly values more than young emotion the wisdom and insights accumulated during middle and elder years.

But Willa's very first literary expression was in poetry; in verse she was able to write throbbing love lyrics, to give vivid pictures of foreign lands and places—as for instance, London, Ludlow Castle, Delphi, The Palatine, Provence; and the moods, elegiac or lyrical, evoked by them. Ferris Greenslet, in *Under the Bridge*, speaks of

> how [Miss Cather's] sense of beauty which found its first expression in poetry persisted and colored all her work. One wonders whether she, like those other poet-novelists, Hardy and Meredith, might in the age of Elizabeth or the Revolution have been poet only.

Yet her ear seems very much less acute in poetry. "Going Home" and my favorite "Prairie Spring" and "Prairie Dawn," "Macon Prairie" and "A Silver Cup," are written in free verse. More characteristic of her poetry as a whole are the regular and sometimes sentimental rhymes and metres of "The Swedish Mother," and "Spanish Johnny," who closely resembles a character in *The Song of the Lark*, Johnny Tellamantez.

SPANISH JOHNNY

The old West, the old time,
  The old wind singing through
The red, red grass a thousand miles,
  And, Spanish Johnny, you!

He'd sit beside the water-ditch
　　When all his herd was in,
And never mind a child, but sing
　　To his mandolin.

The big stars, the blue night,
　　The moon-enchanted plain:
The olive man who never spoke,
　　But sang the songs of Spain.
His speech with men was wicked talk—
　　To hear it was a sin;
But those were golden things he said
　　To his mandolin.

The gold songs, the gold stars,
　　The world so golden then:
And the hand so tender to a child
　　Had killed so many men.
He died a hard death long ago
　　Before the Road came in;
The night before he swung, he sang
　　To his mandolin.

In April, 1923, when *The Century Magazine* began the serialization of *A Lost Lady* (in three numbers) the contributor's column announced:

> Miss Cather belongs to no school and regularly disappoints those who expect that a new book will be like any other.

When Knopf published the novel, in September, 1923, it was instantly appraised as Willa Cather's "best," her "greatest" story. Marian Forrester had the attributes that make a woman seductive to men, including literary critics. She became the toast of New York; in a trice one of the memorable heroines of American fiction. People talked of her eyes, "dark and full of light, set under a low white forehead and arching eyebrows" . . . "lively laughing intimate nearly always a little mocking"; of her "inviting, musical laugh, that was like the distant measures of dance music, heard through opening and shutting doors."

Those who felt that Miss Cather had fumbled in the *longueurs* of *One of Ours* were thoroughly reassured. Here, indeed, was the novel *démeublé;* short, pointed, condensed, episodic. It covered many years of time in the heroine's life. Yet the author had shown such skill one closed the volume with a sigh for its brevity.

The novel is a portrait of a gay but baffling lady of the frontier of the old West, the still young wife of an elderly railroad contractor, whose home outside the small prairie town of Sweet Water was a renowned centre of hospitality to the railroad magnates who travelled on the Burlington.

The setting brings the story into the succession of the Nebraska novels. The period pictured in *O Pioneers!* and *My Ántonia* seems earlier. Yet the foreign homesteaders of those books had come West on the railroad and Captain Forrester, now elderly and retired, had been a still earlier pioneer. His prototype, Governor Garber, according to Mrs. Bennett in *The World of Willa Cather,* travelled up the Republican River in 1870 on horseback, staked his claim in the midst of deer and buffalo.

Willa Cather, working imaginatively, does not make calendared deductions and implications for us. She simply sets us down at the Forresters and we find ourselves in a period piece—the late eighties, perhaps?—when good was good and evil evil. Though written in the beginning of the Freudian age and by an author who now could present a cool cheek to a heroine—make her irresistible and yet not be herself over-dazzled—it had no modern implications. Willa had an infallible instinct for presenting a period in its own terms. She had only, she said, to return to the cottonwood grove where she picnicked as a child to find Mrs. Forrester. She had only—I am saying this—to recall the technique and the moral outlook of her favorite French masters of the novel to portray her: a heroine who does not preserve the moralities, but clings to the amenities, and sometimes surprises us with the nobilities.

Mrs. Forrester, coming to greet a distinguished guest in negligée, brushing her long black hair, lived in another and more romantic world than that of Sweet Water—approached by a bridge that sometimes washed out. James Thurber, as he related in *The New Yorker* a few years ago, went to Sweet Water in search of Mrs. Forrester and also came upon Madame de Vionnet, the lost lady of Henry James's *The Ambassadors*. In an incomparable ironic parody in Jamesian vein, Thurber made a little pointed nostalgic fun of the serious-minded, mid-Victorian way both writers took their naughty heroines.

But that rapt contemplation of a remembered past which had its own moral code and its winter pleasures in Denver makes the novel a document as well as a *chef d'oeuvre*. Willa was more ready than was customary with her to let the newspapers in on the secrets of her new heroine. She told a *New York World* reporter that Mrs. Forrester had been created out of an emotion that reacts on a true artist like food on a hungry person. She had been "teased" (Sarah Orne Jewett's word again) for years!

> "*A Lost Lady* was a beautiful ghost in my mind for twenty years before it came together as a possible subject for presentation. All the lovely emotions that one has had, some day appear with bodies, and it isn't as if one found ideas suddenly. Before this, the memories of these experiences and emotions have been like a perfume. . . .
>
> "To me, the one important thing is never to kill the figure that you care for, for the sake of atmosphere, well-balanced structure, or neat presentation. . . . Sometimes too much symmetry kills things."

Mrs. Forrester's perfume, her place as an *objet d'art* in the middle of her story were the guide to technique. Yet though the writing went quickly—mostly done in 1922—Willa told me that she had to try the novel in three different forms before she hit her mark. One of the drafts was straight, first-person narration by Niel Herbert, the idealistic local boy who fell out of the tree in the picnic grove when trying to reach and kill a bird that Ivy Peters (the villain of the story) had blinded in casual cruelty. This sharp sadistic stroke of Ivy's prepares the reader—as does Mrs. Forrester's eager care for the injured boy, Niel, in her own walnut bed—for the complex developments of the future. Ivy would later be the crass exploiter of a fair wayward victim, Niel would be her defender and protector, even when disenchanted.

The first-person narrative was read by John Galsworthy, who advised Willa (I am indebted to Ferris Greenslet for this bit of information) that it was a serious hazard, in his opinion, for a woman author to limit the observation of a complex, subtle heroine to the mind of a very young man. Miss Jewett had said much the same thing in a letter about that early story "On the Gull's Road." Yet one of Willa Cather's finest books, *My Ántonia,* had just used this favorite device of hers with final success. She did not entirely abandon it in *A Lost Lady.* Though the third person is largely employed, Niel remains the mirror in which Mrs. Forrester's glide to perdition is most luminously reflected.

The portrait of Mrs. Forrester, was, in Red Cloud, recognized as based on the wife of an ex-governor of Nebraska, who had married a beauty from California.

We have learned, recently, that the Forrester-Garber house still stands. It has been described by Mildred R. Bennett and has even been photographed by *Life.* I know one Nebraska pilgrim who found the yellow roses, and entered the deserted mansion of the past, realizing what it meant to a dauntless young girl like Willa Cather, in search of sophistication, to drive out with Mrs. Garber's gay guests from Denver, or to happen into the Red Cloud milliner's shop and find the Lost Lady (who usually bought her hats in Denver) on a stool, twirling about in her ruffled starched skirts, balancing on a toe in a pointed slipper.

With this heroine Willa brought what are usually called her Nebraska novels to a charmed end—for a decade.

In 1923, the year of publication of *A Lost Lady,* the state of Nebraska became conscious that it had produced a very important writer, and the women of Omaha—the Omaha Society of Fine Arts—raised the money for a portrait to be hung in the Omaha Public Library. Willa Cather chose Leon Bakst, the scene designer of the Russian ballet, to paint her portrait. She met him in Paris, and he painted her there in his studio in the summer of 1923. The portrait was unveiled in Nebraska by her niece, then Mary Virginia Auld, at the end of the year. It hangs beside that of John G. Neihardt, "poet laureate of Nebraska."

To let young people know that recognition is given to art as well as to more material enterprises.

But the portrait was a disappointment. Little of the life, richness, and meaning of that fine Cather face came through.

Part Three

—◦◦{ }◦◦—

There is a time in a writer's life when his "life line" and the line of his personal endowment meet. This may come early or late but after it occurs his work is never quite the same.

—*Alexander's Bridge,* Preface to 1922 Edition

—◦◦{ }◦◦—

CHAPTER I

A New Dimension
1924 – 1926

AFTER THE PUBLICATION of *A Lost Lady*, Willa Cather
seemed to draw a long breath of satisfaction and
reflection, then moved quietly forward to take her rightful place in American literature. As the novels of the later
twenties emerged, in quick succession: *The Professor's
House*, 1925, *My Mortal Enemy*, 1926, *Death Comes for
the Archbishop*, 1927, and then, in 1931, *Shadows on the
Rock*, it was clear, even at the time, that a new tide had
washed over Willa Cather and left its mark upon her.
These works of her fifties have quite another form, dimension, and vibration than have her Nebraska books. Their
significance tends to the religious; they seek the decisions
of the world and the spirit on man's tragic fate.

"Manners" figure in them, yet they are lifted to a level
beyond manners. The agonizing problem of mortality, the
oncoming of death, is always present, and we are led to
feel that unusual individuals, like Professor St. Peter and
Myra Henshawe (*My Mortal Enemy*) must wrestle with

them alone and single-handed—as, indeed, they must wrestle with the inevitable march of the twentieth century, which is felt as a menace to their moral poise and well-being.

But Willa Cather's own twentieth century pace is notably leisurely, and her gift of omission so final that the reader is ever beguiled, never pressed or jostled, by the passage of time, even in a novel like *My Mortal Enemy*, *démeublé* to a high degree.

Willa Cather, indeed, seemed very much herself, as the twenties went their hilarious way. Her face had more strength and frank resolution than ever before. Still, at heart, she was deeply aware of post-war life and literary currents, bewildering and new; and did not conceal from her friends her round aversion for the strong, disillusioned young talents that rushed along the literary seas, as if they alone possessed the rights of navigation. I saw her as a fine little French corvette, designed on gracious, firm lines, threading her way through the turbulent waters of the Jazz Age. Though abstractly—and concretely, too—she believed in youth, its creativeness and its fecundity, in her fifties, as she then was, the young hopefuls of her own profession were the "sports." They kept their eyes fixed on the restive present and the unpredictable future, with its confused, pressing world-consciousness. She, whose vision was directed to the past, with its traditional limitations, was sailing by the true compass.

The increase in her literary reputation helped, moreover, to give her a basic confidence in her own direction. Successful, handsome and blooming, even accessible at last, she allowed the world to have its charms for her. Alfred Knopf and his circle of authors and critics—which included her early admirers, H. L. Mencken and George Jean Nathan, then running *The American Mercury* on the Knopf premises—did all they could to persuade her that this was the moment to come into and enjoy her fate as a leading American novelist.

So it was that, shortly after the publication of *A Lost Lady*, a consummate gossip and profilist of the period, Burton Rascoe, pointed up in *Arts and Decoration* the new note of worldly self-confidence in Willa Cather. Her friend Thomas Beer, author of *The Mauve Decade*, who especially admired the urbanity and glitter of her short, singer story, "Scandal," had arranged the meeting at the urbane Crillon. Mr. Beer had deplored in print that Miss Cather had been born, as a writer, into the age when Theodore Roosevelt reigned spiritually, and under him journalism came to an amazing height. Beer rightly enough felt that a story like "The Sculptor's Funeral," or "A Wagner Matinée," was an authentic artist's answer to such challenges. Yet, having myself known Willa first at *McClure's*, and seen how much she was able to learn and absorb from this environment, and how little "superior" to it she felt, I did not commiserate her for her journalistic past. If she could now be courted and reported at the Crillon in a high key, her *McClure's* experience, I knew, was partly accountable.

She had implied this in her Bread Loaf lectures, in the early twenties, and I owe to Mrs. Bennett a quotation from *The New York World* on the subject:

The six years I spent on *McClure's Magazine* in an editorial capacity, I call work. It was during the six years . . . that I came to have a definite idea about writing. In reading manuscripts submitted to me, I found that 95 percent of them were written for the sake of the writer—never for the sake of the material. The writer wanted to express his clever ideas, his wit, his observations.

Almost never did I find a manuscript that was written because a writer loved his subject so much he had to write about it.

Usually when I did get such a manuscript it was so crude it was ineffective. Then I realized that one must have two things—strong enough to mate together without either killing the other—else one had better change his job. I learned that a man must have a technique and a birthright to write—I do not know how else to express it. He must know his subject with an understanding that passes understanding—as the babe knows its own mother's breast.

In an essay on Miss Cather in "A Bookman's Daybook" Mr. Rascoe remarked that she looked as if she might conduct a law practice, a dairy farm, or a magazine with equal efficiency. Nevertheless, he saw in her, in his magazine piece, "a woman intelligently aware of her own genius, who had the will to bring it to fruition"; he further describes his subject as "alert, quick-witted, vigorous-minded and assertive, not at all dreamy, preoccupied, self-isolated or diffident." He speaks of "the forceful masculinity" of her hands, the "blunt decisiveness" of her features; of her "pale blue eyes set wide apart, with eyebrows high enough to give her a look of challenge and appraisal"; of her "mouth with full flexible lips, whose movements are as expressive an accompaniment of her speech as are the gestures of a Latin." Though this ample mouth looks "sullen" in her photographs it is actually not so, but is "capable of severity and stubbornness."

She sits "relaxed without slumping, assured without tension." Her conversation is "staccato with broken sentences," which show that she is "without sentimentality, prudery or false values of any sort." She uses "such good, sanguine words as mutton-head, cub, scamp, ninny, with colloquial effectiveness." Mr. Rascoe managed to extract from her why she was attracted by the singers and actresses who figure in her stories: she finds the stage and the opera "an escape into an amazing world where drabness and time-serving are forgotten in the illusion of adventure."

Robert Frost once said to me that the word "escape" is ambiguous; is one escaping *from* something or *to* something? It seems to me that Willa, if possible, and certainly quite without shame or repentance, escaped both *from* and *to*. The ballet, for instance, interested her vitally as a balanced trial of grace, poise, muscle and temperament in which a unique individual, the ballerina, could excel. The game of tennis fascinated her for the same reasons: she compared Suzanne Lenglen, the superb tennis star of the twenties, to Pavlova, the Russian dancer, a superlative mistress of coördination and aesthetic charm.

When I went to Bank Street, and found, lying about, the English editions of Willa's works, and the numerous paper-bound translations into Czech, into the Scandinavian languages, into French, Italian, Dutch, I knew, from Willa's delight in them, that they were a welcome extension of

her public of readers: tangible proof that the European novelists who had influenced her style—and to some extent the
traditional values her novels unconsciously stressed—were
still meaningful in a sombre, post-war Europe: the same
Europe where our younger American novelists were read
and taken into the *cénacles* and the *cafés*, and under the
wings of prophets of the "modern" like Gertrude Stein,
and Ezra Pound, whom she could not take seriously.

Looked at in perspective, Willa Cather was the eldest—
unless one counts Ellen Glasgow (whom I never heard her
mention) of the "new" novelists of the twenties, whom we
now know to have been the catalyzers of America's literary coming-of-age. She exemplified the aphorism of Ber-
nard Shaw, quoted by Van Wyck Brooks in *The Confident
Years*, that America was "at last producing an art of its
own, instead of merely boring Europe by returning its ex-
ports with all their charm rubbed off."

Willa Cather had never, even in her first Jamesian novel,
Alexander's Bridge, seemed European to a European. It
was her Americanism that counted. In the new growing
nationalism of, for example, Czechoslovakia, *O Pioneers!*
and *My Ántonia* presented a glorious view of a heroic
Midwest, largely transformed by the stalwart contribution
of the Eastern European immigrant who had come over in
the steerage, and stuck out the droughts and the disappoint-
ments of the formative years.

Remembering with what deep piety Willa spoke of
Sarah Orne Jewett, when I first knew her in 1910, I was
struck by the casual way she "placed" Miss Jewett to Burton Rascoe:

Sarah Orne Jewett [he quotes in the interview at the Crillon] was too much cuddled by her family. They'd have kept her in cotton wool and smothered her if they'd had entirely their own way about it. She was a very uneven writer. A great part of her work is not worth preserving. The best—a small balance, enough to make two volumes—is important. She was a voice. She spoke for a small but influential portion of the American people. She was clearly a voice, an authentic voice.

Miss Cather was very much less candid about publicly "placing" her contemporaries. Henry Canby recalls how important it was to him, at the time he was starting *The Saturday Review of Literature*, and mapping its course, to consult her about its shape and direction. She was glad to give blunt and honest advice—in rationed doses, of course; one must respect her seclusion. Her praise or blame was always interesting; but sweeping, prejudiced, he thought. She was likely as not to take up the cudgels against his own favorites among the new writers; perhaps it was just as well he could never persuade her to review them.

She told me how she was being tempted by literary editors like Carl Van Doren, Stuart Sherman, Wilbur Cross to express her critical opinions in journals, and how she was resisting all efforts to bring her into the firing line. There the mood of the detached observer is shattered, she said, especially the mood of the writer who looks inward. Besides, why create enmities? She had done her full stint of book-reviewing in her Nebraska college days and her Pittsburgh years.

But she was free as air in expressing her private views of contemporaneous novelists, and spoke of them in very much the same tone (though not the same words) as does Brooks in *The Confident Years*:

> The burden of the new generation of novelists was a sort of preordained despair, a note of defeat or failure, regression or decay that seemed to express the bewilderment of depolarized spirits, and among their characters morons abounded, with gangsters and mindless and primitive men, and with duped and put-upon children of all ages. While all these types existed in life, the novelists seemed to look for them because they were the opposite of the heroes of romantic fiction—superior beings with developed minds and wills—and because they were too rudimental, too undeveloped to exercise conscious choices on the moral plane. They invariably submitted, without question or protest, to fate. These writers, in their predominant feeling of chaos, had apparently lost sight of the spiritual poles.

Willa never lost her own sense of the spiritual poles, or allowed her major characters to do so. In her dark moments she felt, like the bright young men, that she lived like a bewildered traveller in a garish, unrestful hotel—to use the words of Conrad in *Victory*—but Willa preferred to wear a calm exterior. Once in a while, if I met her for a walk, she would be happy over a new discovery in a familiar author's repertoire:

"Have you ever read *Sea and Sardinia?* Lawrence there used the language of *cubisme*."

"I'm sending you *The Woman Who Rode Away*—you'll be surprised!"

Why was someone who sanctioned the modern in painting so removed from the *avant-garde* of literary America or of literary Europe at this period? The young men of *The*

Seven Arts, The Dial under Schofield Thayer, even with the discerning Alyse Gregory at the helm, and then the unique Marianne Moore: these ignored her altogether. Willa Cather was not, as the French say, *dans le mouvement;* the movement that had pretty well scrapped the Victorian age, which she still idealized. The *avant-garde* were thus as blind to her qualities as she to theirs, though she, too, cared for Proust and saw *Ulysses* as a landmark.

Willa had never, of course, been involved with the vagaries of Greenwich Village, in the pre-war days, and still less with the goings-on of the prohibition era. Sedate, distinguished literary neighbors like Elinor Wylie and the Henry Canbys were pleasing. Mrs. Canby, who lived not far from her, tells how, in her naïveté, before she had ever met Miss Cather, she once made her way to Bank Street, Number Five, in the sacred hours of the morning, though probably near noon, rang the bell in the vestibule: with the purpose of inviting the author of *A Lost Lady* to dinner.

After considerable delay, the buzzer buzzed; Marian Canby, walking into the dark lower hall of the small apartment house and looking skyward, saw no angel but a very dark, dour face, peering formidably over the banisters.

"Who are you, what do you want?"

The editor's wife blushed and stammered out her invitation, whereupon the face above grew kind, warm and ruddy. But the evening was hazardous. Willa Cather, disliking on sight the young English journalist who made up the foursome, retired into one of her dudgeons, and when she found herself alone with her hosts explicitly requested that she might come alone to dine henceforth, unless there were someone who could be guaranteed to her liking.

To salt the social salad she never would agree, unless the ingredients pricked her palate. Fame was already abridging her greatest treasure, time. Writing had, as she said, been her recreation, her holiday, her means of blissfully losing the sense of self for three hours a day. She despised the very word, "publicity," yet found herself making unavoidable concessions to this modern trend in publishing. Nor was it a simple predicament for one who had claimed— and still believed—that money and art had nothing in common, to find her pockets filling. Henry Canby avowed that he was startled when Miss Cather asked his advice about stocks.

Her personal life seemed to go on very much as before; no car, no radio, nor any other time-abridger marred the leisurely pace of Bank Street. She had a jolly, flavorsome peasant cook, who spoke a French patois; and begged her friends to come to her, if possible. Edith Lewis, who now worked at the J. Walter Thompson Company, was always at dinner. One realized how much her companionship meant to Willa. A captain, as Will White of Emporia said (he knew a captain when he saw one, his own mother was a captain), must have a first officer, who does a lot the captain never knows about to steer the boat through rocks and reefs. "It takes two to write a book" was another line of his creed.

At tea one found Willa alone, as before, with the same smoky tea from Boston, the same delicious, buttery crumpets, and crisp *petits fours*, and the same George Sand by Couture—symbol of hopes for humanity's salvation, or

perhaps symbol of a famous correspondence with Flaubert?
—looking down from above the marble fireplace. On the
mantel, now, was a Victorian marble head of Keats by
Amy Whitney, a legacy from Mrs. Fields.

When we were alone, we usually ended by talking of
writing—her writing. She said, still, that her novels were
transcriptions of love for people and places. But now form
seemed to assume greater significance. Her aim was to create a work of art, out of subject matter, new or old, that
had "teased" her, and had left, as she said, a deep impression upon her. Mind and invention were not her tools; the
decisive element was intuitive, poetical, almost mystical perception. Though she rejected Freud, she was a reader of
Henri Bergson. She had spoken, in the 1922 preface to the
new edition of *Alexander's Bridge* of how she had been
enlightened about form "in flashes that are as unreasoning,
often unreasonable, as life itself."

Ever since *One of Ours* she had declared her belief that
"writing" should be so lost in the object that it doesn't
exist for the reader. Self-consciousness was a mistake—the
writer should be just an eye and an ear. Proust was better
when he wrote that way. At this time she thought of prose
as allied to the other arts: the ear, especially, must be attuned to the cadences of music and poetry. Her new book,
she told me (I doubt if she gave its title then—*The Professor's House*, it was) was based on a musical form.

Indeed, she said her unfinished opus had a sonata form,
starting *molto moderato*. There were to be three parts,
every one with Italian musical nomenclature. These did not
appear in the book, and I cannot quote them accurately, but

my impression is that the middle book, Tom Outland's story, was to be *molto appassionata*, as indeed it proved to be in the reading. The cliff-dweller part was based, she said, on a true story that Willa had heard on the Navajo Reservation from a famous family of Indian traders, the Wetherills.

The deep theme of her book, she implied, was the connection or opposition between youth and age, and the way they mutually stirred one another. Somehow I felt that the young hero so close to her heart might resemble those favorite brothers of hers, Douglass and Roscoe, with whom she seemed to be always dashing around the West and Southwest. Anyhow, her rapturous references to Tom made me look up an old *McClure's* article I had kept, in which she commented in a striking fashion on the fecundity of youth:

> The individual possesses this power for only a little while. He is sent into the world charged with it, but he can't keep it a day beyond his allotted time. He has his hour when he can do, live, become. If he devoted these years to caring for an aged parent—God may reward him but Nature will not forgive him.

Another aspect of Willa's life had found a new dimension: the "beyond" in which she worked. Her trips to Red Cloud, frequent through these years, as before, were never for writing. And in New Mexico, there were also too many better things to do, as she usually put it to me. For a time she had considered buying the Robinson house in Jaffrey, below which she wrote part of *My Ántonia* in a tent.

But she needed a further distance, something more primitive, more deeply lonely. Writing not being to her a chore but, in very truth, a vacation and release from care, her discovery in 1921 of the Grand Manan, a wild, beautiful, primitive island off the coast of New Brunswick, her building there with Miss Lewis, in 1925, of Whale Cottage, was a piece of charmed good fortune.

The only picture I knew in her own words, of this beautiful new landscape, this retreat on a speck of green island in the North Atlantic, is to be found in a piece called "Before Breakfast" in *The Old Beauty and Others*, printed posthumously. It has the air of being somewhat a projection of the author's own elderly experience: we find in the story a crochety, tired businessman, Mr. Grenfell, who had a vital desire for solitude (*sans* family life) to rest his soul; and an awareness that his mortal enemy was within his own breast. There is a subtle little touch about how Mr. Grenfell, in his island retreat, found himself viewing the dawn and the abstract heavens as he rose early and started on a before breakfast climb up a cliff where grew a dark spruce wood lighted by early sunshine.

> On either side of the trail yellow toadstools and white mushrooms lifted the heavy thatch of brown spruce needles and made little damp tents.

Even the giant grandfather spruce, gone grey and lying prone, was an old friend which had not suffered change in his absence. Sea-driven, haunted by gulls, with its herring weirs and its springing waterfalls, and its high, grassy headlands, the Grand Manan offered balm and well-being.

Since I did not know New Brunswick and both of us, following our separate ways, did a good deal of coming and going from the Southwest, Santa Fe and Taos would turn up more often in our regional conversation. One summer Willa and Miss Lewis had had for a time the little house of Mabel Luhan's occupied by D. H. Lawrence before he acquired from Mabel the high ranch in the mountains—the ranch he paid for with the manuscript of *Sons and Lovers.* It was much later, in the thirties, that I had the same house, where two major novelists had sojourned and Lawrence had painted a phoenix, his favorite emblem, on a wall.

At this time I spent an occasional week in Mabel's Guest House or in her fascinating Big House, set in sagebrush and hollyhocks, with parrots swinging in the doors, and sage drying on the hearths, and the Indian fields—edged by those golden sunflowers that Willa had written always follow the roads to freedom—stretching on to the many-terraced buildings of the pueblo, under the Sacred Mountain.

Once Willa and I had conjured up The Big House in talk we would go in through the loggia with its great piles of piñon and cedar wood, and find Tony, detached and hieratical, sitting apart, playing solitaire amidst Mabel's Florentine relics; his two long braids delicately pleated with colored tape; his fine two-colored blanket falling in the proper lines, as the white artists and intellectuals tossed the ball of the higher conversation back and forth.

Tony is a man of force, dignity and charm as well as wisdom and intuition, and Willa once said—not to me— when asked why Mabel married an Indian:

"How could she help it?"

Mabel's intuitive eyes would sparkle with pleasure when Tony challenged her Eastern friends. Short, plump, vital, restless and searching, yet ever unseriously smiling, with her bobbed hair cut in a bang on her forehead, and longer over her ears, like a Pueblo woman's, she was pushing all her New York friends to join the Indian "movement": to help defeat the politicians who were trying to destroy the Pueblo lands and ceremonies. But she made no headway with Willa Cather. The tribal side of the Indian meant little to her, even though Mabel insisted that one could not know the Pueblo Indian—no, not even Antonio Luhan—until one knew him tribally.

John Collier and Willa Cather met in Taos in 1926, at the house of these mutual friends Mabel and Antonio Luhan. Neither made the least connection with the other—so both told me, drily.

Mr. Collier's dedicated, dogged personality, his almost mystical insight into the Indian's life and human rights, which was actually to bring about far greater cohesion between the aloof Indian and the American democracy, seemed to Willa Cather fanatical. She had had an overdose of fanatics at *McClure's*, and now that she was so immersed in the art of writing and had given her own conception of the Indian in her own book, she wanted no news about him from the outside—so I surmised.

In the nineteen forties, I gave Willa a little story that had delighted me, about the experience of two white boys on an Arizona reservation during some secret ceremonial. Willa returned it, saying:

"Don't you remember I am not interested in this sort of thing?"

Then I did think back and realized that I had never seen her standing all day on a dusty plaza, or looking down from a flat roof, on the long lines of half-nude, brown

Pueblo dancers, with costumes whose fine design and detail challenged Bakst.

The reader may remember that, after her intensely happy and uplifted experience in the Southwest in 1912, Willa Cather suddenly felt a great, strange cold come over her, while sitting in the sun by the muddy Rio Grande, a sort of "norther," and knew that she must go.

My "norther" came upon me with similar unexpectedness. I was riding back from Santa Fe to Tesuque Valley, over a series of red and shell-pink sand hills, spotted with round, deep-green piñon trees. The Tesuque River, which through the spring and summer must water the crops of the "Anglos," the Mexicans, and the Indians of our valley, was just a dry snake of sand. Winter snows had been insufficient. The cottonwoods were shivering their pale green leaves in a dry wind. The need for water, salt or fresh, squeezed my throat like thirst, and I heard myself say aloud:

"This is not my country."

Within a few days I had closed the Mud House; with the aid of Salomé, my neighbor, had hung the mattresses from the beams to evade the work of field mice; and taken the train East.

I was bound for a many-windowed room that my friend Mary Tonetti had, with her sculptor's touch, and almost with her own hand built onto the little old white house at Sneden's Landing on the Hudson, which she rented to my father for a decade. There in the lush, green, watery, heavy-scented world of Rockland County I was going to begin to write a series of portraits for which I'd been asked by *The New Republic*—Frost, O'Neill, Willa Cather, Amy Lowell, among others.

Before long I had, also, found a winter home, a spacious top floor in an old brownstone house near the East River, Manhattan's other boundary. The colonial furniture I had lived with since childhood, and all my books, could now settle down and take root between the two sets of windows, north and south, and two Victorian marble fireplaces.

Willa, though at the opposite side of town, came to tea, once in a while, sitting by preference on my hard Hepplewhite sofa, which she claimed to prefer to the squashy comfort offered her by the young with their "Davenports." Anyone with Willa's air of clarity and determination, wearing a round hat with a stick-up on the side, and handling a tea-cup with her delicacy, sat rightly on Chippendale or Hepplewhite.

If I spoke of Eugene O'Neill, my new enthusiasm, Willa looked at me sadly. But you're interested in experimentation, I said. You like Virginia Woolf, for instance, who deals with the inner side of things. *The Great God Brown*, *Desire Under the Elms* are dramatic discoveries. And that little Sheridan Square Theatre is just a stone's throw from Bank Street.

She wouldn't consider going there, not for a moment.

O'Neill's stark revelations of lust, fear, weakness, cruelty, even poignant goodness, on the stage, offended her taste. Why spend an evening in Hades when there were still good comedies of manners—even of morals, say Galsworthy's, on Broadway?

My happiest moments with Willa were still those when her own spring, now often frozen over in talk by fame, or busyness, or just taciturnity, broke through and I found, gushing up in her, that old sense of intimacy between herself and her material, that freshness of heart and intense enthusiasm I had first known in her. In her maturity, these elements were often buried deep below the surface. Mrs. Canby told me that any good conversation she had with Miss Cather was preceded by a sort of creaking of the machinery—then Willa got going and everything was warm and free. I was not conscious of creaks, but I did feel blocks —and sudden breaks that swept her on.

Sometimes Willa and I met by chance, at a literary gathering in New York: the one I best remember is a dinner given by Robert Frost's friends—about forty of them—in honor of his fiftieth birthday: March 26, 1925. It was celebrated in an old banquet room, a bit of shabby provincial France, at the Brevoort Hotel. The whole occasion had the charming innocence and sincerity of the unpublicity days. That retiring faun R.F., who still tried for invisibility when he met the world, had brought Poetry with him. The Frost family clump, at the head table, Elinor with her rich fairness and Puritan line, Robert tossing his head back, Lesley and Irma were themselves the early New England spring personified.

No doubt it is with the aid of the old program of the evening that I remember some of the other faces—Carl and Irita Van Doren, Mark and Dorothy Van Doren, Elinor Wylie, Sara Teasdale, Jean and Louis Untermeyer, Ridgely Torrence, Dorothy Canfield Fisher. . . . I vaguely see them. But what I really remember is Willa's large, impressive head, emerging from some rich low-necked gown with a touch of red that greatly became her. She had spent the previous summer in France and I had not seen her for some time.

Her neck, if bare, set this head with its springing bronze hair, which never greyed or curled, in just proportion. The hair was always done at the back of her neck in an unfashionable bun. Her lovely oval face brimmed with affection, her blue eyes gazed upon the hero of the evening as if he were a distant prospect, much admired. Like the *Mesa Encantada*, with a cloud mesa above it—so Willa had felicitously described it—imitating it and mirroring it in the intense blue above.

A reflection of Frost as he then was, before his hair was so snowy and blowing and his skin so rosy-pink and sand-brown from the Florida sun, comes into the portrait I wrote shortly after this dinner. I saw his skin grey as a granite wall, a pasture wall. Or in another light, colored as Carrara marble, with mauve and golden shadows.

In his seventies, Robert Frost's head has the weight and balance of one of those Roman senatorial heads that used to line our Bryn Mawr academic corridors. But the half-century Frost of the Brevoort dinner insisted, sculpturally, on the Greek mode. "A good Greek out of New England," as I wrote at the time. Perhaps a good subject for Skopas who, to the calm, still features of the classic day, added musing eyes, deeply hollowed, and shadows of modern man's unrest.

Aroldo du Chêne, an Italian sculptor who lived at my home, 415 East Fifty-first Street on the ground floor, had seen Frost rather more romantically. But, as du Chêne said, Frost's countenance was changeful, moody. One could not hold him to the sculptural line. Shrewd satiric wrinkles would break his cheeks; malice, wit and blue flame would fly toward the fool who ventured to make a "still" out of life, to freeze a tempest—what words did he use?

Many times that evening did I regret having committed myself to trying to capture in words the imponderable essence of the two unique writers, two first-rate specimens, who preferred the shade to the sun, who did not at all fit into the collective American literary pattern or care to do so; yet had already so deeply affected the American professors and their students; the critics; the elite among readers.

They had certain things in common—there were likenesses in their differences. Frost had never thrown off the effect of having been born in San Francisco in a rough-and-tumble age. Nor Willa Cather the starkness of her migration at the age of nine from a soft green valley to wild red earth. To both, the hardness of the basic struggle for existence was a long memory that purified their approach to the life of the artist. The usual trappings and self-indulgences seemed to them both effete. Both thought of themselves, if I were to believe them, as "roughnecks" who had more or less happened into fame. Both liked a rather bare and timeless world. Both were suspicious of their own emotional, singing side, and imposed on it an elegant and sober line.

Frost had told me how uncertain he was, how floundering in direction as a youth. All he knew was that he "cared to write a little poem"—and to marry Elinor. Willa, far more confident, unencumbered and self-impelled, had early decided to be a writer. But, like Frost, she had turned from one thing to another to make her way—to journalism, teaching, to editorial work. Both of them had come into their first significant recognition in their late thirties. Yet in the life and work of both one could discern an absolute sureness and continuity of literary development.

"Frost," I said in my portrait, "had stuck with piety to the clarification of his own tone of voice, his own form and matter." With Willa it was the same: every novel must be a meeting between the life line and the line of personal development, must be a personal discovery. And they had in common their passionate dependence on the world of nature. They were rocks, they were trees. In common, too, they held valiantly, like a banner, their debt to the masters of the past.

"First heard the voice from a printed page in a Virgilian Eclogue and Hamlet," Frost wrote in my copy of *Selected Poems*. "Influenced by what I have supposed *Piers Plowman* to be. Never read it."

The last quip points up a divergence. Willa could be caustic at her own expense, sometimes savagely angry. But she did not make light of herself. Where R.F., with his glinting humor, wandered along, speculating about what the answer was, Willa seemed to move by will-power and was far more apt to think she knew.

But neither of them ever disappointed me, said I to myself, as I took my coat from the little old, sad French valet, in the lobby of the Brevoort. For the two were parting and Willa was offering Frost, as her birthday present, her recently published selection of the works of Sarah Orne Jewett, the Mayflower edition. In the preface she had compared *The Country of the Pointed Firs* to the tuft of meadow flowers spared by the reaper in Frost's fine poem. She said to Mr. Frost (as he has told me):

"Your success is one of my chief interests."

After this I observed Frost—with someone tugging at his overcoat—hatless, wild-looking, done forever with pretty speeches, frantically herding his family out into the dark night. Willa, on the contrary, stood with stiffly regimented air, waiting for her furs, and bearing coldly with some bold critic who had tagged after her and edged up to her.

She never had the least little bit of small talk, not an iota of ease or light friendliness with a stranger who seemed intrusive. What I thought I heard Willa say, on this occasion, to the gentleman she did not at all encourage to see her to her taxi, was that the Brevoort cuisine was not what it had been: all the best French chefs had been called to the colors in 1914, and had never returned.

In the summer of 1925, Willa went to the Southwest for a time. I received from her a copy of *The Professor's House*, an early printing, and found written in her hand on the flyleaf: "To Elsie hoping she will like Tom Outland's story."

That was the boy she had talked about. The symbolic name, Outland, struck home. Tom Outland's book was the second one, clearly the *appassionata* movement in the sonata.

The story was dedicated:

"For Jan because he likes narrative." (Jan Hambourg, of course, to whom Willa had also dedicated *A Lost Lady*.)

To my mind the haunted story of Professor St. Peter, split between the claims of mind and earth, more than any other novel of Willa Cather's spurs the individual reader's knowledge of life and death and humankind. But many men among the novel's readers have found the professor puzzling. Perhaps a note in a copy of the book that Willa presented to Robert Frost gives a clue:

(Note: This is really a story of "letting go with the heart" but most reviewers seem to consider it an attempt to popularize a system of philosophy.)

St. Peter, half French-Canadian, looking Spanish, with his hawk nose, tawny skin and piercing black eyes and curly beard, seemed, as one knew him, to have some of Willa's own tastes, prejudices, passions. A physical love for a long swim in a blue lake, a knowledge of how to cook a roast of lamb *saignant* with garlic. Moreover he had attachments that had no connection with modern conveniences. He could manage in the shabby old house where he had lived with his wife and two little girls, with a tin bathtub and in the attic study where he had written *The Spanish Adventurers in North America*—if he could just get to France. And in this connection, early in his married life, he had left his family in France to take a voyage to Spain, and had an experience with his creative faculties closely resembling the one Willa had described to me in Bank Street.

. . . Everything seemed to feed the plan of the work that was forming in St. Peter's mind; the skipper, the old Catalan second mate, the sea itself. One day stood out above the others. All day long they were skirting the south coast of Spain; from the rose of dawn to the gold of sunset the ranges of the Sierra Nevadas towered on their right, snow peak after snow peak, high beyond the flight of fancy, gleaming like crystal and topaz. St. Peter

lay looking up at them from a little boat riding low in the
purple water, and the design of his book unfolded in the
air above him, just as definitely as the mountain ranges
themselves. And the design was sound. He had accepted
it as inevitable, had never meddled with it, and it had seen
him through.

Tom, the secondary hero, is so entwined with the professor's life and memories that his presence is felt as a living
element. Actually Tom had died in the First World War
before the novel opens. He (symbolizing always the landscape, light, space, color, distance, of the Southwest; the
cliff city on a mesa where a whole tribe had perished at a
blow as in that little first sketch called "The Enchanted
Bluff") is a ghost, and has a strange effect not only on the
professor and his wife but on his daughters and his sons-in-
law. For Tom had drawn Professor St. Peter's routine and
inner life out of focus. His till then beloved wife was affected by her husband's immersion in this modest South-
westerner, who yet had the kind of "desire," the professor
felt, that leads to achievement of a high order. Desire, the
magical element in creation. St. Peter had had hundreds of
students, but here was a meteor, the first, who could re-
new his own fading youth by its brilliant radiation.

The influence of a meteor can be dangerous; but the
historical work was well along when Tom Outland came
to St. Peter's university; and honored with the Oxford prize
for history when the first book opens. We perceive that
the professor had an unconquerable resistance to moving
into the new house built with the prize money, above all
to working there. An inconvenient dislike, too, for his
bland, clever son-in-law, Louie Marsellus, who had ex-

ploited the dead genius' invention of a bulkhead vacuum, important to aviation. This invention had enriched Marsellus' wife, the professor's elder daughter, who had been engaged to Tom Outland and had inherited his formula. Every single act and thought of Marsellus seemed to smear and falsify the values which Tom had brought to St. Peter.

Tom's early story, Book Two, the middle book, the *nouvelle* in the *roman*, the "outland" that frees the imagination, is a story of youthful defeat. A narrative, simple and direct, yet gradually growing high and intense in key, told in the first person by Tom to the professor. It starts:

> The thing that side-tracked me, and made me so late coming to college was a somewhat unusual accident, or string of accidents. It began with a poker game when I was a call boy, in Pardee, New Mexico.

As a call boy Tom had met an older man, Roddy Blake, a rolling stone, steady only when doing something for the other fellow. Tom and Roddy had agreed to herd cows together and were sent to a remote cabin by a swift river, under the inaccessible mesa. When one of his cows escaped and swam the river, Tom pushed his horse across in pursuit—and discovered a group of cliff cities never before explored.

Now Tom, Roddy and Henry the cook made camp on the mesa and explored the ruins. Tom, the incipient scientist, assembled his finds in an orderly way, reported the discovery to Washington, returned, defeated, to find that Roddy had sold the pots they had dug up to a German archaeologist who had already shipped them off. Henry had been accidentally killed, and there was good money in the bank for Tom's education.

Tom did not feel the pots were his to sell; he was merely their trustee. Roddy disappeared into the distance of the railroad. One is reminded of the bitter and final quarrel of the two businessmen in *Obscure Destinies*. (Incidentally the present Laboratory of Anthropology derives from the Pueblo Pottery Fund, founded in 1922 to provide money for the local purchase and collection of just such fine prehistoric pots from shepherds, cowpunchers and Indians who otherwise sold them to scouts for museums in the East or in Europe.)

In Book Three, "The Professor," St. Peter, having refused to accompany his wife and the rich *jeunes mariés* to Europe, found his whole intellectual capital and his superior emotional susceptibility in a state of passive indifference. Neither work nor money helped him, but he did have the odd experience of meeting, through a bit of dreamy idleness, a new inner companion—the simple earth boy he himself used to be in the Solomon Valley in Kansas before sex, love, mind and his whole mature career "happened to him": a primitive, a solitary, St. Peter's first nature, untouched by tastes, intellectual activities, or marriage. St. Peter remembered that he had seen the same sort of thing happen to his grandfather, believed he himself was close to death, and later was nearly asphyxiated by the old gas stove in the old study. He survived, but as a simple creature of earth.

We have heard of this earth boy before. For was he not the boy S. S. McClure left on the steps of Colonel Pope when he sought his first job in Boston? The boy who went back to the woods when S.S. went into business?

An interesting fragment, "Light on Adobe Walls," in *Willa Cather on Writing*, hints that even the greatest artist may "outgrow" an art and need to revert to earth in age. Even Shakespeare may have turned away from art as "make-believe" and given himself to enjoying, "with all his senses that Warwickshire country which he loved to weakness—with a warm physical appetite."

In this connection, Mildred R. Bennett's book offers confirmation of Willa Cather's own earth passion. Quoting from an interview given to *The Omaha World Herald*:

> "Whenever I crossed the Missouri River coming in to Nebraska the very smell of the soil tore me to pieces. I could not decide which was the real and which the fake me. I almost decided to settle down on a quarter section of land and let my writing go. My deepest affection was not for the other people and other places I had been writing about. I loved the country where I had been a kid, where they still called me Willie Cather."
>
> When [Mrs. Bennett says] she came back to Webster County, Willa liked to go out into the country, climb a hill and let the wind blow in her face. She resented any talking while she was remembering the sensations of the land—the odors to which she was particularly sensitive.
>
> "I knew every farm, every tree, every field in the region around my home and they all called out to me. My deepest feelings were rooted in this country because one's strongest emotions and one's most vivid mental pictures are acquired before one is fifteen."

It would seem that Miss Cather intended both Godfrey St. Peter and Myra Henshawe in *My Mortal Enemy*, the next novel (1926), to symbolize heroic failure against odds. They are opposites, since one died, perversely, of riches and the other, aggrievedly, of poverty. Alike in that both married for love, and in middle life turned restlessly in their yokes, evading, by a sort of right to personal solitude, the usual human sense of responsibility to lifetime relationships; they seem to betray a profound disillusion about marriage as a solution for exceptional people. Myra died on a lonely headland by herself; St. Peter was eventually condemned to live, if live he must, without passion and without joy. In this mental climate, this skeptical pessimism, Willa Cather seems to ally herself with French masters like Flaubert and Stendhal.

But the elders were sages in France and in China—I speak of the past. "If there be a knife of resentment in the heart, the mind will not attain precision." That comes from Confucius, via Marianne Moore.

I find both St. Peter and Myra Henshawe resentful and unprecise in apprehending the working of fate in their lives. But as E. K. Brown, with his rare insight and knowledge, has suggested in his fine critical book *Rhythm in the Novel*, Willa Cather's deepest concern, in these later books of hers, was less with the story and the characters than with the "large background of emotion," with "what calls for the hovering of suggestion rather than for bold and outright statement."

Mr. Brown has explained the symbolism of *The Professor's House* in terms of houses: the old shabby professorial dwelling in the college town; the materialistic new house; and the stripped rock house of the Ancients, the earliest American ancestors, the house of death:

> The common quality between life in the Middle Western college town and life in the Cliff Dwellers' village is

that both kinds of life end in death, we know how to measure them, the ancient and the contemporary. What aspect of dignity, of beauty, would the ruins of the college town possess for Macaulay's New Zealander, if he were to pause on this continent on his way to sketch the ruins of St. Paul's? Great chords are sounding; and as they sound they alter radically the impression we had before we approached the end of the novel.

CHAPTER II

The Historical Novels

1927 — 1931

IN THOSE RUINED cliff houses of the Southwest that Willa loved so well there is always a little low, shut-in storage cave at the back, where the corn for the year of dearth used to be piled away by the Indians. Such a caveful of many-colored New Mexican corn Willa had had in the back of her mind for years. Suddenly she drew on it and was released from the long hunger of the artist to communicate something of moment. The narrative, as she called *Death Comes for the Archbishop,* almost wrote itself, in a very short space of time, and the happy mood of its conception never left her.

A bearded Catholic priest from Belgium, Father Halter-mann, had been one of her earliest guides in New Mexico. Bishop Lamy, a bronze statue of a man of fine dignity, under a locust tree in front of the golden Romanesque cathedral in Santa Fe, had become a sort of silent friend. Yet Willa Cather did not "see" her own story until, on a hot and sleepless night in Santa Fe, at La Fonda, in 1925, a year when she spent the whole summer in New Mexico, she happened on an historic document and a *chef d'oeuvre* in its own right: *The Life of the Right Reverend Joseph P. Machebeuf* by Father Howlett, published privately in Pueblo, Colorado, in 1908. This remarkable book which kept her reading most of the night, led to one of her lightning-like experiences with the creative spirit. By morning she saw her own work of the imagination in complete form.

A form, of course, totally different from Father Howlett's, since it was a crystallization of her own Southwest experience and thought, as well as the precipitation of his narrative in fiction. Meredith's definition of genius quoted in McClure's *My Autobiography*, applies here:

". . . an extraordinary activity of mind in which all conscious and subconscious knowledge mass themselves without any effort of the will and become effective. It manifests itself in three ways. In producing, in organizing and in rapidity of thought."

Two missionary priests, companionable seminarist friends of Auvergne stock, thus became her heroes. Bishop Latour, a man of thought, and Father Vaillant, a man of action, were complementary and, like her Nebraska pioneers, unique in their kind in a period of social change.

It was the French priests' duty first to "subdue," then cultivate a vast, raw, rough, primitive, unlettered land, where the seeds of the authority and tradition of the Roman Catholic Church, as brought by the Spanish explorers, had largely gone wild or blown away in the wind. French manners had something to do with their success. One had to know Willa to realize her power to live into, feel into, an ecstasy of relationship with such characters: with the factual and the sensory world they lived in, as well as with the areas of thought and feeling that tormented or sustained them. The book could never have been written without this rare power of sympathy joined to her genius for storing —and putting into final words at last—the exact memory of sensuous and human and religious experience of her own.

In the summer of 1926, when she was working on *Death Comes for the Archbishop,* Willa spent some time at the MacDowell Colony in Peterborough, New Hampshire— it was her first and only stay there, and a few legends and vignettes remain of this honored guest, who went her own way, as she always did, instead of fitting into the usual pattern.

Colony life is based on breakfast and dinner in common, lunch delivered at the studio in a basket, to permit a long, lonely day of work. This, to most colonists, represents a miracle of freedom for creative work. But Willa, as a lifetime habit, wrote only in the morning, often for only two hours. She liked a hot, hearty lunch. So by noon, I hear, she stole away to an inn that then stood on the Lower Road, taking young, red-haired, witty Mary Colum along to enliven and prick her mind. The Colony lunch was saved for the tea that was equally essential to her.

Dinner is early at the Colony and evenings are long and light and full of sociability, poetry, music, or just croquet. Willa, as Mrs. MacDowell, in her nineties, says with her gay, ringing laugh, was always evading pursuit. Her bedroom was at The Eaves, an old red farm house, with the other women. Some she liked and some she didn't, but few seemed to understand the right to solitude.

An inveterate walker in her leisure hours, Willa soon knew all the paths and woodland lanes of the Colony, and was sometimes spied at the Pageant Theatre, an amphitheatre of stone, almost a cliff, surrounded by great pines. Standing against the grey rock, a tiny, determined figure, she read aloud the paragraphs and pages she had been working on—to see how they sounded. No wonder the prose is so bland and so sensuous.

Willa told me that another person she enjoyed talking with at the MacDowell Colony was the head of the music department in a Midwest college, a composer who based his compositions in part on Indian themes. This was Charles S. Skilton of the University of Kansas. As she had grown up near the Kansas border she and Skilton had something truly in common. "I have a great respect for him," she told me, "and for all such men who live for music, and have no time to themselves. The Colony is made for them! Mrs. MacDowell is their guardian angel."

Mrs. MacDowell tells me that she and Willa Cather, after that year, used to have one good visit every summer, when Willa came to write at the nearby Shattuck Inn in Jaffrey. (There at the inn, sociability was skin-deep, and she could be as aloof as an oyster.)

It must have been in the autumn of 1926 that, during a visit to New Mexico, Mary Austin summoned me to her house in Santa Fe, and I found her in bed, ill, with her heavy dark-red hair hanging in great masses over her shoulders.

"Willa Cather has been here," she said. "I lent her my house to write in.

"You have written a portrait of her in *The New Republic*," she added accusingly. "I could have done it better!" I said I was sure of it. Why hadn't she?

"I know her so much better. . . . I am a Westerner. Look at that chair"—she pointed one out in the next room—"she sat there to write her new novel."

Willa was exasperated when I told her. Not a word of it. She had left her manuscript in a vault in New York when she went to New Mexico. . . . She had stayed at La Fonda and sometimes walked up to Mrs. Austin's in the afternoon to write a few letters. . . .

But the author of *The Land of Little Rain* made this supposed birthplace of a famous book into a legend. "There, in that chair," she used to say for years, "Willa Cather wrote *Death Comes for the Archbishop*." Even Van Wyck Brooks, in consequence, has said so in *The Confident Years*.

With the publication of *Death Comes for the Archbishop* in September, 1927, Willa Cather seemed to reach the pinnacle of her literary career. But her father, whom she greatly loved, died a few months later, and even as her book was published she had to leave her home at Number Five Bank Street, where she had had fourteen years of the happiest work and living.

The house, as so often in New York, was to be turned to other use. Though the city and its traffic had encroached on her quiet; though intrusive feet overhead had forced her to rent—and keep empty—a second apartment over her own, all that counted for nothing when she faced a move. She felt like a turtle that was losing its shell. The psychic pain of stripping off this protective integument was unbearable; she was exposed and miserable.

She spent a few months with her parents in Red Cloud, for the first time in many years. Her Virginia father and she were closely related in feeling, and at this time of glory and renown she was sharing some of her bulky professional correspondence with him, so that he at last understood what burdens and obligations attend fame and success. The sense that his daughter had moved into a first-rate place in American letters had come home to him. His death which followed was shattering to Willa.

I was tied in New York in the spring of 1927, seeing *Fire Under the Andes* through its publication. Then a taxicab accident sent me for six weeks to Bermuda to stay with the Eugene O'Neills. In their pirate's stronghold on Hamilton Bay I read, in manuscript, Gene's new and theatrically startling venture, *Strange Interlude*, which was presented by the Theatre Guild the next year.

Once back in New York, I went soon to the MacDowell Colony, to work at last on *Short As Any Dream*. My studio floor was paved with piles of old family letters of my mother's people dating back to 1810, covered with that touching handwriting of long-vanished spirits of early Maine pioneering days, which set down the concrete facts of daily life with faith in their immortality.

Death Comes for the Archbishop, when it reached me in New York, was almost a miracle. As in first reading *My Ántonia*, the true spirit of the author spoke with resonance, with clarity, with finality. Though I have now re-read the novel many times, the experience is ever full of wonder— like watching the emergence of the lunar moth from the chrysalis. The process and the creature are one, as mood and substance are one and whole in the novel. You see a child of an author's heart being born without a flaw, and in the normal course of nature—and almost fall on your knees. This work, though written in the quiet style of legend, has rhythmic motion, sensuous joy and an uplifted creative tone—the tone of well-being, *bien-être*, spiritual and physical, that always possessed the author in New Mexico.

While her arm wrote and her mind produced, she was feeling as the Archbishop did, even when he was old and near to death:

> In New Mexico he always awoke a young man; not until he rose and began to shave did he realize that he was growing older. His first consciousness was a sense of the light dry wind blowing in through the windows, with the scent of hot sun and sage-brush and sweet clover; a wind that made one's body feel light and one's heart cry "Today, today," like a child's. . . .
>
> Something soft and wild and free, something that whispered to the ear on the pillow, lightened the heart, softly, softly picked the lock, slid the bolts, and released the prisoned spirit of man into the wind, into the blue and gold, into the morning, into the morning.

The "primary ecstasies" as Professor Paul Tillich calls them—saying that nobody can experience the higher ecstasies without knowing the primary ones—are central to the story.

Willa Cather renders them with unimaginable charm and conviction: the light dry wind of the Southwest; the refined and ancient art of cookery, which Father Joseph practises with relation to an onion soup, a salad and a roast in his preparation of Christmas dinner for his Vicar; rest and recuperation after illness and physical hardship; as in the month-of-Mary chapter, when Father Joseph renewed his devotions and his prayers, in a retired budding garden, where he experienced the rewards of both divine and human companionship. The very foundation-stone of the story is a primary ecstasy: the almost jocund togetherness of feeling, from childhood to age, of the two from Auvergne, largely, in New Mexico, separated by their gifts and tasks and temperaments; yet bound by their common memories—especially the memory, thrice cited in the novel, of the poignant secret departure from Riom by diligence, of two seminarists not yet twenty, who had to break the ties of blood.

In a letter to his sister Philomène, cited in the Ohio part of Father Howlett's biography, Father Joseph Machebeuf explains why he is leaving the American Midwest where he has lived since 1839. Father Lamy had made the request that, as Vicar General, he accompany the latter, now named Priest of Agathon and Vicar Apostolic of New Mexico:

> In the quality of an intimate friend upon whom he could depend, as well as an assistant upon whom he could lay a part of his burden. From these two vicars [Father Lamy had said] we shall try to make one good Pastor.

Arriving in 1852 in New Mexico, history is their backdrop, or their creation. They make it as they go and they do a great deal of going, on horseback or muleback, usually alone or with a native guide, to discover unlettered parishioners, Mexican or Indian; to deal with refractory priests, who had somehow married and acquired progeny because their church had been out of touch with Rome for a couple of centuries. In these long, hazardous, intensely sensuous journeys an encounter with the noxious datura—a rank plant with startling white blooms like lilies is as dramatic as one with an "historic" figure like Kit Carson. Jean and Joseph are always in touch with the cosmic and the pristine. The perpetual presence of a world of nature, still hardly born to civilization, is of the essence of their experience. Willa Cather, to whom such an encounter with landscape and sky was a "primary ecstasy," seems to endow Bishop Latour with her own sensitive apprehending and to make his religious practice a service to beauty as well as to God.

For instance: Father Latour and Eusabio, his Navajo Indian friend, are riding from the Navajo country in the west to Santa Fe:

> The weather alternated between blinding sandstorms and brilliant sunlight. The sky was as full of motion and change as the desert beneath it was monotonous and still —and there was so much sky, more than at sea, more than anywhere else in the world. The plain was there, under one's feet, but what one saw when one looked about was that brilliant blue world of stinging air and moving cloud. Even the mountains were mere ant-hills under it. Elsewhere the sky is the roof of the world; but here the earth was the floor of the sky. The landscape one longed for when one was far away, the thing all about one, the world one actually lived in, was the sky, the sky!
> Travelling with Eusabio was like travelling with the landscape made human. He accepted chance and weather as the country did, with a sort of grave enjoyment. He talked little, ate little, slept anywhere, preserved a countenance open and warm. . . . The Bishop was rather surprised that he stopped so often by the way to gather

flowers. One morning he came back with the mules, holding a long bunch of crimson flowers—long tube-shaped bells, that hung lightly from one side of a naked stem and trembled in the wind.

"The Indians call rainbow flower," he said, holding them up and making the red tubes quiver.

This seems to be a description of the scarlet Pentstemon which grew on my Tesuque hillside.

The villages, too, Indian and Mexican, as Willa described them, were much as I knew them: Mora, Arroyo Hondo, Taos itself, Acoma, Isleta. The saints' legends and Catholic tales subtly inserted in her narrative were indigenous to the villages. For example, the lovely legend of Our Lady of Guadelupe or the salty one of Fray Baltasar, the fat Spanish priest who overdid gluttony and was joyously tossed off the cliff of Acoma by the Indians. I have seen the story of Our Lady of Guadelupe acted as a mystery play in a Mexican house in Santa Fe at Christmas. Willa Cather, of course, improved upon the legends.

Father Joseph's letters to his cloistered sister, Philomène, who, like himself, had renounced the world but still loved it and felt curious about it, were bursting full of tiny facts, descriptions of native customs and humorous-pathetic episodes which the novelist used and again improved upon— for instance the story of the gift of the two white mules from a Mexican to a French missionary is straight Howlett. But beyond and behind was the communicative *emotion* of the letters which spoke to Willa's heart. Thus the author's encounter with two Catholic priests *in a book*— she uses their real Christian names in the novel, but changes their surnames—was at least as great and spontaneous a human experience as her chance meeting with Flaubert's niece at Aix-les-Bains. These were men, as was Professor St. Peter a man, whom she would have immensely enjoyed in life. She believed in her luck in such matters but was perhaps glad when a lucky encounter had only literary consequences.

Father Joseph humorously characterizes himself: "The levity and inconstancy of my character"—"When I undertake a thing I give myself to it, and cannot accommodate myself to anything unconnected with it." He describes in full the odd little carriage he had had constructed before setting forth to Colorado in the days of the gold rush. We get to know that he was a puny little fellow, who was also a dynamo of energy; his nickname was Blanchet, Whitey; also Trompe-la-Mort, Death-Cheater, because he never died as expected, though often seriously ill. He called himself the Vicario Andando (Travelling Vicar) who lived on the Camino Real, the King's Highway. His salvation was— he discovered this in his early youth—"rest in action." His religious motto was *Auspice Maria*, but *Deus providebit* would do as well, for he was always out of pocket, and wherever he went stayed in the homes of the humble. Father Latour, however, washed his hands in a silver basin, wore fine linen, and lived inwardly, making few friends, because his nature was in essence withdrawn and thoughtful.

Willa Cather never allowed the facts of history to block the suavity of her narrative. Unobtrusive paragraphs here and there, often at the beginning of chapters, relate the personal story to the general course of events. Yet history is not altered except in the minor ways a novelist may choose to increase the values inherent in the story.

Here are a few hints of how the author used her source material. In the novel we see two priests, after a very long and dangerous journey, by sea and overland, entering The Villa (Santa Fe) *alone*. In the *Life* they are met by a thousand people. Both biography and novel tell us that Father Latour, no sooner there, had to turn about and travel on horseback to Old Mexico and back, three thousand miles in all, to get confirmation of his credentials. In Howlett's book, he is accompanied by an envoy, but in the novel, goes and comes on his horse—*alone*. Again, in the novel, the Archbishop attends Vaillant's funeral—he is now Bishop of Denver—and then returns to prepare for his own death. From a footnote, we learn that it was the other way about.

When, in the chapter called "Gold Under Pike's Peak," we find Father Joseph in his famous carriage, hurrying to look after the sinners of the Gold Rush, the parting of the two priestly friends seems sad but bearable—Father Joseph will surely return. Yet in fact the history made by the two vicars jointly is over. It ends in 1860, historically, and has lasted but eight years. The lives of the two will stretch on, separately, for almost another twenty years. Miss Cather, calling on what has been between them, minimizes the separation and brings Father Joseph back to Santa Fe for frequent tender visits. She speaks of Blanchet as a "promoter," but it is the biographer, Father Howlett, who informs us, in full, that his subject Father Machebeuf, became Vicar Apostolic of Colorado and Utah, first Bishop of Denver; that he had built, at his death, one hundred and four churches, attached to his diocese sixty-four priests, and brought into Catholic schools three thousand children.

To overemphasize this tempestuous, extravert life, would have been to weaken the spell of Archbishop Latour, to lose the sense of good manners and consideration the author showed in relation to this pious, withdrawn prelate, whose nature refused too much exposure. Latour is, after all, the main character, as the reader has known since he met him as a young priest, lost among oven-shaped, conical sand-hills after a long, thirsty horseback ride. His plight, his reasonableness, his prayer before the cruciform tree win one's sympathy. Though in this first chapter, considerable past history is abridged, one never loses contact with the hero; when Father Latour and his tired animals reach *agua segreta*, hidden water, and a group of hidden Catholics, forgotten for two centuries in a green valley, the moment is unique.

In the later part of the book, with his lively associate no longer bouncing in and out—"I am always the one to whip the cats, *fouetter les chats*," Joseph, who had the chastising to do, comments somewhere—Bishop Latour becomes more and more retired. With the aid of a young French architect he has already built his golden cathedral, in the Midi-Romanesque style. This building Willa Cather, who loved all things French, fervently describes more than once, in its dramatic setting.

Mary Austin felt differently. In her autobiography, *Earth Horizon*, she uttered a word of censure, along with the claim, to which I earlier referred, that *Death Comes for the Archbishop* was written in her house:

... after Willa Cather came to write *Death Comes for the Archbishop*, and I had to go to the hospital. Miss Cather used my house to write in, but she did not tell me what she was doing. When it was finished, I was very much distressed that she had given her allegiance to the French blood of the Archbishop; she had sympathized with his desire to build a French cathedral in a Spanish town. It was a calamity to the local culture. We have never got over it. It dropped the local mystery plays almost out of use, and many other far-derived Spanish customs.

The old Bishop finally retired—first to a little country place he bought at the head of the Tesuque Valley where his small private chapel stands today (I know it well), under the foothills of the Sangre de Cristo Mountains. Here the old priest planted fruit trees and domesticated wild flowers, including the wild purple verbena—an exquisite, colorful libertine, which I cherished also, a couple of miles down the same valley.

Eventually the old Bishop moved back to his former study in the house of the new Archbishop, where he wished to die.

During those last weeks of the Bishop's life he thought very little about death; it was the Past he was leaving. The future would take care of itself. But he had an intellectual curiosity about dying; about the changes that took place in a man's beliefs and scale of values. More and more life seemed to him an experience of the Ego, in no sense the Ego itself. This conviction, he believed, was something apart from his religious life; it was an enlightenment that came to him as a man, a human creature.

The happy death of the thoughtful, mild old priest differs strangely from the tortured struggle, and almost fret-

ful will-to-death of Professor St. Peter. Bishop Latour sat
maturely in the middle of his own consciousness, feeling
that none of his previous states of mind and awareness
were lost or outgrown: the whole picture was there and
he visited every part of it, knowing that he would soon be
done with "calendared time."

As he drew his last breath, the Bishop was remembering
the moment in a green tilted French field, when he was
trying to comfort a brother of the soul, torn in two before
his eyes by the desire to go and the necessity to stay.

Thea, too, had known this fateful rending that grips at
the exile's heart, at the station when she left home for good.
So had Willa, and how little had she forgotten it!

In an open letter to *The Commonweal* Miss Cather spoke
of *Death Comes for the Archbishop* as comparable, in its
lack of accent, in its stress on simple direct human experiences, seen in the light of a supreme spiritual experience,
to the frescoes by Puvis de Chavannes of the life of Sainte
Geneviève, at the Paris Panthéon.

David Daiches in his *Willa Cather, a Critical Introduction*, points to the opening of Book One of *Death Comes
for the Archbishop*: "One afternoon in the autumn of
1851 a solitary horseman . . ." as similar to an opening by
Scott or Fenimore Cooper "or any one of a dozen minor
historical novelists of the nineteenth century." But, after
all, was *Death Comes for the Archbishop* of less delicate
and inventive texture than *To the Lighthouse*, or *The
Death of the Heart*, as he informs us? What does Rebecca
West say of the same book?

The most sensuous of writers, Willa Cather builds her imaginative world almost as solidly as our five senses build the universe around us. . . . She has within herself a sensitivity that constantly presents her with a body of material which would overwhelm most of us, so that we give up all idea of transmitting it—and she has also a quality of mountain-pony sturdiness that makes her push on, unfatigued under her load and give an accurate account of every part of it.

In the enforced move from Bank Street in the autumn of 1927 with Miss Lewis, Willa had chosen the Grosvenor as a haven. This discreet small hotel on lower Fifth Avenue was to be a temporary refuge only. But, in fact, four years elapsed before they left it. Both Willa's and Miss Edith Lewis' mothers were taken ill and must be visited in distant places. Mrs. Cather was in California, near one of her sons. But there was another reason for the delay in finding a satisfactory home, which Willa frankly stated to me: she could not decide what to do next.

She was half inclined to live in the country: why endure these urban restrictions and complications? But Miss Lewis was still working in the city and wanted to go on doing so. So, obviously, it must be an apartment. But where? Any decision that she almost reached was followed by a recoil. So they would wait until next year and tackle the matter again. . . .

But the enigma of life and death hovered in that rather gloomy hotel room of hers where we were drinking tea. Willa, with her depth of feeling for the father she had lost and the mother who was so ill, turned to me for the compassion and insight one old friend does try to bring another. She was vibrating, almost physically, with a sense of enigma.

Born a Baptist, baptized into the Episcopal Church in 1922, she had yet been impelled to enter deeply into the faith and the consolations of the Roman Catholic Church in *Death Comes for the Archbishop*. Now, to her concern, Catholics were writing her, believing her one of them. Priests, especially, wanted to visit her and talk with her. She had had to refuse them and was sorry. No faith, she feared, could save one from the great spiritual duality of our time—the conflict between the brave ideals of our pioneer ancestors, and the mounting materialism and industrialism of the post-war world.

The creative writer, we were agreed, has a momentary refuge from the duality that pulls modern man or woman apart but it lasts only for the absorbed duration of the work in which he is engaged. Then comes the dismal moment when the book goes to press—one has produced a dead thing, it seems. How does one deal with the soul, the spirit, lamenting and tortured? The book will not give the answer.

I can see Willa, putting on her fur coat, with a sad downcast face; we had decided to walk down to Washington Square, where I would take my bus uptown.

Just before we were ready to go, to my utmost surprise, she turned to me and in a very sensitive way asked if I thought psychoanalysis would help her.

She knew that I had begun analytical psychology with a pupil of Dr. C. J. Jung of Zurich. Willa wondered how this would affect the writing of the novel on which I was working.

When writing the portrait of Dr. William Alanson White, of St. Elizabeth's Hospital, for *Fire Under the Andes* I had asked him the same question. In his opinion, a writer should not write and analyze at the same time.

The material came from the same source—the unconscious.

"The unconscious," Willa mused, "the unconscious—" (I can hear her dubious tone.)

"You meet the unconscious with a vengeance in O'Neill's *Strange Interlude*, I remarked, recalling to her that I had been to the opening with the William Alanson Whites and Mary Austin. At dinner, between the two parts of the play, we had had a discussion about the validity of this bold experiment, which presented the inner comment of the actor-characters (in words) as well as their social reactions and replies.

Dr. White thought it was a fine dramatic experiment to put into words the split between what a character wanted to seem and what he actually was and felt. . . .

Willa hotly said that every play that amounted to anything contained secret reactions, inner feelings that diverged from what was actually being said and done by a protagonist on the stage. That could be expressed by action, by facial expression, by tone—it did not need to be inserted as spoken dialogue. . . .

Here she disappeared under water, and I knew she was no subject for psychoanalysis. But I had known it anyhow.

She wanted to know the title of my novel before we parted and as she herself had a genius for titles I was pleased that she cared for it: *Short As Any Dream.* It was an episodic family novel, a story of my mother's Maine people, starting with my great-grandmother, Nancy.

That we had in common, the grandmothers whose voices, reading us so simply the classics, echoed down the years. When my little novel came out in September, 1929, Willa wrote me a rare letter. I had, she said, understood how to portray a stream of blood. . . . Would it have been better to make the observer a delver in genealogical records, rather than to bring the author as a descendant of the family into the prologue? She would have done the opposite. But that was a detail, she said, warming me with congratulations from her mind and heart.

In November I sailed for Europe: my first visit since the First World War. I was bent on hearing in Zürich the seminar of Dr. C. G. Jung, the only modern psychologist I could discover who believed that the word "soul" could be spoken with reverence in our time. I stayed two years in Switzerland with visits to France and England: a period that, in Willa's life, corresponded with her visits to her sick mother, and her writing of *Shadows on the Rock* and the death of Mrs. Cather in 1931.

Willa had been, she told me, faced with a troubling inner division of her powers at this period. She kept her new book (figuratively speaking), in a kind of underground place, to which she could retire for a few hours of concentrated work. Even in California near her very sick mother, seeing her daily, she had such withdrawn hours when she could at least read French memoirs or Parkman's histories bearing on the period of Frontenac. As the Pueblo male retires from the teeming village to the kiva or underground chamber, so she could find herself as an artist in her hidden imaginary retreat on the rock of Quebec, and emerge from it with the power to bring something vital to the life that clung to hers.

When *Shadows on the Rock* came at last to hand in 1931, I was again in the captain's house at Sneden's Landing. My New York apartment, while I was in Europe, had gone the usual way of change and transformation. The depression was also upon us.

Near at hand was my old friend, Mary Tonetti who now, by choice, lived alone with her dogs at Pirate's Lair, a black house to which no road led, near a marsh, full of tall grey sedges and grasses where a heron sometimes stood. Autumn lasts till Christmas on this sleepy, misty shore.

In the evenings I read the story of the Rock which I had never seen. The book faded into the Sneden's opalescence, and I paused often to hold imaginary conversations with the author. It was clear that I should have fewer real ones, now.

This was Willa's tenth novel, her twelfth volume of fiction. It was again Catholic, again historical, and again revealed that devotion to and insight into French culture that had been almost a quality of her mind through the years. But by contrast with her nineteenth century missionaries the late seventeenth century French exiles on the rock of Quebec looked minute, fixed, immobile, almost puny; in a state of suspension. They were conservationists, not builders or discoverers. The Roman Catholic Church and the French King had done the whole trick for them.

Observed from above, as Willa was ever doing—setting

her rock in wonderful vistas of weather and sea and forest
—the whole citadel, stuck over with churches, nunneries,
spires, and bishops' and governors' residences, ringing with
bells, had the feel and look of a single religious and noble
house of prayer and obeisance. Into this pious enclosed
space her hero, once a *petit bourgeois* of Paris, a philosophic
apothecary in the service of Frontenac, fitted in a docile
way. He cherished the flame of the *foyer*, even after the
death of his wife; fearful that the breath of the great forest,
and the cry of the savage, could extinguish the precious
image he had borne overseas.

Writing to Wilbur Cross, who had reviewed *Shadows
on the Rock*, Willa Cather, about this time, elaborated her
aim as an artist. She had tried to develop her book

> into a prose composition not too conclusive, not too
> definite: a series of pictures remembered rather than ex-
> perienced; a kind of thinking, a mental complexion in-
> herited, left over from the past, lacking in robustness and
> full of pious resignation.

The old gusto of this author appeared when she described her clear-cut child-heroine, flavoring and serving
her father's soup; cooking his roast; presenting his dessert
(he preferred gooseberry to all jams); helping lay down
his wild doves in lard for winter eating; saving the parsley
from freezing on cold winter nights. Cécile had the finesse,
address and compassion of a much older woman, coupled
with a disarming innocence. This French interior is painted
with the strokes of a Dutch master. The obscure family, with all its detail of living, is clear as if seen behind
glass in a museum.

"*N'expliquez pas*"—leave it to my imagination,—said Cécile coaxingly to a nun who was telling her a legend which seems to the reader a refrain on harpsichord or lute. That is bedrock Cather. So is the little girl's zest for steep walks in all seasons and weathers, to points of majestic beauty. So is Cécile's love of the nomad Pierre Charron, relative of Tom Outland, the typical Cather wanderer-adventurer; the New World Frenchman who shot the rapids and explored the great lakes. But Charron's deep love story—in the past —is that with the aristocratic Jeanne Le Ber, whom he pursued even as she sequestered herself in church and convent. Here was an almost concealed *nouvelle* in the *roman*—I could have wished it to be the *roman* itself. One can have more than enough of a child heroine, however sage and efficient.

The driving force of *Shadows on the Rock* as of *Death Comes for the Archbishop* seemed to me the author's scarcely conscious pioneer longing to press on to a new frontier. New Mexico, New Brunswick and Quebec were not places where fate had situated Willa Cather, or where professional interests had taken her. They were psychic homelands that her love and adventure had eagerly sought and embraced—almost fragments of her soul.

Compare her to Faulkner, who has written only of one region, or to Sarah Orne Jewett, and she seems a nomad: prey and reward of her own diversity.

If so the leap from the limelight of *McClure's* in 1912— leap symbolic and actual and no more desired than dreaded —into the small quiet room where nothing happens outside the sole inhabitant, had been salvation, no less. This had really happened chiefly through the influence of New England—as a mental climate—at a critical period.

And now, at a moment when, below the surface, her own life was sad and in a state of flux and change, the most distinguished, intellectual New Englander of his day, Mr. Justice Holmes began to take a deep joy in her work. As a young man the Justice, too, frequented the delicious literary parlor at 148 Charles Street. His reading of belles lettres, old and new, had never ceased to be extensive, in spite of his immersion in the law. His judgments were pithy. Touched with fire, as he had put it, in his service to his country as a young Union officer in the Civil War, Americanism—for lack of a better word—became his over-all, under-all concern. He was always working for it, in his "opinions" in the Supreme Court, always listening for the sounding of the chord that revealed American life as a profound and passionate thing.

Beverly Farms
July 25, 1930

My dear Mr. Greenslet:

"My Ántonia" came duly and has been read. Every word of it. It lifts me to all my superlatives. I have not had such a sensation for a long time. To begin with I infinitely respect the author's taking her own environment and not finding it necessary to look for her scenes in Paris or London. I think it a prime mark of a real gift to realize that any piece of the universe may be made poetical if seen by a poet. But to be more concrete, the result seems to me a wonderful success. It has unfailing charm, perhaps not to be defined; a beautiful tenderness, a vivifying imagination that transforms but does not distort or exaggerate—order, proportion. It is a poem made from nature from which only a genius could make it: that being read establishes itself as true, and makes the reader love his country more. I thank you deeply for having opened this door to me.

Sincerely yours,
O. W. HOLMES

SUPREME COURT
OF THE UNITED STATES
WASHINGTON, D.C.

March 24, 1931

MY DEAR MISS CATHER:

A month ago Mr. Greenslet sent me a copy of "Death Comes for the Archbishop" and suggested that I might write a line to you. Circumstances have delayed my reading but I heard the last words from my secretary last night and avail myself of Mr. Greenslet's suggestion to tell you the pleasure I have had. I think you have the gift of the transforming touch. What to another would be prose, under your hand becomes poetry without ceasing to be truth. Among the changes of old age one is that novels are apt to bore me, and I owe you a debt for two exceptions, both of which gave me delight.

Very sincerely yours,
O. W. HOLMES

Holmes' handwriting alone made a letter from him a rare honor, Willa said. When, after the Justice's death, the *Holmes-Pollock Letters* were published, it touched her profoundly to find that Holmes had recommended her to a

great Britisher, Sir Frederick Pollock—also no mere legalist.
My Ántonia and *Death Comes for the Archbishop* Holmes
adjudged "great." *Shadows on the Rock*, no, a minor work.

In 1931 Miss Cather received an honorary Litt.D. from
Princeton University. This pleased her partly because she
was in very good company: Charles A. Lindbergh and
Robert Frost, two great admirations. She told me about the
occasion, about how much she had enjoyed meeting Mrs.
Lindbergh. But there had been a bit of trouble about the
loud speaker.

Every recipient of an honorary degree, after accepting
his parchment roll, was expected to walk to the microphone
and respond. When it came to Willa Cather's turn she
refused to go! So the microphone must and did go to her
instead. Her subjective recoil from the devices of publicity was automatic.

I never heard the sound of a radio in her apartment.
Once she proposed a spoken record. That was the romantic
voice of Edward the Eighth, abdicating his throne for love.
She played it twice over for me in her handsome Park
Avenue dining room.

There was another unexpected public episode in connection with the presentation of the Prix Femina Américain, in
1933, to *Shadows on the Rock:* Willa had demurred at accepting publicly this prize, with an attendant ceremony.
Of course she cared that French and Canadian people were
moved by the shadows she had cast on that great rock.
But the good literary life, as she saw it, did not include such
appearances. Under pressure to consider Fame something

she must give time to, she yielded the point, with the strict proviso that there be no photographers. This was agreed; but all at once, the vandals were pointing their lenses at her and flashing their lights. And there was Willa Cather, who expected others to keep faith, shrinking into a frozen statue.

Her reaction was symbolic: for the vital, easy, eager, curious, friendly participation in life one had first known in her had been a mood of youth. She was not yet sixty, nor completely withdrawn; would never completely withdraw, but she had reached the point where she determined that her life as an artist should and must be a guarded thing. During the fourteen years she had yet to live and work, her face lost some of its round warmth, except when an old affection welled up in her. But it wore very often, a look, as memorable as her former vital, heartening smile: a delicate look of remembrance.

CHAPTER III

Look of Remembrance
1932 – 1939

I<small>N</small> 1932, Willa Cather published *Obscure Destinies*, a book of three short stories. This major book, written on the edge of sixty, as the dates show, and during the rather sad, unsettled period between Bank Street and Park Avenue, proved a new milestone. Though there was so much continuity in Willa Cather's work, both in substance and in background, the mood and spirit of her writing had again subtly changed.

In her central story, "Old Mrs. Harris," she returned very quietly and unobtrusively, with the eyes of an elder daughter observing the past, to the roots from which she sprang. Dated 1931, New Brunswick, it must have been the means she found in a moment of deep grief, to "let go with the heart."

Old Mrs. Harris, an innocently sacrificed old woman, taken for granted by a whole crew of young children— by a gay, oblivious, high-handed Southern daughter; by a courteous son-in-law who is trying his best; even by Vickie,

the eldest child, full of rebellion and high personal determination,—accepted her humble fate in her little cluttered
downstairs room. There the children's overshoes, the ve-
locipede, the baby buggy, and the sewing machine were
also stored.

Only the old Southern servant, who bathed and rubbed
the old woman's feet at night, and the cat Blue Boy which
jumped on her knees, and the cultivated Jewish neighbor,
who stole in with an offering of coffee and cake, seemed
to realize her separate existence. She was embarrassed
when it was discovered; was lonely and tired only when
the glowing tide of child life did not wash about her.

The adolescent Vickie in the story seems frankly autobiographical; and in the last story in the volume, "Two
Friends," the author in the first person tells another story
as it appeared to her as a still younger child. This quiet
reminiscence, written in Pasadena in 1931, concerns two
small-town, Midwest businessmen—one the local banker
and storekeeper, the other a cattleman. Because they had
symbolized success and power, they had given the narrator
a sense of spiritual anchorage and connection with a wider
world.

The little girl had a lively curiosity about the person-
alities and the talk of these local potentates, and would walk
through the general store of a winter evening, watching
the two able men playing checkers behind the wire screen-
ing. On hot summer nights, when their chairs were moved
out to the brick sidewalk by a clerk, the girl would sit on
the edge of the sidewalk, throwing jacks and listening—
to Mr. Dillon talking, and Mr. Trueman making an occasional teasing, stinging answer. The listener, sitting by

the dusty road which drank up the moonlight, finally heard a quarrel between her two idols, about Bryan, that in a cruel, senseless way broke the friends' long friendship.

The first story, "Neighbor Rosicky," written in New York in 1928, concerns a Bohemian farmer who had a special gift for loving people. This was like an ear for music, or an eye for color, his American daughter-in-law felt. Polly had had a good deal of trouble in getting used to the Bohemian ways of her husband, Rudolph, until her father-in-law had a heart attack in her house, and she had held old Rosicky's pale brown, nimble gypsy hand as he lay on her bed.

This hand brought Polly to herself and into the Rosicky family. The tender little scene will go down in American letters as one of Willa Cather's classic pages; like the last pages of the second chapter of *My Ántonia* when Jim Burden makes his first solitary contact with the Nebraska wild land; like the pages in the first book of *The Song of the Lark* when Thea discovers her inner self and its secret purposes; or like Alexandra's triumphant return to the Divide, singing. All these "classic" pages had to do with the creating of a deep relationship through a gift of love. Soon I learned that the "Neighbor Rosicky" of the story had some identity with the living Bohemian farmer who introduced himself at a hospital by saying: "I am the husband of My Ántonia."

Perhaps it was in part that I was then living in a quarter of New York where the cloud of the depression rested very darkly that I found myself so resistant to visiting

Willa on Park Avenue—a street that I had never liked because it seemed created all of a piece by snobbery, not by
evolution, like most New York city streets which grow
out of the little neighborhoods that cling about them and
give them character.

Willa had said so much across the years to the effect
that smug success and easy money were not real aims in
human life; about the hostility of comfortable, self-satis-
fied people to any serious effort of the artist, that I wondered how she would tolerate the masked faces she would
meet going in and out.

If Neighbor Rosicky ventured into this lobby with its
repressed attendants in uniform, whose chief job seemed
to be to tend an excluding telephone board, would he
reach his goal? Grandma Harris, even Mr. Trueman and
Mr. Dillon, in this setting would remain indistinguishable.

Still, when I reached Willa's front door upstairs and she
opened it herself, as of old, and met me in the eager, warm,
unchanged way with which she greeted old friends, I was
reassured. Saying that she had not really cared for Park
Avenue in advance but she had been persuaded that it was
the right place for her, and it was proving comfortable and
convenient, she led me from the sizeable hall down a little
corridor to her bedroom, where my coat was soon laid out
on a calico patchwork counterpane, surely of Red Cloud
make. This little room seemed bright and inviting and
individual, and I hoped she wrote there—for how could
Willa, so connected with primeval nature, write in the
luxurious sheltered cave of the connecting main rooms—
spacious but not spatial. Noiseless but with no view or sun.

For all the windows faced the blank north wall of the Colony Club.

But that, Willa said happily, was the virtue of the place: she had taken it because the walls and floors were thick and the windows far from the roar on the Avenue. No heels ramped and tramped above. No radio sounded.

A maid stealing in a little anxiously out of the kitchen department with a tea tray seemed to be entering a buffer state, a home that had not yet taken on the vibrations of life. It does require time to turn a conventional apartment into a *foyer*, Willa lamented.

At least there was a fireplace (though not arranged to draw up to) and gradually, seeing among the new tables and chairs, more formal than those in Bank Street, the orange tree, the freesias, the George Sand engraving, the head of Keats, and the charming little paintings of the Mediterranean shore by a friend of Miss Lewis who lived in Capri, I dared to look straight at my hostess, thinner than of old, sitting quietly in her new armchair, bearing the accretion of her years and her works.

"I love your new book, Willa," I said. . . .

"That little listener, and the road drinking up the moonlight. . . 'Nothing in the world,' " I quoted, " 'not snow mountains or blue seas, is so beautiful as the soft, dry roads in a farming country, roads where the white dust falls back from the slow wagon-wheel.' Isn't there a line of Frost like that? It's poetry anyhow. . . and it reminded me of the moonlight in 'The Bohemian Girl'—why haven't you re-published that story?"

She thought it never quite fitted in any collection yet conceived—certainly not in this one.

I had noticed on a table a melting even angelic photograph of young Yehudi Menuhin, of whom she had spoken sometimes since his appearance at the age of twelve at Carnegie Hall. She had a rapturous admiration for his musical gifts and, she now told me, had met him in Paris in 1930 with his family. At last it seemed she had a youngster in her life, marked by fate for genius and a great career as a violinist. Yehudi for Willa opened vistas into the world of the masters of music to which her own passion had ever led. She made a story of this prodigy and his fascinating and gifted little sisters, and of his parents, as if she had at last, by proxy, a family exactly to her taste. Not at all like her beloved Cather family with its pioneer tradition; in this brilliant Jewish milieu, erudition and art were primary, and everything else of secondary importance.

Willa seemed disturbed that I was living in temporary quarters, without my Lares and Penates, and writing pot boilers for popular magazines, instead of the novel that was to follow *Short As Any Dream*. She had felt I should never stop writing novels and damned the depression and fetched the dry sherry from the dining room, with three glasses, in case Miss Lewis came home from the office. Whether Willa ever served cocktails, though she lived into the cocktail age, I doubt, though her drawing room—it really was that, big enough to house a party of thirty—looked a little lonely for two ladies drinking their dry sherry together.

As I got ready to go, Willa began, as she always did when lonely, talking rapidly of her nieces—of the twins, Roscoe's sweet daughters, and Mary Virginia Auld, another favorite, the one who had unveiled the Bakst portrait in Omaha. (This niece worked in the circulating room in the New York Public Library and before long confirmed her aunt's worst suspicions by saying that she was constantly asked for the commentaries on D. H. Lawrence by Mabel, Frieda and Brett, and *never* asked for *Sons and Lovers* or any other novel by Lawrence himself.)

What next for you, Willa? I asked, hesitantly. She had something in mind. But so many tiresome engagements . . .

We were in the hall by then and she gave me, as so often in parting, a fond look that was almost a plea.

We are friends, old, old friends—even if I do live here and have so many dull things to do—for Fame—even if we do disagree about the Roosevelts.

"New York is a wild that one has to tame anew in every new neighborhood," she murmured as the door closed. . . .

In the spring of 1933 when the Roosevelts took over the White House, John Collier, in whose group I had been fighting the battles of Indian defense against the government for ten years, was appointed Indian Commissioner. Secretary Ickes, also a fighter for Indian rights, was now at the head of the Department of the Interior, and it seemed that many reforms hitherto impossible would be tried out. So I returned to the Pueblo and Navajo country in the summer of 1933, began to work, sending in reports of economic and social conditions among the Pueblos, first informally, and finally on a government appointment. From 1933 to 1936 I was largely in New Mexico, living either in my house in Tesuque, or in a "one-room" adobe I rented from young friends in Santa Fe. When I went East, to see my father or for other reasons, I rarely found Willa on Park Avenue: she would have gone to Europe or to the Grand Manan.

She wrote me now and then and I remember discovering *Lucy Gayheart* shortly after its appearance in 1935, on the Harvey House bookstand in Lamy. This particular Harvey House, being small and at a junction, rarely full, had been a great favorite of Willa's; it was a happiness to read her book under the Spanish arcade of the little patio, grown with vines, and feel in touch with her again.

Lucy Gayheart, the small-town Midwest girl who, unlike Thea, loved her small town; who, as a pianist, had a musical gift not an overwhelming one, was, I saw at once, no replica of Thea. Lucy's talent took her also to Chicago, to the musical and urban environment we had come to know through the author's eyes in *The Song of the Lark*. Thea had genius and also the will-power of the prima donna. Lucy, the accompanist to a singer, lived not by will-power but by sensitive adaptation, by thoughts and feelings, that, as always with fantasy and dream, are entangling rather than liberating.

The modern career girl might well say of Lucy: "She can't be like that." But Lucy was like that—that is, involved, in a selfless, dreamy, idealistic way, with her distinguished, egocentric, middle-aged singer, who was married, disillusioned and cautious. Perhaps only a woman writer, who has received a thousand confidences from women connected with the arts, could make so subtle a romance of an unequal human relationship doomed from the start. In the end the hero drowned, in the grasp of one who, unlike Lucy, did exploit and demand: his male secretary. And Lucy, so unaware, in her supersensitive adoration, that passion has its dark shadow, drowned, too, in a flight over thin ice.

Beyond the clear, delicately sketched portraits of Lucy's gentle father, her fumbling sister and other townsfolk, including Tom Gordon, a young banker whom she might have married, there lies this almost allegorical shadow cast by a solitary, immature passion. Suffering and ecstasy are bedfellows, here, and in no other novel has Willa stressed in just this way the *lacrymae rerum.*

In 1936, when I had to choose whether or not to accept a government appointment in the Southwest on a more permanent basis I decided to seek my Eastern roots again.

I arrived in Boston in time to see Dr. C. G. Jung receive a degree and make a learned address at the Centennial of Harvard University. After this I made my way to a windy, gull-haunted, wave-dashed island in a blue sea off Brunswick, Maine—Bailey Island—where the tall, broad-beamed Swiss psychologist, with his white head and ruddy cheeks and robust laugh, was to give a seminar to a gathering of the Jungian clans. This was an utterly fascinating and rewarding return to the "inner world," among a group of friends some of whom came from the far West.

There is something about the hard, swift efficiency of New York that is terrifying after a long immersion in the Southwest where nobody seemed, even in the thirties to be driving to a fate or pushing to a goal. Everybody, Indians, Spanish Americans, even Anglos, seemed then to live at the slow, grazing pace, the pace that Willa had loved from her Virginia childhood. She speaks of this pace in her essay on Thomas Mann.

The potent, lush, black-bottomed soil of Rockland

County lures all primitives—artists and writers, too. Sneden's Landing has sweet invitations to the irrational and the dream, and ever varied rhythms of running water. Mary Tonetti had invited me to spend a month in a ground-floor studio apartment directly on the Hudson.

The "out" was that it was warmed in winter by an enormous coal stove. Mary hoped that I might decide to stay and rent the place. To that end, she presented her Italian handyman, gardener, dog-tender, who would look after me.

Ernesto and Mary, I quickly saw, had tacitly agreed that there should be one American community ruled by feeling rather than efficiency. One place where artists got the right conditions for work, where dogs came into their own and lived to a great, great age. One place where the relation between man and the vegetable kingdom was recognized also as binding.

When my friend brought this Italian peasant to my door, Ernesto gave a succulent earthy laugh, which came from his stomach, and said confidentially:

"Miss Serga, Fascismo no getta me!" That was his great pride. He had escaped from Mussolini. The two police dogs, one yellow-brown, one white, crowded up to him, licking his hands, pressing their hairy bodies spasmodically against his legs, leaping high to touch his brawny shoulders, uttering fond, painfully apprehensive cries.

Mary lived at Pirate's Lair, down the rocky path along the Hudson, toward those floating bastions of dark rock, the Palisades, swimming out of the great blue living river which flowed like the very stream of life toward the great city.

Apparently I had decided to stay the winter. My writing table was installed, my fire was burning and I was already working on an Indian story.

It was pleasant to write near a friend who stopped in for a cup of tea or coffee, and then, in her grey floating garments, or her tweeds, her face ruddy and young, her head noble and white, pursued her own jobs, while aqueous echoes, glancing from shore to terrace, enveloped her.

Sometimes she decided to go to the city, perhaps to see her friend Kit Cornell in a play. She made no bones of climbing the long hill to the bus, though she was tall, elderly and built on Demeter lines.

Ernesto would watch her out of sight, holding the whining dogs in leash, and then he'd say to me: "When she go, *fifty* people gone."

He never forgot to leave a lighted kerosene lantern on the wall in front of my bedroom window, and if I waked at one or two in the morning I would see from my bed the tall, cloaked figure clasp it to her arm with a gesture of comfort.

Someone has thought of me.

It was in this environment that I received, just at Christmas time, Willa's book of essays, *Not Under Forty*, which established her distinction as a literary essayist with a felicitous gift for portraiture. She had sent the English edition, published by Cassell, and on the flyleaf had written:

These are true stories, told just as they happened.

It was interesting that she called them "stories." In her prefatory notes she referred to the contents as "sketches" and she frankly addressed them to the middle-aged. She asserted again that the world broke in two in 1922—or about that time—and that the persons and prejudices recalled belonged to yesterday—except for Thomas Mann, who is very much, she said, one of the forward-goers—did she mean the *avant-garde?*—and yet goes back a long way; and so satisfies the backward, of whom she was one, and for whom she had written.

I eagerly scanned the contents to see how she had selected the pieces and how many of them I knew.

First came "A Chance Meeting," published in *The Atlantic Monthly* not long before. This essay records the wholly unexpected encounter of the author, then in her sixties, with a very old French lady, a widow, staying alone with her maid at Aix-les-Bains. Willa had stopped often at this old-fashioned French watering-place with its opera house and formal squares, but never had she dreamed of finding the niece of the great Flaubert there—the niece Caroline, who sat like a mouse in her uncle's study as a child; the niece he wrote to, in a famous printed correspondence she had long since read; the niece who had been her uncle's literary executor. Willa took Madame Franklin-Grôut very much at her own valuation and the meeting between the two of them seemed to have been planned in Willa's heaven, and came to her with a sense of fate.

Next in the volume was "The Novel *Démeublé*," her own declaration of faith as a novelist made in 1922 in *The New Republic*—hardly "backward" in trend at the time, and indeed never "dated" or abandoned as a faith. After this, with a brief introduction, the delicious essay on Mrs. James T. Fields called "148 Charles Street"; then quite

naturally, a sketch of Sarah Orne Jewett, a part of which
had been written as preface to her own selection of Miss
Jewett's stories, the Mayflower edition.

The new material is Willa Cather's quintessential estimate and picture of Sarah Orne Jewett as "a lady, in the old
high sense"—which was in her face, her figure, her smile,
her carriage, her gift of conversation, and her gift for literary style. Willa Cather pointed out that Miss Jewett was
not what we now call a "career" writer: her gift with her
pen was one of her many personal qualities, and grew out
of her life and environment—the Maine country village,
where she lived aristocratically.

The sketch of Katherine Mansfield, written in 1925, was
the result of an unusual shipboard meeting of Willa Cather
with a man who had known this gifted New Zealander as
a child. Both touching and critical, it reveals a true literary
kinship that has been little stressed. In analyzing Miss
Mansfield's own method, in "Prelude" and "At the Bay,"
which interprets the struggle for individual life that under-
lies everyday behavior in a happy family made up of husband and wife, children and grandmother, Willa Cather in
some sense forecasts her own "Old Mrs. Harris." On top,
the group life; underneath, secret, passionate and intense,
the real life that marks the faces and gives timbre to the
voices of the individuals.

The only essay I had not read was that on the two first
Joseph books of Thomas Mann. That, expressed in terms
of thought, is the most original and eloquent, of the critical
contributions, and brings forth, as nowhere else in Willa
Cather's writing, her own profound debt to the great Bible
stories which her pious elders taught her as a child.

Willa heard of my way of living in Sneden's with surprise and concern. She urged me to come into the city, to have tea with her, or dinner with her and Miss Lewis.

When I did this I was sometimes led into discussing values I saw in the New Deal that Willa condemned. I told her what it had been like in my New Mexico valley in the autumn of 1933: all the men from the Mexican village standing idle on the bridges; if working at all, paid by the ranchers only in produce—in fresh meat or milk. A whole family of brothers depended on the few dollars I paid their little sister for housework. But by the time I left, all the men were laboring on needed highways at WPA wages.

No good! Willa believed in the early American virtues, courage, sturdiness, tough endeavor. Nobody, young people especially, should be helped, no artist or writer either. Endowments, frescoes for public buildings, travelling fellowships be damned. During the ten years before she received the Pulitzer Prize, she said, she did plenty of pot-boiling articles and average short magazine stories—let them be forgotten.

It was harder and harder, I discovered, for professionals in her own literary world to see Willa. Henry Canby of *The Saturday Review of Literature* would try, only to find her guarded by lions of every description.

If one is to believe the preface to the revised edition of *The Song of the Lark* which appeared also in 1932, Willa, because she was an artist, was now denied most of the gentle, spontaneous joys of every woman's life.

The life of nearly every artist who succeeds in the true sense (succeeds in delivering himself completely to his art)

WILLA CATHER

is more or less like Wilde's story, *The Portrait of Dorian Gray.* As Thea Kronborg is more and more released into the dramatic and musical possibilities of her profession, as her artistic life grows fuller and richer, it becomes more interesting to her than her own life. As the gallery of her musical impersonations grows in number and in beauty and that perplexing thing called "style" (which is a singer's very self) becomes more direct and noble, the Thea Kronborg who is behind the imperishable daughters of music becomes somewhat dry and preoccupied. Her human life is made up of exacting engagements and dull business detail, of shifts to avoid an idle gaping world which is determined that no artist shall ever do his best. Her artistic life is the only one in which she is happy and free, or even very real. It is the reverse of Wilde's story; the harassed, susceptible human creature comes and goes, subject to colds, brokers, dressmakers, managers. But the free creature, who retains her youth and beauty and warm imagination, is kept shut up in the closet, along with the scores and wigs.

Thea was, of course, an interpretative artist—not a creative writer. But Willa had said: "nearly every artist." Can a free female creature be shut up only for and with her work, without a serious spiritual penalty?

In the autumn of 1937, Professor Jung again came over from Switzerland, this time to give some lectures on religion at Yale, and to continue the Bailey Island seminar in New York. I needed contact with ideas, libraries, friends and connections in the city, so took a one-room apartment on East Seventy-third Street. It had a fireplace and a long row of southern windows, giving in part, on a quiet monastic garden. I could raise spring bulbs and not feel too city-bound.

Willa now approved of me, and though much farther east, I was relatively in her neighborhood. Sometimes we met by chance at the Society Library, which had always been "her" library and had long since moved up town. I did not then belong but dropped in to do research. She looked shorter and smaller to me, and more remote and when I read Alfred Kazin's appraisal of her I felt he had said something for me, better than I could ever say it:

> Her distinction was not merely one of cultivation and sensibility, it was a kind of spiritual clarity possible only to those who suffer their loneliness as an act of the imagination and the will.
>
> It was as if the sense of loss felt by a whole modern American generation had suddenly become a theme, rather than a passing emotion, a dissociation which one had to suffer as well as to report. She *seceded* as only a bare and exquisite sensibility could secede, with dignity.

In 1937-1938, Houghton Mifflin published a unified autographed Library edition of Willa Cather's complete works in twelve volumes. Knopf coöperated, and *Sapphira and the Slave Girl* was added in 1941. The edition, beautifully designed by Bruce Rogers, and printed on fine paper, was for bibliophiles above all. In several cases, two volumes are printed in one. Most have frontispieces, which are either portraits or snapshots of the author, some rather unfamiliar; or facsimiles of some significant manuscript page of the particular book. The familiar Steichen portrait in the middy blouse, perhaps the best Cather photograph extant, is there, and another pleasing informal photograph taken with a police dog, in the garden of the Hambourg's villa at Ville d'Avray.

Most interesting to me was the facsimile of the corrected manuscript page (deletions in brackets) shown in *Shadows on the Rock,* as follows:

> When the sun came up over the Ile d'Orléans, [like a bridegroom issuing from his chamber] the rock of Kebec stood gleaming above the river like an altar with many candles, or like a holy city in an old legend, shriven, sinless, washed in gold, [shining like the righteous in their Heavenly Father's house.]

The deletions, as Mr. Greenslet pointed out, are all to the advantage of the text, and when I saw them I remembered how in my *McClure's* interview, Willa insisted that all good writers accepted cuts, there were plenty more good phrases where those came from.

In the case of *Lucy Gayheart,* the theme—as I see it—of this nostalgic work is written out in longhand on the heavy white paper with the initials W.S.C. as she used it in the later years of her life. (She had dropped the Sibert in signing her books, but kept it in her personal life.)

> Some people's lives are affected by what happens to their persons or their property; but for others, fate is what happens to their feelings and their thoughts—that and nothing more.

But Willa Cather did not revise her works as a whole in this edition, as Henry James did in the celebrated New York edition of his works, or add any new prefaces. In cases where textual changes had already been made, or

prefaces added, the later revised form was used: for instance *April Twilights*, revised in 1923, from the original
Badger edition of 1903. *Alexander's Bridge*, revised in
1922, with a valuable preface; and *The Song of the Lark*
revision of 1932 with another important preface—these you
will find in the autographed edition. One book, *Not Under
Forty*, appears with a new title: *Literary Encounters*.

In the late spring, in May, at the end of the thirties,
Willa and Miss Lewis came to dinner with me in East
Seventy-third Street. One cannot entertain formally in a
one-room apartment, but Pauline Goldmark was there also,
and along with the spring blossoms from Sneden's and the
fresh spring silks of the three ladies, there was a moment of
happy communication again. Willa was always simple,
concentrated and affectionate at these now rather rare
meetings—every bit of her was present, once she got to the
point of making the initial effort.

She was then engaged with Sapphira, and told us that
she had discarded some six pounds of manuscript, dealing
with the Shenandoah Valley background.

As often among old friends who are getting older, there
was a death to speak of. Isabelle Hambourg had died in
Sorrento in 1938. Willa told us that Jan Hambourg, after
his wife's death, had sent over her own letters to Isabelle,
and that she was burning them up, as quickly as she could.
Every Sunday Miss Lewis took a bundle of them to the
apartment incinerator.

There was a kind of finality in this cremation that
brought a chill of regret and dismay. Willa had sometimes

said that a book at its best was life—life burned, cremated. But a lifetime of letters, a deep communication between two friends, cremated? What remained was surely an essence, something for the heart alone.

CHAPTER IV

Not Too High, Not Too Wide
1940 – 1947

IT WILL ALWAYS BE consoling to Willa's friends that the forties, during which they lost her, opened triumphantly with the appearance of her only Southern heroine, Sapphira Dodderidge Colbert. This masterful, devious, proud, resolute woman, whom we meet in middle age, with dropsical legs and confined to a clumsy wheeled chair, is a heroine we shall no more forget than Alexandra or Ántonia or Thea. But she is rather coldly observed, not created out of poignant love and admiration; one might sense that her creator was fascinated, rather than emotionally involved. The words in which Sapphira is described are not fervent, though they are exquisitely accurate, and every one in its place.

Willa Cather did like powerful women, but here, with no moralizing (but with a good bit of documentation) she reveals how subtly tyrannical and malevolent a well-bred, well-endowed outdoor Virginia woman of 1850, who has ridden horseback and directed her farms and slaves, may become when physically ill and spiritually and socially frustrated. Like Myra Henshawe, Sapphira had a devoted, capable, subservient husband. Henry Colbert, the miller of Belgian descent whom she married (nobody knew just why), was a good miller, a reliable businessman. She had brought him along with her slaves from Loudoun County, where she had been born of British emigré parents with money and traditions. Like Myra, again, Sapphira had chosen to desert a richer past, and to take a husband who was her superior only in the tender and gentle things of the heart, which, strangely enough, meant less to her than personal power.

Thus *Sapphira and the Slave Girl*, Willa Cather's last novel and final work was, in a sense, another study of an unequal marriage, viewed in the middle years. But it is also a story of the underground, half darksome, half lightsome world of slavery, just before the Civil War, and in a unique family and regional setting, where sympathies were divided. Henry Colbert was not a slaveholder, and his and Sapphira's only child, their daughter, a young widow, with two small children, who had lost a beloved husband and now nursed her poor neighbors, was as actively engaged in helping slaves escape by the underground railway as any *McClure's* reformer who dealt with later versions of human exploitation.

The region where this humanly divided family lived was a sparsely settled area below the North Mountain, between Winchester and Romney, in the Shenandoah Valley. Here the reader begins to get a whiff of a fragrance that is of the quintessence of this book. This, the seat of the novel, is the very locality where the author was born and lived to the age of nine. A haunting and spontaneous savor of time and place encloses the characters. Their separate lives in the brick house, at the mill, in the slave quarters, and on the mountain above them are permeated and activated by half-hidden Virginia earth meanings, that burst into flower and draw them in their various directions. One has the reminiscential sense that one has "been there before."

In my own case, this sense was enhanced by a memory of accompanying Willa, in imagination only, in the summer of 1913, to this corner of the Shenandoah Valley. She was taking a driving trip there with Isabelle McClung and described her adventures in some detail. Gore, her birthplace, had proved tiresome, and the people she had loved as a child were dead. But nothing could diminish her exuberant joy in walking for six miles at a time through the great forest trees, preferably in the rain—the trees of the North Mountain.

So, though not inspired by such joyous apprehending and awakening as gave us *O Pioneers!* and *My Ántonia*, Sapphira's story emerged with great solidity. It is a sort of document, a kind of "historical" novel which owes everything to mature imagination. The author had again taken that ride she described in the essay on her two first novels: on a horse that knew the way, on a fine morning when she felt like riding. But she was older now, and guided her beast with a gloved hand, touching his flanks, now and then, with her riding whip, almost as Sapphira must have done when bent on an errand.

The rider knew, moreover, at what brick house (Willowshade Farm) she would dismount at teatime, and whom she would find, sitting with dignity in her wheeled chair, in the parlor, with a sedate colored housekeeper, Till,

Nancy's mother, at her back. Family legend stored in a Nebraska attic, and a very special, sentient awareness of a particular locality had given her all the needed clues.

The story Sapphira (perhaps not a Cather) whispered in the ear of the author had, Willa said, many twists and ramifications. They came flooding upon her. But, in her zest for the novel *démeublé*, she threw out many, many pages and chapters, to give Sapphira the central place. Thus, since Sapphira was cold and calculating, the story warms the reader only in its peripheral human relationships. Willa excelled, I believe, in her rendering of those primal, delicate, unquestioned, unconscious aspects of love as occurred between the miller and the slave girl, between Ántonia and Jim Burden, Father Vaillant and Father Latour. Psychologists call them "projections," and they are innocent as life itself until punctured by a rapier like Sapphira's. The black girl, catching the import and implications of the sophisticate, as primitives do, escaped with desperate fear and Sapphira's own daughter's aid to guide her to a better haven through the underground railway.

In the Epilogue to the book, twenty-five years later—therefore let us say in 1875—we meet a little girl just over five—here some literary liberties have been taken—who, sitting waiting with other relatives, is deeply attentive to the return of the slave girl Nancy, now dignified by marriage and a career as a British housekeeper in Canada.

This child, as I said in the Introduction to this book, was little Willie Cather. The novelist who grew out of her told me, not long before she died, that she had, she felt, made an artistic error in bringing herself into the story. But I like her there myself. I like to see her being affected in childhood, as potential genius often is, by a mysterious visitant. Elizabeth Roberts told me once that her novel, *The Time of Man*, derived from her seeing two people, a man and woman, driving by in a wagon on a sandy Southern road.

The world we lived in had now moved on, with the Second World War, into a menacing period of change. Willa feared and hated the psychological repercussions of change, even in peacetime, and was increasingly troubled by the heroic and tragic disasters of the war. Moreover, she was increasingly subject to illness, and the limitations resulting from illness. With her dearest friends, in and out of her family, dying and taking with them irreplaceable values, she had little spiritual margin with which to resist physical weakness and sorrow. Her seeming withdrawal from vital participation into a mold of almost rigid quietness resulted. She is saving herself for her work, I thought, and I believe she tried to do just that. Nevertheless, no other new books appeared in her lifetime.

Willa did, however, consent, with a little coaxing from her publishers, to have a number of her greater novels printed in the Armed Services Editions. At first she resisted this extension of her public, and the mass mail that resulted made great demands on her time. She answered letters from enlisted men personally, when they seemed to require it.

Once during a meal in a small restaurant, where the radio was kept quite horribly turned on, Willa Cather heard several chapters of *My Ántonia* read by an unknown voice which keyed them up in an emotional, elocutionary way, instead of respecting the muted and sober quality of her text. So when she was asked to permit that some of her novels be recorded for the blind, under the auspices of the Library of Congress, she refused until Archibald MacLeish could assure her that her books would be read simply. Five of her best novels have now been made available as "Talking Books" and can be had from branch libraries: *My Ántonia, The Song of the Lark, One of Ours, A Lost Lady, Death Comes for the Archbishop.*

But this was an exceptional permission. In general Willa Cather stuck to the view that her books should be read only in the regular editions issued by Alfred A. Knopf and Houghton Mifflin. She thundered against the trend to anthologize, to cut books to small pattern for magazines, to reproduce fragments in "portables." It's a sorry comment on our times, she would say, sarcastically—why waste energy wading through a long novel if you can know the author from a single excerpt? All her own books continued to sell steadily. She would never autograph copies sent her by strangers, on the ground that to do so interfered with the publisher's right to special editions.

And as for the movies—she had consented once, just once: *A Lost Lady* had been filmed in the early thirties and the result was so dismaying that she not only refused all future movie commitments in her lifetime but saw to it, in her will, that her works should not be given on radio, television, or any other scientific invention of the future.

Willa had apparently exhausted her own desire to write material based on memory and reminiscence of youth, and certainly had no interest or gift for writing of contemporary life. When she talked with me, as she did, of her friend Sigrid Undset—that great rock of a Norwegian woman who, during the war, established herself on Brooklyn Heights where she could see the battered ships come in from their dangerous voyages, and keep in touch with the Norwegian underground—Willa spoke with warmest admiration of *Kristin Lavransdatter* and *Gunnar's Daughter*, books whose inspiration comes from the Sagas and the early Nordic time. Here, too, was heroic man, pioneer man, exposed to untold danger and peril and resisting and conquering it, creating a new spiritual world. But Mrs. Undset's novels of modern Norway were of no interest to her. She was not concerned with the present status of marriage in Norway—any more than with the divorces of the Midwesterners coming to take their chances in her city of New York; or with the poetry of T. S. Eliot.

As friends grow older, meetings are often deferred by illness, and letters often chronicle deaths too hard even to talk about. Willa still lived on Park Avenue (where I hesitated to telephone often) and I was again living at Sneden's Landing, or, rather, at Palisades, on top of the long hill from the Hudson and in a village, near post-office, library and New York bus. At the Blacksmith's Shop I had a ground-floor studio apartment with a big garden which Mary Tonetti had helped to design. It had a pebbled space like Professor St. Peter's garden, and looked into a fine patch of woods, filled with birds and wildflowers, and always golden-pink in sunset light. But Willa somehow believed that I was in the wilderness.

She would anxiously ask how I was getting through a

cold snap, though I had told her I had an oil burner (with war-limited oil) and a fine brick forge-fireplace, relic of a real forge which Mr. Dumkin, the then village blacksmith, kept red-hot in my first Sneden's years.

Willa would conclude by saying solicitously that she did hope I would be spending the winter with one of my sisters —for the country was so hazardous for a woman by herself —unless she were one of Miss Jewett's lone women which (she said) I certainly wasn't. That always amused me, since Willa herself (like me) was the last woman in the world to give up an individual life. Both my sisters had families; one was an editor and the other an artist. Willa had two sisters left in the West, but now she was so far from well she rarely saw them.

In 1942, Willa spent the whole summer, a very hot one, in the city itself—an unaccustomed thing for her—recuperating from a gall-bladder operation. When she and Miss Lewis got away to Williamstown for a month, it rained; and on her return she found three pounds of personal letters, from all quarters of the globe, awaiting her. A fine orthopaedic doctor, Dr. F. R. Ober of Boston, who since Dr. Lovett's death had kept my war ankles in trim, had brought Willa's arm to terms in 1941. But after those letters were answered she was back again with Dr. Ober's brace.

And in 1943, after a summer with Miss Lewis at the Asticou Inn at Northeast Harbor, she came back to find three nieces whose husbands had been pulled into the war, waiting to find places to live, and one had a small baby. Life kept on making its claims, even if one did not answer the telephone.

In 1944 when she was given the Gold Medal by the National Academy of Arts and Letters, and was sitting on the platform, she watched her old friend and boss, S. S. McClure, then in his eighties, receive an award and, before all the dignitaries, dashed across to throw her arms around him, with a touch of her old verve and spontaneity.

But in the middle of that very same summer, when she was again in Maine, her brother Roscoe, president of a savings bank in Colusa, California, died of a heart attack. Douglass and Roscoe, the two brothers just younger than herself, had from childhood been her beloved companions. Douglass had already and recently died—he was the one with whom she had done so much jaunting around the Southwest, in the fateful summer of 1912, when *O Pioneers!* was born. He—then a railroad man—was the one who read and advised her about the railroad and brakeman episodes in *The Song of the Lark*.

Roscoe, three years younger than Willa, had been perhaps even closer, and she had spent many summers with him and his wife and his children in Wyoming, and made camping trips on horseback with them into the mountains. She used to let me think—and now said again, under the stress of grief—that though she was working in New York and seemed to be living there, the most actual and joyous part of her life had been spent with Roscoe in the West. She told me that they had exchanged frequent letters, that he had been East to see her in winter. It was a major grief, which transformed the whole shape of things—and she wanted me to understand it.

In the posthumous volume, *The Old Beauty and Others* a very eloquent quasi-autobiographical story of a young teacher, "The Best Years," confirms this relationship between an elder sister and her younger brothers as of basic significance in Willa Cather's life. (Strangely enough, as she was writing the story at the Asticou Inn at North East Harbor, Mt. Desert, where she spent some of her later summers, she received the news of Roscoe's death.) If, as David Daiches says in his critical study of Miss Cather, she had a "masculine consciousness," wasn't it because so much of her intimate life had been lived with boys and men of her own blood and been seen through their eyes by projection?

Lesley (of "The Best Years") comes back from teaching her first school to see her family, which consisted entirely of brothers:

> The boys were much the dearest things in the world to her. To love them so much was just . . . happiness. To think about them was the most perfect form of happiness. Had they been actually present, swinging on the two trapezes, turning on the bar, she would have been much too excited, too actively happy to be perfectly happy. But sitting in the warm sun, with her feet on the good ground, even her mother away, she almost ceased to exist. The feeling of being at home was complete, absolute; it made her sleepy. And that feeling was not so much the sense of being protected by her father and mother as of being with, being one with her brothers. It was the clan feeling, which meant life or death for the blood, not for the individual. For some reason, or for no reason, back in the beginning, creatures wanted the blood to continue.

This again reminded me of a passage from "The Namesake" (1907): the story of an American sculptor, living in Paris, who describes whence came, from what family memories and what Civil War past, his statue of a Color Sergeant:

> It was the same feeling that artists know when we rarely achieve truth in our work: the feeling of union with some great force, of purpose and security, of feeling glad that we have lived. For the first time I felt the pull of race and kindred, and felt, beating within me things that had not begun with me. It was as if the earth under my feet had grasped and rooted me and were pouring its essence into me. I sat there until the dawn of morning and all night long my life seemed to be pouring out of me and running into the ground.

In the opening poem of the first edition of *April Twilights*: "Dedicatory: To R.C.C. and C.D.C." (Roscoe and Douglass) Willa Cather imagined these two brothers of hers and herself gathering from the world's four quarters in an April twilight, stealing to a moonlit tryst like the happy shadows of three playmates who once lay on an island in a Western river and planned together their own world conquests, as the moon rose.

The nostalgic poem was suppressed in later editions. There was no Cather left in Red Cloud after Willa's mother's death. She never went back there after 1931.

In 1945 I had a serious eye trouble which confined me to bed at the Blacksmith Shop for several months. Cold and wintry months they were, except for the warmth that came to me from neighbors, friends and relatives; and from Ira, my Dachshund, who from the foot of my bed shared my troubles, or busily greeted visitors at the front door. When I heard an especially rapturous scurry of paws and wail of impetuous joy I knew that Mary Tonetti was soon coming in; her blowing white hair hung with snowflakes, her ruddy cheeks, too, and her red sweater. She would sit in my great-grandmother's chair, pools forming about her snowshoes on the floor, Ira on her capacious knees, telling me how the men were getting on with their plow on the woods road, and planning how some friend I longed to see, like Willa Cather, might be transported to Sneden's.

Willa had written and telephoned me, urgently promising, in her voice of youth, to come out to see me in the early spring—I promised her Dutchmen's breeches and dog-tooth violets. But when the frogs began their ardent keening in the woods, Mary died.

It was after that that I realized that those who are forbidden to read have a store of pictures behind their own eyelids. I would glimpse Willa as she was in 1917, on the campus of the University of Nebraska, in that blazing summer when she received her first honorary degree. The sun was molten, ripening the corn and wheat, and all the "old girls" in their white dresses and the English professors in their white ducks were making much of her. She was radiantly happy and handsome, but it was time to go back, she said, shaking off their clinging hands and their possessive glances.

Sensing that perhaps she, like Mary too, would not be here for long, I began to recall the life essences, the people, the symbols, the pictures, the colors that Willa had meshed so lightly in her prose. I would catch a glimpse of Bishop Latour, riding below the *Mesa Encantada*, on his white mule, with an Indian guide; discover Mrs. Forrester setting forth in the snow for that sleigh ride with her lover; suddenly see old Mrs. Harris, nursing the misery that came upon her after the children had gone to bed.

One night I had a dream about Willa. She was standing at the corner of a fine, brown, small field, watching a stalwart young Roman in a white robe drive a primitive plow behind two white oxen (I had seen such beasts plowing a classic field at Fiesole, in the early thirties). This field Willa Cather guarded was rich, and limited by walls, and the young man, paying no heed to the literary watcher, dug deep the rolling furrows, and sang as he worked. Willa's sentient awareness of him was quiet and silent, but as I stared at her, her little round straw hat dropped down over her face like a countrywoman's felt. The wind was blowing and as she clutched a shawl about her, the Latin field became the great Nebraska plain, with winter coming on.

Willa Cather died suddenly, unexpectedly, on April 24, 1947. She had been in good health and she and Miss Lewis had had an especially jolly lunch and talk together. Though they had gone their own ways and lived their own lives, their companionship was deeply founded and delightful.

Willa Cather was in her seventy-fourth year and, in spite of all, had been preparing another collection of short stories. The longest of them lay incomplete on her desk. For this reason *The Old Beauty and Others* published in 1948, will always seem a little meagre. "The Best Years" and "Before Breakfast" have the true Cather tang that lingers on the literary palate as unique. But the title piece, a sort of recurrence of the lost lady theme, seems, after Mrs. Forrester's story, dim and faded.

This book was followed, also in 1948, by the volume *On Writing*—a distinguished collection of spontaneous opinions, beliefs or revelations forced out of a novelist by some need to explain a purpose in her own work or a criticism of another. Prefaces, open letters, explanations—few theories. All of the essays and letters had previously been published, save the interesting controversial fragment, "Light on Adobe Walls," that ends the book. Some, like "The Novel *Démeublé*," had been included in *Not Under Forty*. Nevertheless it was worth while to re-gather the pieces, for they do resemble, as Katherine Anne Porter suggests, a notebook in which a great author has freely avowed her errors and her faiths.

Willa Cather was buried in the Old Cemetery, Jaffrey Center, New Hampshire. The New England pioneers who incorporated this village in 1773 are said to have "raised" the framework of their enormous church, known as "the Old Meeting House," on the day of the Battle of Bunker Hill. The Old Meeting House stands on a height and dominates the intimate village square, with its old spreading trees, charming old houses, some white, some rosy brick. Beyond the high white edifice, toward Monadnock Mountain, the Old Burying ground slopes steeply down, like Thornton Wilder's graveyard in *Our Town*. There lie the early settlers, under their delicately engraved grey stones and monuments. Willa's grave, with its pure white, graciously curved headstone, is the very last near the lower fence with no other between it and the view, and seems to hang suspended above a flat, blue space of sky and level, forest-grown plain stretching to the long humped Roman profile of Monadnock.

"Don't you feel she must be lonely here?" asked a young writer who was with me on one occasion when I visited the grave from Peterborough.

No lonelier than she was anyhow, I answered, when she committed herself to the impersonal life of the novelist which seemed to mean much more to her than her personal life. In Jaffrey she had worked on some of her finest books, and her spiritual home, so I imagined, was, indeed, the place where she wrote at her best.

The words carved in a lower corner of the stone seem almost to be *spoken* in a low, familiar voice:

> . . . That is happiness; to be dissolved into something complete and great.

The quotation concludes the fervent, earthy chapter of *My Ántonia* in which the little boy first observes and experiences the prairie after he reaches his grandmother's homestead near Black Hawk. Jim was entirely happy, walking through the red, blowing grass to the edge of the world, feeling the "motion" in the country which seemed "somehow to be running." He sat down among his grandmother's pumpkins on the warm earth of the draw bottom.

"Perhaps we feel like that when we die and become a part of something entire, whether it is sun and air, or goodness and knowledge."

Mary Austin, another Western woman, who adopted the Southwest as her final home, dying a few years before Willa Cather, requested that her ashes be scattered on a mountainside of the Sangre de Cristo range. But Willa, with similar individualism, and very much less drama, chose the contained peace of her adopted New England village. One can easily imagine Mrs. Fields and Miss Jewett stopping by to leave a bunch of pinks and larkspur from the South Berwick garden. They would both have appreciated the beautiful northern New England prospect; a landscape as soberly poetical as one of Miss Cather's prose paragraphs, from which all excessive ornament or metaphor has been stricken by a firm pen.

Many times in the last three summers I have stopped at this grave and increasingly rejoiced that Willa should have chosen to lie forever in a place where the works of man—village, church, graveyard, outlying farms—are related harmoniously and intimately to the universe around them. What she loved in the ancient cliff cities of New Mexico and Arizona was the sense that there man and nature and earth were one. Jaffrey, too, surrounded by outlying farms and topped by an impressive, ancient church, is, like Acoma pueblo, a kind of hilly citadel.

The inhabitants of Jaffrey Center today are relatively few. For when the Boston and Maine Railroad came through and the mills were built along the river, most of the citizens moved to East Jaffrey. That is, of course, why "summer people" bought some of the old houses at the Center, and why the Old Meeting House has now become a community center, where atomic scientists and others discuss the agitations and hopes of the modern world.

Did Willa know how many of these Jaffrey New Englanders are Roman Catholics? Some have French Canadian names. Even the Shattuck Inn, where she wrote some of

her finest pages, now is housing a school of the order of
the Sacred Heart of Jesus and Mary, for Catholic boys
destined for the priesthood; and on the village street, in
Jaffrey Center, the Sisters of Notre Dame are teaching
New Hampshire boys and girls.

If on her grave that bears no religious emblem or references, a young priest laid a wreath for Father Latour
and Father Vaillant, I am sure that Willa Cather would
rejoice. If a young veteran of the Korean War, which she
missed by dying in 1947, stopped by—a man with an Asian
outlook, one of those constrained to hail and accept (as
Thornton Wilder said in his Alumni Day address to Harvard students in 1951) "that painfully emerging unity of
those who live on the one inhabited star"--she would surely
receive him as a new Tom Outland.

Willa Cather did not, however, write only for youth and
age; only for Episcopalians or Roman Catholics; only for
Nebraskans, New Englanders or Virginians. Perhaps she
wrote chiefly for classicists. "The Poet's Testament," found
among George Santayana's papers after his death, is the
poem I would choose to read at her grave:

> To trembling harmonies of field and cloud,
> Of flesh and spirit was my worship vowed.

Acknowledgments

THE FIRST PERSON with whom I talked of Willa Cather, from the detached standpoint of the writer—or of the semi-detached writer who was also a literary friend—was her future critical biographer, Mr. E. K. Brown. In 1949, Professor Brown sought me out in the Hudson Valley, and again in 1950. We had long half days together and utterly engrossing talk. I had already done some research in the hospitable Barnard College Library and had a tentative draft of Part One of this book which Mr. Brown read and encouraged me to publish, as his book (he said) would not be based on personal impressions. Until his death—a shock and a serious loss—we carried on an intermittent correspondence, with an exchange of queries on dates and facts.

Since then Mr. Leon Edel, his distinguished successor in the biography, and Mrs. E. K. Brown have been especially helpful and kind. Mr. Edel read my completed manuscript and offered valuable suggestions. To him and to Miss Edith Lewis, who in her capacity as Willa Cather's literary trustee read several parts of my manuscript, I wish to offer sincere thanks and appreciation. The critical biography by Messrs. Brown and Edel and Miss Lewis' *Willa Cather Living* were not, however, published in time to be used as source material for this book. But I was fortunate to be able to see both books in time to verify certain dates and details.

I want to offer thanks to authors or literary executors who have permitted me to make quotations from the following works: to Mrs. Z. B. Adams for *The Letters of Sarah Orne Jewett;* to Paul Reynolds for Henry James, *Notes on Novelists;* to Burton Rascoe for *A Bookman's Daybook,* and quotations from *Arts and Decorations;* to Pauline C. Drown for *Mrs. Bell;* to Van Wyck Brooks for *The Confident Years;* to Mrs. E. K. Brown for *Rhythm in the Novel.*

Special thanks are offered to several books that may be thought of as memoirs: to the late Rev. Father W. J. Howlett's *Life of the Right Reverend Joseph Machebeuf, D.D.,* the chief source book for *Death Comes for the Archbishop,* which I found in 1939 on the bookshelves of Miss Catherine Farrelly in Santa Fe; to *The World of Willa Cather* by Mildred R. Bennett, of Red Cloud, who was the first to collect and publish Nebraska photographs, stories as told by Willa Cather's childhood friends, and also revelatory newspaper interviews that she so freely gave in this environment; to *Writings from Willa Cather's Campus Years* by James R. Shively; to *These Too Were Here* by Elizabeth Moorhead, a memoir bearing on the Pittsburgh years.

In addition I have had help or documentation from various friendly private sources: from Mr. F. B. Adams, Jr., of the Pierpont Morgan Library, who, with the consent of Mark De W. Howe, Justice Oliver Wendell Holmes' literary executor, has generously permitted me to print two letters from the Justice, bearing on Miss Cather's work; from Witter Bynner of Santa Fe—his recollections go back to days when he and Miss Cather were on the staff of *McClure's*—who has provided a letter from Henry James, with the permission of William James; from M. A. De W. Howe, literary executor of Mrs. James T. Fields, who has given wise comment on Mrs. Fields and Miss Jewett, and has allowed me to include a letter of his own to Willa Cather; from Mrs. Graham B. Blaine, who has guided me to places of the author's predilection in Jaffrey; and from Mrs. Marian MacDowell of Peterborough who has joined her "Colony" reminiscence; from Marian and Henry S. Canby; Ferris Greenslet; Alvin Johnson; Philip James and many others.

To all of these I am appreciatively indebted and also to several generous friends, who have read my manuscript, in part or as a whole: Esther Bates; Pauline Goldmark; Ferris Greenslet; Alyse Gregory; Elizabeth Winsor Pearson; Thornton Wilder.

E. S.

The following publishers have granted permission to quote from the books, newspapers and magazines listed:

Alfred A. Knopf, Inc.: "Going Home," "Prairie Spring," "Spanish Johnny," and "Dedication" from *April Twilights; Youth and the Bright Medusa, One of Ours, A Lost Lady, The Old Beauty and Others, The Professor's House, Death Comes for the Archbishop, Obscure Destinies, Lucy Gayheart, Shadows on the Rock* by Willa Cather. *On Writing* by Willa Cather, with a Foreword by Stephen Tennant.

Alfred A. Knopf, Inc. and the Willa Cather Estate: "The

Profile," "The Bohemian Girl," "The Namesake" and "Plays of Real Life" by Willa Cather.

Houghton Mifflin: *The Song of the Lark, My Ántonia, O Pioneers!, Alexander's Bridge* by Willa Cather. *Under the Bridge* by Ferris Greenslet. *Earth Horizon* by Mary Austin.

Dodd, Mead & Company: Excerpt from *The World of Willa Cather* reprinted by permission of Dodd, Mead & Company from *The World of Willa Cather* by Mildred Bennett. Copyright 1951 by Mildred Bennett.

Harcourt, Brace and Company, Inc.: *The Autobiography of Lincoln Steffens* by Lincoln Steffens.

The Viking Press: *The Strange Necessity* by Rebecca West.

The New York Herald Tribune: Interview, *New York Herald*, December 24, 1922.

The New York World: Interview.

Nebraska State Journal: "Concerning Thomas Carlyle," by Willa Cather, March 1, 1891.

World-Herald (Omaha, Neb.): Interviews.

Newberry Library Bulletin: "Willa Cather: The Benjamin D. Hitz Collection" by E. K. Brown, 2nd Ser., No. 5, Dec., 1950.

Index

A NOTE ABOUT THE AUTHOR

Born in Winchester, Massachusetts, on April 23, 1881, Elizabeth Shepley Sergeant grew up in a New England that looked back to the literary "Golden Age" of Hawthorne and Lowell and saw the emergence of new creative writers like Amy Lowell and Robert Frost. After attending school in Boston, Miss Sergeant studied at Bryn Mawr College, receiving her A.B. degree in 1903. (On Bryn Mawr's seventy-fifth anniversary in 1960, she was one of seventy-five alumnae honored with a citation.) Miss Sergeant's career as a writer has spanned more than fifty years. During World War I she was the Paris observer and correspondent for the *New Republic,* and was seriously wounded on a deserted battlefield. Since then she has lived in New Mexico, France, and Switzerland, where she studied analytical psychology with the late Dr. C. G. Jung. Miss Sergeant now lives and writes in a house overlooking the Hudson River, and spends some of her summers in New England. In addition to numerous articles and sketches, her published works are: *French Perspectives* (1916), *Shadow-Shapes* (1920), *Fire Under the Andes* (1927), which included the first literary portrait of Willa Cather, *Short as Any Dream* (1929), the present memoir, first published in 1954, and *Robert Frost: The Trial by Existence* (1960). Her translation of *Lectures pour une Ombre* by Jean Giroudoux, published in this country as *Campaigns and Intervals* (1918), introduced that writer to American audiences.